THE NEW Paris

THE PEOPLE, PLACES & IDEAS

FUELING A MOVEMENT

LINDSEY TRAMUTA

PHOTOGRAPHY BY CHARISSA FAY

ABRAMS, NEW YORK

To Cédric: Thank you for introducing me to your Paris,
and joining me for the journey as I discovered my own.

Contents

the foundations
of a
NEW PARIS

"The old Paris is no more
(the form of a city changes faster,
alas, than the human heart)."

—CHARLES BAUDELAIRE

*I*came to Paris with many of the same motivations as the countless dreamers that came before me. As a student of French language and literature, I arrived at the end of 2006 seeking a taste of the textbook reverie I had spent so much of my university life back in Philadelphia studying. The works of George Sand, Charles Baudelaire, and Victor Hugo, among those by literary expat figures like Ernest Hemingway and Gertrude Stein. Both their use of the language and their relationships to the city planted the seeds of curiosity. I wanted to experience the quality of life, itself a thing of legends, and the stories I hoped (no, *knew!*) would unfurl before me with each street, quartier, and Parisian encountered. To a great extent, I came to know that it was real. Like most wide-eyed new visitors, my viewpoint was narrow. In my colorful imagination, Paris functioned as a one-trick pony on an immaculate stage of perfectly packaged historic marvels—a picturesque trophy city. If we were to trust our twee vision, Paris appears more like a simulacrum of a city—a living museum that trades on its past to woo travelers eager to experience *Paris*, the iconic destination.

If I returned after that first summer of intense study and linguistic immersion in Paris and laid down roots shortly thereafter, I did so for its true colors as a livable, everyday city that is as grimy as it is chic, as maddening as it is edifying. Where uniform, Haussmannian boulevards belie an erratic beauty that doesn't cleave to the picture-perfect city of our imaginations but rather reveals the capital's diverse character. Even the less pleasant and seldom publicized realities—trash-strewn sidewalks, offensive odors, and all the various imperfections that intrude on the tourist's idyll—are part of that character. These are the truths I was only able to see after pulling back the veneer and opening myself up to what existed beyond the fairy tale. Ten years later, the city's imperfections are among the many reasons I stay.

The trouble with such an internationally fetishized public image, though, is that the city becomes a prisoner to its own deified history, hemmed in by its former successes. Few tourist cities have the weight of such an image and heritage to shoulder. So to protect its legendary reputation, the city has historically turned inward and resisted change. Or at least, it certainly felt this way when I moved to Paris in the middle of the new millennium when the notions of progress and an embrace of cosmopolitan ideals were noticeably elusive. As other world capitals garnered attention in the media for innovations in technology, business, and even the culinary arts, Paris's image as change-phobic and voluntarily disconnected from the global world was cemented even further. Mediocrity (or a bad

---

PAGE 1 The rue de Nil in the 2nd arrondissement is home to an array of new restaurants and shops. PAGE 2 Inside Clown Bar. PAGES 4–5 Meringues from Aux Merveilleux de Fred. PREVIOUS SPREAD Floor tiling at Folks and Sparrows Café. OPPOSITE View of the Sacré-Coeur from the 10th arrondissement.

"This isn't the Paris of monuments; it's the Paris of nonchalance, of real Parisians."

—GILLES BALLARD, COFOUNDER OF MEDECINE DOUCE

Rive gauche at golden hour.

case of resting on their laurels) in many areas of life, from gastronomy to business and tourism, had become the accepted norm—why mess with something that works? Some have called it complacency, others have pointed to a *malaise*, tied to past failures, declining French influence, and conflicting values,[1] that has stunted substantive change across the country as a whole. "We have in mind this great nation of ours: the major power in Europe under Louis XIV and Napoleon I, the biggest allied standing army in the first world war," Dominique Moïsi of the French Institute of International Relations told the *Economist* in 2013. "Now there's a sense of 'What happened to us?'"[2]

To be sure, old-world charm and numinous beauty, both reliably immutable, have served it well, as evidenced by the 29 million visitors that descend upon it each year. But the Paris of yesteryear wasn't enough anymore. Not for locals and not for the growing set of travelers who wanted and expected more from the places they visited.

ESTABLISHING THE LEGEND: THEN AND NOW

As the most idealized city in the world, Paris has no shortage of travelers willing to heap plaudits on its many treasured gifts—bridges, unparalleled vistas, grand boulevards, squares and parks, iconic museums, an unshakable aura of romance—chiefly the things that elevated Paris to urban supremacy centuries ago, turning it into a utopia where persisting blemishes like theft, litter, pollution, and societal disparities were overlooked for the sake of preserving the fantasy. If we look at the way Paris emerged as Europe's first modern city over the course of the seventeenth century (aided in part by Louis XIV's vision of the city as a pleasure ground, which quickly swept across the globe), it's easy to understand how this folklore of greatness became the prevailing narrative, still widely accepted today.

The creation of the Pont Neuf bridge, completed in 1606, initiated the universal perception of Paris as a wondrous spectacle to be seen and admired. It marked the first time that Parisians and visitors could marvel at the magnificence of the Seine River and the city's monuments with an unobstructed view. With that bridge came reserved space for pedestrians, modern sidewalks, social mixing, and the enduring notion that one could walk for pure pleasure—the early *flâneur*, a modern urban adventurer who walked to see and be seen. Then came the first public mail delivery system, public transportation system, and street lighting. Later, postcards were used to spread these modern images of the city, solidifying its identity as a progressive place and birthplace of significant conveniences and innovations in urban planning. Paris was, says author Joan DeJean in her book *How Paris Became Paris: The Invention of the Modern City*, the center of the European cultural world,[3] a sentiment confirmed by late seventeenth-century guidebooks, which presented "a city bristling with creative energy, a cultural magnet, an incubator of the kind of ideas that could revolutionize urban life."[4] When cast as the most stylish and romantic capital in Europe, the lore of Paris as we know it today was born.

The list of advances continued into the mid- to late nineteenth century, which saw the popularization of the bicycle and marked the first public screening of a motion picture by the Lumière brothers at the Grand Café on Boulevard des Capucines. Georges Auguste Escoffier's *Le Guide Culinaire*, published in 1903, established the building blocks of cooking, like the five mother sauces and various stocks (though his contributions go beyond recipes to include restaurant kitchen hierarchy and logistics developed in Paris), which are still referenced today. The 1940s brought more sartorial contributions, namely in the form of the now-ubiquitous bikini by Louis Réard (on proud display at Molitor, see page 244) and the pencil skirt by Christian Dior, while World War II ushered in a new era in café-going that united intellectuals and artists of varying socioeconomic classes over the shared trauma of wartime.

There was the arrival of the nouvelle cuisine movement in the 1970s, provoking a seismic shift in the world of French gastronomy, the effects of which are still discussed by chefs across the globe; the 1982 launch of the Minitel, the forerunner to the Internet; the 1998 birth of Silicon Sentier, the epicenter for Internet start-ups (which currently boasts the largest concentration of tech start-ups in France); the first partial face transplant in 2005 (then the world's first successful full-face transplant five years later); and, shortly after my arrival, the launch of Vélib', the city's much-lauded bike-share program that directly inspired those developed in Chicago, New York, and London (Autolib', the car-share iteration, followed several years later). France ranked first in the 2014 Deloitte Technology Fast 500 index for Europe, the Middle East, and Africa, which identifies the region's fastest-growing companies, and Paris finds itself among the world's cities with the most female-launched start-ups. In 2015, "Une Journée Sans Voiture" marked the first time cars were banned for a day in dense traffic zones to raise awareness for sustainable transit and the need to fight pollution. Transforming the city into a pedestrian and cyclist's paradise, the initiative was the perfect example of Mayor Anne Hidalgo's capstone preoccupation, the Paris Piéton project, which attempts to transform Paris into the world's perfect walking city by considering Parisians' expectations for a better pedestrian experience: comfortable, shared spaces, more greenery, and more water sources like fountains (and today, one Sunday of each month on the Champs-Elysées is a day without cars). And after much anticipation, the Halle Freyssinet, the world's largest digital business incubator, financed by France's most disruptive figure in tech, Xavier Niel, opened its doors in 2017 in the 13th arrondissement (in a restored historic monument, no less), hosting a thousand start-ups and permanently anchoring Paris as a driver of digital innovation.

These were among many marquee achievements that demonstrated how the city excelled in public works and cultural initiatives, from gastronomy to the arts. When I moved to Paris, however, micro-level improvements felt few and far between, and locals struggled with multiculturalism and resisted the growing presence of international concepts. But perhaps the city wasn't so much trailing behind as it was following its own course, at its own pace. As an American whose country was built on change and whose continuing modus operandi is further, faster, better, Parisian progress felt not only slow but at a standstill. The reality, however, is that the "new Paris" is, in fact, a state of being that has defined the city at numerous points in its history—high points on a trajectory of ups and downs. Now, the city's singular talent for improving urban living thrives again, and a new openness has taken root at a grassroots level.

OPPOSITE Evening stroll on the Quai de Valmy, along the Canal Saint-Martin.

The terrace at
Clown Bar, home
of innovative neo-
bistro cooking and
an impressive natural
wine selection.

THE NEW PARIS

I have not only observed the city's evolutions with studied interest, but I have felt the prevailing debate shift from "how can Paris (and the rest of France) protect itself from globalization and preserve its past?" to "how can the city honor its past, while embracing and innovating in a global world?" Polarizing discussions of education, economics, race, creed, national identity, and immigration dovetail with a newfound energy that has drastically revamped the city's social fabric.

My goal in writing this book is to further shift the perspective of the city beyond the hoary clichés that have circulated blithely across lands and generations. Today, the Paris long-adored for its medieval vestiges, religious relics, Seine-lit bridges, old-time brasseries, and corner cafés finds itself on unstable ground and of value for so much more than its storied past. It is yet another seminal time in the capital's history.

A wave of creatives in industries such as food and wine, coffee and pastry, fashion and crafting has infused a more dynamic, open-minded sensibility to the local landscape and fostered this "new Paris"—both a contemporary destination bursting with spirited energy, and a new movement anchored on the knowledge that to grow as a city and compete with thriving international capitals there must be a forward-looking focus on innovation and creativity, building upon the past along the way.

While the first intimations of this "new" Paris predated the economic crash of 2008, particularly in food and drink, with such debuts as the bistronomy cooking movement and craft cocktail bars, the winds of change forged forward from the consequences left in its wake. The economic crisis, or *la crise*, as the French still refer to it today, brought the realities of a fragile job market and dwindling opportunities into sharp focus, especially for young people. Their paths wouldn't be clearly paved, and many would attempt entrepreneurship as a way to control their futures.

In the throes of *la crise*, the buying power of the ultrawealthy remained largely unscathed, but for everyone else, dining out and treating oneself to any superfluous purchases required careful consideration. At the time, I was nearing the end of my graduate studies and facing a truly precarious job market. Around me, people were scrambling to determine the most judicious next move. In the realm of business, no brands, save for luxury labels, seemed spared by the effects of the economic downturn, which has had an enduring impact on their bottom line, even years later. Companies laid off their employees in droves, construction projects halted, shops shuttered, and many restaurant owners started cutting corners to scale back spending, to the detriment of the customer. In dining, that sadly meant using frozen ingredients purchased at wholesale giants or reheating premade dishes, certainly not living up to the universal dream of fine, gourmet dining in Paris.

Feeling defeated, disillusioned small-business owners jettisoned their moral compass when they felt backed into a corner by the state's steep labor costs and social security charges (which include health care and pensions), which were much less of an issue when times were flush. *La crise* was indeed a crisis—of values. In the midst of all this, I found myself wondering if I was the only one gravely disappointed by what appeared to be a collective shoulder shrug. *C'est comme ça!* That's just the way it is, everyone appeared to say.

Fortunately, that attitude didn't last long, and I learned I wasn't alone. This instability birthed a reaction, a response from creative and passionate people, French and foreign, who asked themselves the tough, but necessary, questions about their futures, which were no longer failsafe within the confines of the careers-for-life tradition that defined previous generations. Rather than slavish dedication to an antiquated model—one chef king with a team of small fish in a big brigade who fight for recognition—people of all ages began breaking out on their own, leaving desk jobs or unsatisfying careers to test their mettle at more fulfilling pursuits, many of which are manual, as you will see in The New Shopping & Crafts (page 192).

But it isn't just the maladjusted or corporate-fatigued that have gone independent or fought to make changes in their fields. Most of the individuals featured in this book are on a determined quest for deeper meaning in their lives and looking to add real value to the lives of other Parisians. For some, that meant starting their own business after years of training, deciding there was no better time than now to take the plunge. Others have found their calling in entirely new territories.

Clément Brossault, my favorite local cheesemonger (seen at right), for example, left behind his suit-and-tie banker life to pursue a tangible path that wouldn't leave him questioning his contributions to society each day. In 2012, he traversed the country's major cheese regions by bike to meet producers, *affineurs*, and dairy farmers, learning their methods of production and building relationships along the way. Upon returning to Paris, he opened his shop in the Goncourt section of the 11th arrondissement, his own neighborhood and one lacking in artisanal *fromageries*. He maintains a zero-plastics policy (no plastic shopping bags, all cheeses are wrapped in recycled paper) and makes deliveries exclusively by bike, an ethos that has resonated with locals looking to consume better and more responsibly. Clément is but one of countless examples of people whose ideas and efforts are driving a much broader movement worldwide, where the status quo is questioned, not blindly upheld. These are individuals who profoundly want to elevate the city, and they have already made great inroads in leading it beyond its assumed role as time capsule. Now, it is a dynamic, vibrant place bursting with energy and ideas, a city open to what the rest of the world has to offer it and far more cosmopolitan in attitude than ever before.

This awakened an inventive side to the city, the one that resists being defined solely by the untenable duo of magic and myth, and the place I love and am proud to call home. I became part of an entirely new epoch in its narrative, built on ideas and inspiration from beyond its borders.

DRIVING THE CHANGE

So what's behind all of this? For starters, the world is getting smaller and easier to navigate. The Internet has broken down informational barriers that made other cultures feel distant and inaccessible without physically visiting them. What happens in Johannesburg or Tokyo can have reverberations on the other side of the globe in record time. Then, of course, we cannot disregard the impact of social media and unfettered access to an unending stream of information, making all of us more informed. We can discover how others travel, where they go, how they innovate,

Clément Brossault, owner of Fromagerie Goncourt, sells artisanal cheeses and runs his business in an environmentally conscious manner.

A new angle on the old Paris: rooftops in the 10th arrondissement, an area that has seen many exciting developments in recent years.

and even how they cultivate talent. It's never been easier to follow what's happening in food, art, culture, and fashion in other countries than it is right now.

As more Parisians travel, thanks to low-cost flights and inexpensive train tickets, the more they are exposed to ideas from farther afield, encouraging them to challenge the systems in place that have traditionally favored an old vision of Paris. Those who don't or can't travel needn't search very long for images, updates, and stories from their friends and family who can, shared in real time across all imaginable channels. We can vilify the Internet for many things, but exposing people to positive and inspiring developments in other places and cultures is one of its many gifts.

A number of societal shifts are also at play. The always-on-the-go lifestyle so common to Anglo-Saxon cultures is infiltrating Paris, resulting in more goods and services geared toward quick consumption (that also means that the much-bandied-about two-hour-long, wine-soaked lunch break is fading). And while eating for speed is an unfortunate development, the (perceived) dearth of time has raised expectations for the experience of gathering around a table with friends and family for a shared meal or round of drinks. More discerning than ever, locals are seeking out quality on and off the plate.

Parisians have also followed the global swing toward a heightened concern for personal well-being. P.D.E.—public displays of exercise, like running and cycling, with all the right gear to boot—have gone from *faux pas* to *à la mode*. Add to that a newfangled interest in kale, vegetable-driven restaurants, cold-pressed juices, detox cures, gluten-free baked goods, and vegan lunch joints, appropriated as *la cuisine healthy*, and you've got a new lifestyle.

But more than anything, disillusionment drove many to enact change. A collective *ras-le-bol* (fed-up frustration) of being hoodwinked by large, soulless corporations or hierarchical structures was a sentiment echoed by nearly all of the people interviewed for this book. The change they've wrought is a testament to their tireless work and fervent belief that we all should be consuming less—and consuming better.

In essence, we're seeing the rise of the creative class, much like the one that developed in the United States at the turn of the millennium, where the abiding philosophy prioritizes authenticity, sustainability, sharing, and personal growth over money or status.[5] But the movement has been given a Parisian spin. Now, the sounds of coffee grinders, cocktail shakers, and creative conversation fall on the ears like an incantation for opportunity with an undeniably French accent.

For this book, I spent months interviewing veteran chefs and rising culinary stars, award-winning pâtissiers, world champion mixologists and craft beer brewers, self-taught fashion designers, jewelry and soap makers, gallery owners, and interior designers to glean their thoughts on this newfound energy and understand how they contribute to the movement. Enriched, enlightened, and excited to share bits of their stories, I am more convinced than ever that the French penchant and talent for savoir faire, technique, and tradition isn't just respected by this creative class—it is the thread connecting them.

As we now know, passion begets passion. To see others finding their footing as their own bosses or working on projects they love is a powerful source of inspiration for those oscillating between ripping off the Band-Aid of familiarity and trying to survive on the eroding corporate route.

Of the seventeenth- and eighteenth-century advancements that contributed to the construction of the capital, Joan DeJean writes, "Eyewitnesses to modernization appear to have experienced no apprehension at the idea that their city was changing around them. Instead, they seem to have been so exhilarated by the prospects they saw opening up that they were eager to broadcast the story of Paris's rebirth and to celebrate the revolution brought about by modern urban life."[6] I can only imagine the enthusiasm those same people would feel were they to live the city's cultural reinvention again now. And just as they felt compelled to share these changes widely, so do I today.

There is a false notion that the old Paris of centuries prior must be mourned as it shares ground with the new. Traditionalists comb every new opening, development, or trend as an augury of how the new guard is forcing unwanted change upon the local landscape. I prefer to see this shift as the next chapter in the city's monumental story. Part of the city's road to achieving greatness—the kind that would live up to Charles de Gaulle's vision for the country's "exceptional destiny"[7] overall—is grappling with what ails it and building upon the foundation laid by centuries of invaluable contributions to art, architecture, food, fashion, and technology. It's also about finding constructive ways to address prevailing issues of immigration, security, and national identity in the wake of recent terrorist attacks that shook the capital.

If Paris is a storybook city today, it is for more than the sum of its stellar monuments. It is for the people, places, designs, and ideas, many within these pages, that enrich the everyday, always with a focus on honoring the past while building for the future. They are emblematic of a spirited movement that has expanded the very symbolism and perception of Paris as a destination, where the new coexists beautifully and respectfully with the old.

I hope that the next six chapters peel back some of the layers of my vibrant city in motion. When it comes to food and dining, fossilized ideas about what French cooking should be and what should exist in the Paris food scene are put into question. Coffee in Paris has become a craft of its own worth getting excited about, the pastry and confectionary trade has evolved to reflect shifting tastes and products, and former fringe neighborhoods have become unexpected hubs for shopping. Even cocktails and beer have, quite literally, shaken and stirred up the scene.

By the time this goes to print, hits bookshelves, and arrives in your hands, the "new Paris" wagon will have continued to barrel ahead. Finally, a decade after I arrived as a young, impressionable Paris lover with grand hopes and expectations for my adopted city, I am both enamored by its storied past and humbled and excited to be a part of writing its future.

The guide I have provided at the back of the book includes the addresses of places mentioned throughout each chapter and a host of other favorites that are driving the "new Paris" movement forward. To stay updated about ongoing changes, new developments, and more stories, visit www.thenewparisbook.com.

OPPOSITE Métro station Barbès-Rochechouart, seen from the rooftop of the renovated and revitalized Le Louxor Cinema (see page 231).

the new
FOOD & DINING

"Where Paris was once a magnet for literary minds, today it attracts a huge talent pool of international chefs. And that makes it a more interesting place to eat, even if it's not what people are expecting."

—MEG ZIMBECK, FOOD WRITER AND FOUNDER OF PARIS BY MOUTH CULINARY TOURS

*W*hen my husband and I bought our apartment east of the Bastille in the 11th arrondissement in 2008, we were already familiar with the neighborhood. Our previous residence, where we lived together for two years, was located mere minutes away on an eerily quiet side street that linked the heavily trafficked avenue de la République and the rue Oberkampf, a popular market street lined with butchers and bakers, cheese- and fishmongers that bustled during the day as locals weaved their way in and out of shops picking up the week's provisions. Following the street north toward the 20th arrondissement led directly through a warren of dingy dive bars, kebab shacks, pizzerias, Laundromats, and night owls; it was a tremendously popular nightlife locale among college-age students and young professionals but had potential to become much more.

Of the vivid memories I have of frequenting that street as a new resident, it was a peculiar ramshackle bar that struck me as the last vestige of an older Paris—a Paris that would soon come apart at its seams. It occupied the corner of rue Gambey and rue Oberkampf, between my local dry cleaner and my then-preferred boulangerie, and only ever seemed to attract the same two elderly men who, already inebriated, spent the morning hunched over the counter nursing glasses of cheap red wine.

As I walked up and down the street, passing the bar twice on some days, I wondered how much longer a place like that could survive, devoid of patrons and crumbling from wear. Just as soon as I had directed the question to the cheesemonger across the street, the "for sale" sign went up on the bar, and within months, the window announced the arrival of *Top Chef France* finalist Pierre Sang. The chef set up his first eponymous modern bistro on that corner with a sleek open kitchen, a novel practice at the time, and a surprise/no-choice menu crafted from ingredients sourced from the street's many merchants. The same is true for his second space, located a few doors down on rue Gambey, which opened in 2014 with more Korean-inflected dishes as a nod to his origins. And that's only on one side of our home; the young chef–bistro boom has reverberated widely.

I can't help but think that my foray into food writing was facilitated by my location in the epicenter of new dining. Le Chateaubriand, Le Dauphin, Septime, Le 6 Paul Bert, Yard, Pierre Sang, Le Servan—I have seen the city's best spots sprout around me, in farther reaches of the 11th arrondissement and in nearby neighborhoods on the city's east side. (Sometimes it's not so

---

PREVIOUS SPREAD The dining room at Verjus, where American fare with a Southern twang is served. OPPOSITE The small plates at Le Mary Celeste, an oyster and small-plates cocktail bar, have mixed origins. The menu features a refreshing, idiosyncratic style, one not reliant on tricks, but rather predicated on using the best of France's bounty for dishes that are decidedly un-French. You might even say they are detached from any one cultural marker. For Parisians, the regularly rotating menu provides just the right dose of the exotic.

On the success of Verjus, chef Braden Perkins says, "We were lucky, we arrived onto the scene in the wake of a burgeoning movement."

bad being priced out of moving to a new neighborhood!) This is a significant departure from the state of the food scene when I moved to Paris more than ten years ago.

There exists an outmoded but widespread idea that all food in Paris is good, or at least superior to most places in the world, by virtue of its legendary contributions to cooking. And for the longest time, particularly before my plans to move to the city came to fruition, that's the story that was trotted out by my friends who had already visited Paris. But shortly after I arrived, the tone changed for the worse. Paris was then pegged as a laggard in an international dining landscape brimming with ambitious concepts and inventive chefs. With accolades bestowed on emerging culinary hotbeds like Spain, Denmark, and Japan, the once grande dame of dining was teetering on decline.

The reasons for this are manifold: The old guard was desperately trying to preserve the culinary traditions tied to national identity but was egregiously out of touch with evolutions in food trends and evolving tastes for greater diversity on the plate. Their blinkered attitude toward change was swiftly tarnishing the capital's longtime reputation as a gastronomic beacon. As the French food journalist Anne-Laure Pham explained to me, the French are extremely nostalgic and like to hold on to the familiar, making progress slow and fraught. "We are really attached to our rituals, namely the act of eating at a table, seated together, and taking our time to go through the full trio: *entrée*, *plat*, *dessert*. Not all of us adhere to this ritual on a daily basis, but many French people consider it the only respectable way to eat."

On top of this, the proliferation of cheap and poorly made convenience food meant that there was even greater disparity between the ways Parisians were eating. You'd be hard put to find a "good" meal in Paris for less than fifty euros, and that didn't even include wine. At that rate, dining out to eat well was an infrequent luxury for the average middle-class Parisian who was priced out of the city's most reputable establishments. Haute cuisine dining (and its many iterations—molecular cuisine and nouvelle cuisine) was buttoned up, ceremonial, and unrelatable for a growing set of the population, myself included.

The city had also experienced its fair share of food scandals to stoke a mini revolution. After countless news reports and television investigations broached the question "What's really in the food you're eating?" and a particularly damaging incident in 2013 involving horse meat unfit for public consumption finding its way into the food chain (this came after the revelation that tons of horse meat had been mislabeled and sold as beef in prepared meals across Europe), transparency and provenance became paramount.

So what has changed? Most notably, the scene went from a chiefly two-pronged offering— upscale, haute dining experiences on one end and affordable brasseries and bistros of questionable quality on the other, with a smattering of forgettable fast-casual chains—to casting a much wider net to cover that gaping hole in the mid-range category, with modern bistros (neo-bistros, as you'll read more about on page 29) offering unprecedented value for gastronomic-level quality. Bistronomy, as the dining movement has been monikered, was paved and prepped by a handful of key chefs, beginning with chef Yves Camdeborde in 1992, who was able to emancipate himself and

Verjus has drawn customers and critical acclaim by giving traditional American food tropes a fresh spin, using French ingredients and even incorporating Asian flavors. The second restaurant from Braden Perkins and Laura Adrian, Ellsworth, which opened in 2015, was born of a desire to have more space to work with whole animals and smaller producers, and begin exploring techniques such as fermentation and curing. They make their own sourdough bread, butter, cheese, labneh, vinegar, and charcuterie for both restaurants and reduce waste by using leftover parts and pieces for dishes in the Verjus wine bar. Lamb belly from Verjus will become lamb bacon for Ellsworth, for example.

his cooking from a rote system that had kept him, and many others, in the shadows, before soaring into ubiquity in the period between 2007 and 2016.

With greater access to quality ingredients, the dining public is more and better informed than ever before and has higher expectations for what they will be served in a restaurant. The culture around eating has also changed. People have less time to spend at the table, which explains the rise in to-go joints and takeaway prepared foods in the front of the supermarkets. But when they do sit down for a meal, they seek out rich experiences.[8] These experiences may come from a food truck or a high-priced tasting table. Adept at moving seamlessly between the high-end and the ultracasual, Parisians today have an abiding expectation of quality. And the food entrepreneurs and chefs in these pages have heeded the call.

Cheap eats have evolved as well to become a full-blown category of their own that we might call Quality Fast Food or Gourmet Comfort Food, marching to the drumbeat of new ventures that take locals beyond low-brow associations of foreign street food totems.

With its reputation for superior produce and technical excellence, France continues to attract a diverse group of gifted chefs. And it is largely thanks to these foreign and French-born young talents who either trained or worked outside of the country that energetic revival has been spurred, reinventing and even democratizing modern French cuisine in the process. Because of their contributions, the city has regained its serious culinary cred and, in the process, diverted mouths east from the left bank, once the reigning hub of stuffy fine dining, to the dynamic and culturally diverse right bank. Paris's resurgence as one of the world's culinary capitals also marked a turning point in Parisian perspective: Locals were finally ready to embrace outside influences, on all levels of the food chain.

THE RISE OF THE NEO-BISTRO

To understand the emergence of the neo-bistro movement, often referred to as *bistronomy*, and why it has been symbolic of energetic change across the food sphere, it's important to first note the distinctions between brasseries and bistros, the two most well-known Parisian dining categories.

Brasseries, elaborately decorated, bustling establishments that offer nonstop daily service from morning to night, were predominantly opened by Alsatians who fled to Paris after the Franco-Prussian War of 1870 to 1871, bringing with them local traditions (the first, Bofinger, actually opened in 1864). In fact, the word means "brewery," and beer was the drink of choice, served alongside Alsatian specialties like choucroute garnie (sauerkraut, sausages, and smoked meats), steak, sausages, and simple grilled fish. In their heyday, brasseries were the beating heart of the Parisian social world, as much places to be seen as to dine at any hour of the day. But their success didn't last.

Longtime local Alexander Lobrano, author of *Hungry for Paris,* recalls a precipitous decline in quality at the start of the 1990s, when most of the marquee brasseries like Balzar, La Coupole, and Bofinger, among others, were snatched up by two big restaurant groups. Mediocrity and flippant attitudes swiftly came to define them. Of this shift, Lobrano writes, "The problem was that behind the scenes, it was accountants, not cooks, who edited the menus and order sheets and who eliminated expensive kitchen staff by enthusiastically embracing almost every industrial shortcut devised by France's booming food service industry.... Every year, it seemed, there was less real cooking going on behind the swinging doors, maybe just a bit of grilling, frying, and reheating."[9] These unfortunate practices coincided with the home "cooking" trend of microwavable frozen meals that began in the 1980s and accelerated in the 1990s; restaurateurs and home cooks alike were rejecting the well made and homemade for convenience.

That mediocrity is still pervasive in brasseries today. They've rested on their laurels and still attracted clients for so long that they subscribe to an attitude of "Well, why should we change? We're still working!" As I discussed this phenomenon with my friend Arash on a walk one day, he pointed to one such brasserie and said, "This is one of the places that when you come in as a tourist, you say to yourself, 'Oh, this is so Parisian. I want to have this experience.' I just want to scream, no you don't! Don't eat that! Don't put that in your mouth!" I couldn't help but laugh because I've seen people fall for the postcard-brasserie trap countless times, but it isn't where anyone is going to have the awe-inspiring culinary experiences they so desperately want.

Even the more recent Brasserie Barbès, built just beneath the métro tracks of the Barbès-Rochechouart métro station—an ethnically diverse neighborhood with a largely working-class and immigrant population—hews to the tradition of style over substance, with prices (like eight euros—nearly nine dollars—for a pint) that exceed what the average Barbès local can afford, and indifferent service. Worse, the owners swooped into the neighborhood posturing that they were going to improve the area (by which they meant gentrify it) and attract monied Parisians from other arrondissements.

Though traditional brasseries are, for the most part, a dying breed, not all hope is lost. Charles Compagnon, a thirtysomething restaurateur and sommelier with rugged good looks and a shrewd vision for what the food scene in Paris should offer, has been leading the charge with an honest update to the brasserie. Only, his interpretation combines elements from several dining categories—all-day service (morning, noon, and night, much like a brasserie), pared-back decor (no tablecloths, exposed stone walls, servers in relaxed wear, like most neo-bistros across town)—with thoughtful, market-driven dishes that go well beyond the Alsatian fare served at traditional brasseries (see an example on page 32). Le Richer, the first of his neo-brasseries, replaced a bistro of the same name that I frequented back in 2009 when I was working a block away. At the time, this stretch of town, where the 10th arrondissement blurs into the 9th, was a dining no-man's-land. The bistro, designed to look like a New York steakhouse, trafficked in style but doled out frozen French fries to accompany rubbery steaks with no flavor. When Compagnon took over the space, selected because it was the most affordable placement he could find, the neighborhood came alive.

Then he followed in 2014 with Le 52 Faubourg Saint-Denis several blocks over, named for the street that it shares with Turkish butchers, Kurdish sandwich joints, Indian spice shops, African hair salons, and the family-run grocer Julhès, a neighborhood institution. To date, it's where I have taken my friends and family when they come to visit, and no one has ever left disappointed.

Charles Compagnon, owner of Le 52 Faubourg Saint-Denis, L'Office, and Le Richer has reinvented and refreshed the traditional brasserie formula.

"What we're seeing is the democratization of the *beau* and the *bon*."

—JULIE MATHIEU, EDITOR IN CHIEF
FOU DE CUISINE AND *FOU DE PÂTISSERIE* MAGAZINES

LA MARIS

BIÈRE BLONDE PALE AL

A comforting fall dish at Le 52 Faubourg Saint-Denis with a bottle of their house craft beer.

Compagnon's stint working for the James Beard Foundation in New York City and the many years he spent with the Costes brothers, the masters of atmosheric restaurants and lounges with stiff service, were formative and served to show him the dos and don'ts of the food world. With his restaurant group, which includes three eateries, his own specialty coffee roaster, and his own label of craft beer (brewed in Germany), he has single-handedly raised the bar for the mid-range dining space.

Where the brasserie was lively and fast-paced, the bistro was more intimate and predicated on hearty, just-like-*maman*-made slow-cooked dishes such as pot-au-feu, roasted chicken, cassoulet, sweetbreads, and regional stews like braised oxtail or boeuf bourguignon, brought to Paris by Auvergnats, Lyonnais, and others who settled in the capital during the nineteenth century. Those who come to Paris today seeking a traditional, "quintessentially French" experience are typically expecting old-fashioned versions of the bistro, kitted out in checkerboard tablecloths, zinc countertops, leather banquettes, and handwritten menus. It's easy to understand the format's appeal; it's French comfort food that warms the soul. But bistros too fell victim to the same cost-cutting and time-saving shortcuts as the brasserie to the detriment of taste and quality.

The neo-bistro, then, builds on the format but with a radically different style born out of bistronomy, a veritable food movement that changed the game for chefs and diners alike. A portmanteau of bistro and gastronomy, bistronomy[10] unofficially began as one chef's reaction to the ever-stultifying haute cuisine beholden to the Michelin Guide and defined by inaccessible prices. When Yves Camdeborde left the grand kitchens of Le Ritz and Hôtel de Crillon, where he spent the early part of his career, behind him, he effectively freed himself from the Michelin grip and its attendant rule book on etiquette and perpetual innovation for innovation's sake (versus a result of personal volition), becoming the guardian of a new movement that valued affordability and a relaxed setting.

In opening his modern bistro La Régalade in 1992 in the far reaches of the 14th arrondissement, then a culinary wasteland, Camdeborde eschewed traditional French food tropes, high price tags, and the strictness of gastronomic cooking, partly because that's all he could afford to do. His dishes were entirely driven by quality products and whim in a space that allowed him the flexibility to emerge from the kitchen and engage with diners. It was antielitist, from the democratic pricing to the refreshingly imperfect decor and simplicity on the plate. But simple meals and relaxed hospitality didn't mean Camdeborde and his team—which included chef Stéphane Jégo for twelve years before he went on to open his own neo-bistro, L'Ami Jean—took shortcuts; the plate was still marked by the exacting technical precision he acquired in top kitchens. And that is true for the chefs who have become part of the movement and for whom Michelin stars aren't the badges of honor they used to be.

Bistronomy lacks a neatly defined meaning because that would imply there is a strict model to follow. Instead there are a set of values that are common to the genre, and a spirit. For one, the dishes and their flavor combinations may seem incongruous at first glance but are worked to harmonious effect. As Katrina Meynink explains in her book *Bistronomy*, "It's a mix of high and low where street food–inspired lobster rolls might sit alongside dishes involving consommés, mousses, and the sort of soufflés that would make Escoffier cry."[11] The plate may look pared back, but there is a strategic layering of ingredients, and serious technique is at play. What's more, chefs aren't afraid to experiment with unexpected (and in some cases, long-neglected) products and preparations, from offal and duck heart to smoked oysters. Less theatrical than the kind of cooking many neo-bistro chefs were trained in at more high-minded restaurants, simplicity and lightness trump embellishment for the sake of esthetic. The trend in carte blanche (surprise/no-choice) menus with dishes that vary daily or weekly has forced producers to adapt their ways of working to accommodate the eternal quest for freshness. And for the chefs, this means they're presented with a creative challenge day in and day out that keeps the process exciting.

"Ten years ago, only triple-starred restaurants could offer quality like this, and it cost nearly ten times more," says journalist and restaurant owner Bruno Verjus. "Producers would reserve their best, most rare products for haute cuisine restaurants, so the variety of fish, fruits, and vegetables at the heart of menus today was simply absent from modest tables before." The rarefied is no longer reserved for a dining elite. Neo-bistro chefs aren't seeking approbation from other chefs or the Michelin top brass as they typically are in fine dining establishments. Instead, their goal is to keep challenging themselves for you, the diner. And that tilt in perspective has brought a marked improvement in service.

On the inside, unfettered environments—a blend of industrial meets beatnik bistro—have supplanted the very carefully designed and immaculate dining rooms typical to bistros and restaurants. Chefs with modest budgets looked to low-key sleeper enclaves (usually in the eastern arrondissements) and former fringe neighborhoods for cheap spaces and low overhead costs, putting the bulk of their money into sourcing top-shelf ingredients. These spaces are often characterized by open kitchens, which allow the chefs to receive direct and instant feedback from diners, exposed stone or brick, original parquet floors or tiles, Spartan decor, and a noticeable lack of the usual linen adornments. Even the serving staff takes a pared-back approach, ditching the button-ups and suits for distressed aprons with jeans, tees, and casual footwear. The atmosphere is meant to be comfortable and inviting but not sway attention away from the food. Fresh, high-quality produce, responsibly sourced fish and meats, affordable wines, and relaxed (but no less attentive) service are the style's compass points. With antiqued bistro chairs and booths and reclaimed farm tables, the old very much blends with the new.

For chefs like Eric Trochon (a Meilleur Ouvrier de France, or Best Craftsman of France, a prestigious honor awarded to a select group of artisans from more than two hundred trades; see page 149 for more information) of Semilla, one of my very favorite neo-bistros, and Freddy's wine bar, bistronomy is also about refreshing the classics. For example, instead of a traditional

OPPOSITE Tatiana owns Le Servan with her sister Katia, who you will find managing the dining room. The concept? Simply to run a restaurant where their friends and family could afford to eat, with a rigorous focus on seasonality. It's modern French cooking inspired by their mixed Filipino-French backgrounds.

"People lost themselves in the race to earn money and high-profile success, so even the bistro needed saving. Now, we're in a golden period of dining."

—TATIANA LEVHA, CHEF AND CO-OWNER OF LE SERVAN

Le Fooding and ⎯⎯ *Omnivore* ⎯⎯

IF THERE IS ANYONE OR any one publication that supported the upstarts in all of these food categories it is Alexandre Cammas and his dining and drinks organization *Le Fooding*. It was the first to praise the foreign chefs who flocked to France to open and run restaurants and has fervently challenged the rigid perspective that French food must be prepared and imagined by French chefs. It punctured the Michelin bubble and offered a look at what was happening in dining on a democratic level. Its mission, according to Cammas, was to infuse a much-needed dose of "cool" into dining.

The changes in food, he says, go well beyond a revolution of the plate. "We've got 'normal' people at the helm of most of these restaurants. These chefs are curious, they've traveled, they're informed, and they're intrepid, not at all threatened by foreign top chefs. They want to be the best in *their* world, not the best in the world." As such, the annual *Le Fooding* guide and its companion website have gone to great lengths to showcase the gastro-bistro chefs changing the face of French cooking, the emerging culture of wine bars and cocktail dens, and the booming, and no less important, subculture of street food and simple eats, by organizing food festivals and pop-up events. Today, landing a review from *Le Fooding* can heavily influence the success and longevity of a new business.

Similarly, the abiding mission of *Omnivore,* the food and beverage guide and first French culinary road show to have international reach (events, master classes, and demonstrations are held in Moscow, Shanghai, Montreal, London, Istanbul, and New York City), is to support the world's rising stars in cooking, baking, mixology, and other areas of gastronomy. With an emphasis on emerging trends and the tales of the diverse cast of talents behind them, the *Omnivore* food guide and annual awards have become the barometer of culinary innovations not only in Paris but in the country at large.

blanquette de veau, a veal ragout with rice and cream, for the menu at Semilla, he cooked up a lamb blanquette with green tea ragout for a lighter twist.

And then there is the elevated role that pastry and dessert have been given in neo-bistros, a course treated as no less important than the others. Where the norm on a bistro menu leaned toward recipes that tasted as homespun as they looked—by-the-book *tarte aux pommes*, *tarte au citron*, mixed berry crumble, or crème caramel, to name a few—today's young chefs run to plated desserts that modernize the classics and highlight their deft handling of seasonal products.

L'île flottante (floating island), a classic dessert composed of soft meringue islands floating in a sea of custard, was given a fresh update at Le 52 Faubourg Saint-Denis by a dedicated pastry chef who stuffed the meringue mound with diced pineapple, covered it in a crunchy corn tuile, and finished it off with a scoop of lime sorbet. And at Dessance, plated desserts make up the entire menu. Owner Philippe Baranes wanted to distance diners from the notion of dessert as an excessively sweet and heavy end to a meal (and the abiding fear of sugar altogether) by offering a tasting menu around creations that play up the sugars naturally present in fruits and vegetables. Each dessert is made *à la minute*, in an open kitchen that overlooks the dining room, by pastry chef Christophe Boucher, formerly of the refined tables of Le Grand Véfour and Ledoyen. These might be a savory dish with asparagus, wild garlic, sea buckthorn emulsion, and a velouté of warm parmesan; a vegetal platter of Jerusalem artichoke with shiso pineapple sorbet, smoked meringue, and buttermilk; or a hearty dessert of salted caramel *bretzel* with lemon sorbet. For the average Parisian accustomed to the ritual of starter-main-dessert, the idea of an entire meal composed of dessert took some getting used to, but what is well executed and clever ultimately attracts regulars.

Shortly after the doors opened at Le Chateaubriand in April 2006, the media was calling French-Basque chef Iñaki Aizpitarte the city's "It" kitchen star, the self-taught man to watch who was furthering what chef Yves Camdeborde had begun nearly two decades prior. He entered off-the-cuff, market-driven cooking into a creative repertoire that would serve to inspire a young generation of chefs (the so-called Génération Iñaki) and established his restaurant as a destination on a previously uninteresting swath of the 11th arrondissement. Dining at Le Chateaubriand was an adventure; while Aizpitarte's dishes weren't always faultless, they were never dull or predictable. What's more, his spot and those that followed in the same vein did away with the vertiginous pricing structure that had made fine dining inaccessible to many wallets. The ambience may have been casual and informal but the food was as ambitious and creative as ever.

That his restaurant ranked eleventh in the world and number one in France on the annual S. Pellegrino World's 50 Best Restaurants in 2010 gave ballast to the idea that *la cuisine bistronomique*,

OPPOSITE Yard, a neighborhood bistro par excellence, was opened by Franco-American Jane Drotter in 2009 and has had a loyal following ever since. Situated in an old ironwork shop, an Anglo chef diligently turns out sophisticated and hearty dishes from an open kitchen: stewed lamb with fennel and almond-and-cheese sauce and house-made duck raviolis, for example, which pair beautifully with a well-edited natural wine list. The Backyard, just next door, is the more recent addition to the street, serving wine and tapas-style small plates.

which had been transmuted into whatever the chef's whims dictated, was a culinary subset worth respecting and celebrating. The lore of Aizpitarte's earnest auteur cooking keeps visitors lining up for a table and chefs around the world intrigued, some of whom request his talents for guest stints in other kitchens. But an even greater testament to his impact is that he remains just as relevant and creative today as when he first opened his doors. He was truly a harbinger for the ripples of change that would follow. "I think the best thing about Iñaki is that he's…Iñaki: the vanguard. He has a unique and personal talent for mixing it up with products he respects, and he does what he wants, whether people like it or not," food author Adrian Moore told me when I asked him why Aizpitarte's approach remains so special, even today. "He doesn't care, in a good way. Or he cares too much. He's the ultimate culinary outsider and the consummate insider. He's of his time."

It wasn't only Aizpitarte's cerebral cooking style that caused a frenzy in the food world. Emerging at the same moment was chef Daniel Rose, arguably the Frenchest of American chefs. The Chicago native, a resident of France for the last eighteen years, pursued cooking school at the Institut Paul Bocuse in Lyon as a means to stay in France (an excellent window into French culture, he insists) before opening his modern and slightly radical French restaurant, Spring. "I was leaving space for improvisation, which I thought was missing from all of the other experiences I had had in France, but using all the very French techniques to do it," Rose explains, describing part of what made his approach so unique at the time. He joked that with his first iteration of Spring he didn't know what he was doing or how to manage staff so he did it all himself, limiting himself to just enough ingredients to feed the twelve people he had room to accommodate (and they'd all receive the same sequence of dishes for a shockingly low price of thirty-six euros).[12]

Unusual though the format may have been, Rose's approach was lauded by French journalists who reaffirmed that his instincts in the kitchen were right. In his review for *Le Figaro*, journalist Emmanuel Rubin called Spring *"un restaurant qui ressemble à la vie,"* a restaurant that resembled life, by which he meant the energy in the dining room amplified everything he was tasting. It was joyful, generous, beautiful, even a bit dangerous—securing a bank loan, already a challenge in itself due to risk, at a time when chefs weren't deviating from tried-and-true formats was pressure Rubin could sense and appreciate.

Unlike some of the chefs of his generation, Rose has never subscribed to abandoning all signs of the past. In fact, his cooking style is very much anchored in traditional French technique, and that includes Escoffier's famous five base sauces (regulars have come to expect Rose's ginger beurre blanc sauce, served with the fish course) as well as components like wild rabbit civet, *choux farcis* (cabbage rolls), or potage Dubarry.

It could be argued that by virtue of cooking only what is in season and with little advance notice of what ingredients they might receive on a given day, this new generation of chefs has largely done away with the signature dish. This was the topic of my conversation with Jean-Claude Ribaut, one of the most esteemed food authors and columnists for *Le Monde*, on a trip south to Les Baux-de-Provence to celebrate the seventieth anniversary of Baumanière. He recalled the *soupe aux truffes* by Bocuse, the *tarte aux pommes* by Alain Passard, the caviar bar by Anne-Sophie Pic,

The most French of American chefs, Daniel Rose.

"French cooking did not get exported all over the world, and to New York City, where it became very much *the thing*, because it was bad. It happened because it was delicious and the people who were making it were onto something. My job is to figure out what that is and then update it. Through updating it, you're eliminating the things that are less interesting or unnecessary."

—DANIEL ROSE, CHEF-OWNER OF SPRING, LA BOURSE ET LA VIE, AND CHEZ LA VIEILLE

"It's not only about the technique, which we *can* learn in Japan, but we come to France for the culture, the philosophy, and the terroir. We can pursue things further in France. We can't create our own signature in Japan. We're supposed to follow the rules."

—RYUJI "TESHI" TESHIMA, CHEF-OWNER OF PAGES

A refreshing verbena dessert with fresh figs and white chocolate sauce at Pages.

the *gigot d'agneau* by Jean-André Charial, and the *saumon à l'oseille* by Troisgros, each as legendary as the chefs themselves. "Emblematic dishes come with experience," he told me when I asked him what he thought of this modern wave of young chef–driven dining. "They can't impose them."

Rose has managed to create a comforting consistency that still allows for improvisation—the format of the service never deviates from the following sequence: apéritif, first course (usually cold or raw, light and refreshing), second course (usually fish and *gourmande*: cream, butter, concentrated broths enter here), third course (always meat in two preparations), and desserts (always three and always one meant for sharing). "Creativity must be formatted in some way in order to create a functioning restaurant—or at least one where more than three people work," he adds. As for the lack of a signature dish, Rose chalks that up to "an intense bulimia of creativity that marks many young chefs' new mode of operating. Even at Spring, I can identify classics even if they have only been made once! Asparagus with oysters and veal jus vinaigrette, roasted pigeon with almond purée, and sweetbreads with crayfish and lemon preserves."

Both Aizpitarte and Rose had the culinary bona fides to lead such a movement, despite doing so unwittingly. At the time, it was almost unheard of for twentysomething chefs to consider opening their own restaurants. They would first think about becoming a sous-chef and then, as Rose told me, when they were thirty-five, they could either find a sponsor (as in another chef) or have enough legs to obtain a bank loan, but only after spending a solid number of years working for someone else. As the generation of young chefs that has emerged in their wake has shown us, that model has been flipped on its head. They are ambitious and daring in a way that could only have developed from seeing the successes of two relative unknowns.

The arrival of this movement has, in turn, produced an even more present and vocal food-conscious public, unwilling to capitulate to the assembled-defrosted-reheated reality of many corner bistros and brasseries. The standard has changed and puts pressure on everyone to do a better job. Call it hipster or call it conscientious cooking—its impact is real and palpable.

The pendulum hasn't exactly swung back to high gastronomy in Paris, but some of the city's most esteemed, award-winning chefs, like Alain Ducasse and Éric Fréchon, have certainly taken a few cues from the younger generation. In fact, the omnipresent neo-bistro food movement in Paris has done more than carve out a new culinary genre (that has fanned out well beyond the east of the capital and into other French cities like Lille, Bordeaux, and Marseille); it has demonstrated that seasonal, skilled dining needn't be fussy or come with pressed tablecloths and stuffy service.

JAPANESE CHEFS IN THE SPOTLIGHT

Peek behind the curtain (or, in many cases these days, have a front-row seat to an open kitchen) and you'll likely find a brigade of Japanese cooks running the show.

It isn't that unusual. Culturally speaking, there has been a longstanding, mutual admiration between France and Japan, and nowhere is that more evident than in cuisine. The two gastronomic cultures, each strong in its own right, have complemented and even informed one another greatly, and that continues to be true despite all the changes that France's food scene

Septime,

A Vanguard of the Bistronomy Movement

"Bistronomy is the best thing to happen to French cooking in the last twenty years. What we do now is evolve it, keep it moving forward."

—BERTRAND GRÉBAUT, CHEF AND CO-OWNER OF SEPTIME

CONSIDER THE FACTS: A former graphic designer finds the sedentary computer routine (*métro-boulot-dodo*) dull and seeks change. He finds himself, along with his roommate, directing their focus toward an entirely differently world—that of hospitality. He arrives at cooking because, quite matter-of-factly, he loves to eat and drink good wine, and comes from an epicurean family. That attraction drives him to see what kind of future he could have on the other side of the food world. He makes the leap without even knowing if the career will be the right fit for him.

After training at Ferrandi, the French School of Culinary Arts, an internship with the father of veggie-driven cooking, Alain Passard, at L'Arpège, and a first gig chez L'Agapé, the former designer, then twenty-six, scored his first Michelin star. I could only be speaking of Bertrand Grébaut, now thirty-four, who opened his own restaurant, Septime, before the age of thirty and earned another Michelin star in 2014.

Very much a product of the Iñaki generation, Grébaut approached cooking with a profound understanding of bistronomy's pillars and how his values—micro-seasonality, creative cooking, *la naturalité* (naturalness, which puts more emphasis on grains and vegetables than meat)—could come to life and be appreciated within the idiom. His visual arts background has lent an esthetic sensibility to his dishes, which are big on composition and color.

The opening of Septime La Cave (wine bar and cellar) and Clamato, Grébaut's seafood annex next door to Septime, allowed him and his team to have a little more fun and offer menus that appeal to an even wider variety of budgets. A visit to Brooklyn's Maison Premiere, known as much for its seafood small plates as its creative craft cocktails, inspired the format. "In France, we have a strong fish tradition, but brasseries have typically been the only places to eat seafood, and they're no good," he told me. So he took a more modern approach, pairing food with simple, classic cocktails like the Bloody Caesar or Gin & Tonic, both of which have gotten the imprimatur of the city's leading barmen.

Diners who used to come to Paris almost exclusively for a meal at Guy Savoy or at the Plaza Athenée have added Le Chateaubriand, Frenchie, Spring, and Septime to their dining itineraries, which has only helped to legitimize what the chefs behind them have worked so hard to cultivate.

OPPOSITE An amuse-bouche at Septime. Wood, exposed stone, and natural light are key to the pared-back decor.

has experienced. France remains the ultimate destination to acquire the grammar of any culinary education. Japanese chefs come to learn and perfect their craft with fervor and train in the highest culinary temples like Bocuse, Ducasse, L'Astrance, L'Ambroisie, or Hélène Darroze. Many work as sous-chefs in Michelin-starred restaurants, but more than ever they are reinventing bistro codes and developing their singular style in their own spaces.

Some of the Japanese chefs at the city's top affordable tasting tables like Pages or Nakatani chose to carry on the crisp, iron-pressed tablecloth tradition when they opened their own restaurants. Ryuji "Teshi" Teshima of the restaurant Pages, named for the idea of a blank page where anything is possible, says that it's a way to honor his training and the culinary culture that has long inspired him. In his own space, however, he's able to emancipate himself from the Bocuse and Escoffier schools of cooking to explore and establish his own style. "I can cook like that and reproduce it perfectly a thousand times. But it was time to get over it, to stop functioning that way, and create my own cooking." Alongside his wonderfully talented wife Naoko Oishi, who oversees pastry, they've managed to strike the right balance between formal and experimental, executed with tremendous heart.

Others have come to detach themselves from that overly ceremonial, formatted training to explore their creative sides, mixing Japanese and French cuisines. Taku Sekine is one of my favorite examples. After working with Alain Ducasse in Tokyo for three years before transferring to Paris, he realized he wasn't satisfying his growing need to experiment with flavors and concepts. "Grapefruit and veal together? It wouldn't work in high-end restaurants, like a lot of other flavors I was curious to pair together. I realized I had gone as high as I was going to go and that [gastronomic] world was no longer for me." He recalled watching Australian chef James Henry and Parisian chef Romain Tischenko, both bold and daring in the kitchen, emerge and popularize the anti-gastronomy movement. That's when he knew there was a place for him.

In creating Dersou, the restaurant he owns with mixologist Amaury Guyot (of the cocktail bar Sherry Butt), he brought with him high technique and an open mind. And when he travels the world, he takes local cooking classes to continue expanding his range and inform his cooking.

But he doesn't have to be away for long to realize how lucky he is to be running a restaurant in France. "No Annie Bertin, no Dersou!" the chef posted to his Facebook page around the time I was writing this book. It was accompanied by a photo of a box full of twenty-five herbs in vibrant greens and purples. Taku had just received his daily delivery from every chef's dream woman, Annie Bertin, and her organic farm in Brittany and was imagining all that he could create with such a bounty. "And this, one of the reasons to stay in France," he added.

The quality of the products available here, rivaled perhaps only by those that define Californian cuisine, it seems, is all the convincing foreign chefs need to drop everything and bring their talents to France.

OPPOSITE At Dersou, the food and drink are intended to complement each other: raw mackerel, tomatoes, tomato juice, red berries, shiso sprouts, and purslane leaves, paired with a cocktail made of vodka, fino sherry, blue poppy seed, hazelnut syrup, and bergamot syrup.

"I wanted Taku's food to be paired with premium cocktails made with pure ice that we carved ourselves and a fine selection of whiskeys. This kind of place didn't exist in Paris when we opened."

—AMAURY GUYOT, MIXOLOGIST AND CO-OWNER OF DERSOU

ABOVE Chef Taku Sekine and mixologist Amaury Guyot of Dersou, named Best Table of the Year 2016 by *Le Fooding*. OPPOSITE A dish of roasted pigeon, girolle mushrooms, radishes, beetroot, and hibiscus beetroot sauce exemplifies chef Taku Sekine's boundless love and respect for French ingredients and is meant to be paired with a cocktail that complements, never overpowers, the flavors in the food.

RETURN OF THE CLASSIC BISTRO

For those with great affections for more classic French bistro dishes, not to worry, they're making a comeback as well. There are a handful of chefs turning their attention back to heritage dishes, simplifying and sprucing them up with better ingredients. That means establishments with visible roots in the type of fare the great culinary voices like Julia Child, James Beard, and Richard Olney spent much of their careers writing about: artichoke and foie gras salad, pot-au-feu, whole-roasted chicken, and oysters.

"There was all this excitement about the new generation of chefs, and rightfully so, but my impression today is…well, I'm still kind of hungry! I still want those little things that are more old school, comforting, and more French," says Daniel Rose, who opened La Bourse et La Vie in 2015 and Chez la Vieille in 2016, both odes to the classic bistro, to give people that nostalgic experience with substantive dishes that resembled the elevated home cooking they dreamed of having. "This has become rarer for reasons of economics—it takes a long time to cook these dishes in a country with crushing social charges—and fashion: Food television has persuaded thousands of people that cooking is all about creativity, not about cooking the same dishes over and over again with real passion and precision; so traditional bistros have become rarer and rarer," Alexander Lobrano shared with me. Add to that the fact that few places executed the dishes with any care anyway, and they faded for the sake of expediency and spectacle.

Bistros like Rose's are anything but show-offish. They're meant to nourish you like you're at home but with all the advantages of dining out—great service, a lively atmosphere, and soul-warming dishes that serve as a reminder of the beauty in simplicity. They're also a lesson in how the old can merge with the new in magical ways. A few institutions, like Le Bistrot Paul Bert and Yves Camdeborde's Le Comptoir, have been keeping the tradition alive for years, but it is thanks to a handful of newcomers that the classics have gotten a much-needed reboot.

A paragon of the old-fashioned bistro, Le Bon Georges is the passion project of Benoît Duval-Arnould, who left the food and beverage corporate world to revive a dying dining breed. A self-proclaimed *amoureux* of the land and responsibly produced goods, Duval says his obligation as a restaurateur is to defend and promote the local terroir. "I'm not militant about using French ingredients at all costs, but I do want to extend the hard work of farmers and producers. It just so happens we're blessed with the good stuff here."

That emphasis on quality products drove Thierry Dufroux of Bistrot Belhara, tucked into a quiet corner of the 7th arrondissement, to break out onto his own and showcase true French

---

OPPOSITE The exterior and interior decor of Le Bon Georges might appear somewhat caricatural, where totems of the classic bistro such as vintage wood tables, chairs, and stools; chalkboard menus; and old wine, beer, and spirit plaques color the walls like yesteryear, yet there is something resolutely of-the-moment about the space that Benoît Duval-Arnould has created. Dishes run to the lighter side of traditional, but the flagrant difference is in the quality of the ingredients used (eggs from a farm outside of Paris, beef exclusively from Polmard, lamb from Hugo Desnoyer, fish from small boats in Saint-Jean-de-Luz—all of which are visibly marked on the chalkboard menu).

savoir faire. "I was instilled with the utmost respect for products, the right cooking method, and impeccable seasoning. Tradition and modernity aren't incongruous, that's what I wanted to demonstrate with my neighborhood bistro." He only works with seasonal products—asparagus and morel mushrooms in the spring; tomato, basil, and marjoram during the summer; game, cep, and girolle mushrooms in autumn; scallops in winter—for dishes that are light and modern in esthetic but delivered by a staff steeped in the old world. If the batch of revivalist bistros popping up across town are any indication, the old can very much merge with the new.

LE STREET FOOD AND QUALITY FAST FOOD

To anyone reared on an ethnocentric interpretation of Paris as a capital for all-French excellence, the arrival of a plucky American chef from Los Angeles with the sharp determination to give Parisians the burger experience they were missing (and in a truck, no less) sounds like apostasy. But lest you question the appeal of greasy, messy cheeseburgers and crispy French fries to the French, bear in mind that they are the second-greatest consumers of hamburgers in Europe (after the UK and ahead of Germany). The fast food giant McDonald's (or *McDo* in local parlance) has found in them a loyal audience; France is the company's second most profitable market after the United States. Most of their success can be attributed to the way they successfully localized their offering, advertising their use of regional meats and cheeses for a more French interpretation of *le burger* (that is, after years of getting the cold shoulder from the population who disliked the effects of globalization on their country and specifically, all American imports).[13]

With her celebrated burger truck Le Camion Qui Fume and no-nonsense approach to quality hamburgers, Kristin Frederick not only arrested the city's attention but also pioneered a movement that saw hundreds upon hundreds of comfort-fast-street-food entrepreneurs apply for permits to get their own food trucks on the road. She was the ultimate avatar of what was to become gussied-up comfort food in Paris. I will never forget racing to Place de la Madeleine, where her very first truck was stationed at 11:30 A.M. on Fridays, to get my hands on a piece of American nostalgia done right—the next big thing in Paris. This was the same woman I had met one year prior at a food event I was hosting and whom I incredulously questioned if Parisians would take to her concept. "I'm confident they're ready for it," she told me then.

Shortly after her heavily publicized and wildly successful launch, bureaucratic challenges and complicated negotiations on securing permits to station the truck ensued. Restaurateurs and the previous mayoral administration were calling foul, saying that food trucks produced unfair competition to restaurants that pay commercial rent and higher taxes. With her truck off the road for several weeks while the issue was discussed, it seemed like her concept might be short lived. Hurdles were overcome, trucks were added to the fleet, and perseverance became her weapon to ensure trucks and mobile units had a permanent place in the local food landscape. That was five

OPPOSITE It's all tacos, tostadas, and good vibes at Luis Rendon's taqueria, Café Chilango (TOP). The street food queen, Kristin Frederick, in one of her Le Camion Qui Fume trucks (BOTTOM).

"We're only seeing the beginning of a street-food movement that is spreading all over France. People are excited to try new things, so long as the quality remains high."

—KRISTIN FREDERICK,
FOUNDER OF LE CAMION QUI FUME

Hero

THE VIBE MAY BE LAID BACK and fun but the details at Hero are exacting, from plate to design. Selected for her inexperience working in Paris, Swedish designer Jeanette Dalrot was tapped by the Quixotic Projects trio for the interior, and she brought not only fresh eyes but also fresh style to the scene. A large, communal wash basin takes pride of place at the center of the dining room as a clear indicator that forks and knives are in rare supply: Here, guests eat with their hands. Faded pink banquettes, gold sconces, hand-painted wallpaper, handcrafted lamps covered in old book pages, and wall projections, which include clips from Korean music videos, establish a singular

sense of space on the top-floor dining room. On the lower level, American designer-artist Adrian Rubi-Dentzel built a custom wood chef's table, a signature piece meant for a lucky few.

"Did Paris need Korean barbecue? Probably not," said Josh Fontaine about Quixotic Projects's fourth project, Hero. "But we try to bring interesting and fun experiences to the food scene that add value." For the Parisian diner, the menu at Hero may read like a map into the unfamiliar—ssamjang pork buns, yangnyeom chicken (gochujang sauce, sweet and sour garlic sauce, or plain), kimchi, and rice cakes—but Korean comfort food has found a willing audience.

years ago, and today, her *petit empire* has expanded to four trucks, one boat, one physical burger restaurant, and ancillary businesses like Huabu, her American take on Chinese food, and the gourmet popcorn she supplies to movie theaters.

She was the catalyst not only for a new format and style of no-frills, simple-but-delicious dining but also for a whole new culinary subculture. For a time, traditionalists perceived every new opening or development as a sign that this new generation of food entrepreneur was imposing change where there needn't be any. But the nomadic movement took on a life of its own, and detractors were hushed as more businesses emerged over the next five years with varied focuses—Breton crêpes, falafel, empanadas, tacos, dim sum, vegan hot dogs, gourmet kebabs, bao buns, bánh mì sandwiches, fish and chips, Thai noodles, Korean fried chicken, even Texas barbecue—and a more laissez-faire approach to food. It didn't have to be American comforts, though that was the direction many of the places pursued initially; it just had to be simple and good.

But arriving at this point wasn't an easy road. The city's arcane system for securing permits and prohibitively expensive labor laws struck a discordant note among food entrepreneurs. Some have bravely powered through the bureaucracy to spark change in the food scene, with Frederick as their tireless locomotive. For several years, she has served as the president of Street Food en Mouvement, an organization that bridges the broader food industry and quality street food entrepreneurs and supports the development of such new businesses, driving change through fierce campaigning and negotiations with the city. As evidence of her success: Fifty-six permanent parking permits are now available, spread primarily across eastern and western arrondissements where there was a dearth of quality fast-food options. The inherent cost to such licenses in addition to the costs of maintaining and storing a truck may not make the format a sustainable option, but there is no doubting its utility in testing the market nor its power as a launchpad for new businesses.

Behind most of these street-food success stories, including Frederick's, was a legion of killjoys. "It will never work!" or "You'll never be able to get Parisians to eat that!" and the common "You left your job to do what?!" went the refrain. But a little bit of moxie was all it took to rise to the challenge. Mexican chef Luis Rendon, co-owner of Café Chilango, a taco, tostadas, and coffee bar in the 11th arrondissement, first confronted the alarmists when he entered the kitchens of Candelaria, the city's first taqueria and clandestine cocktail bar. When people told him and the trio of brains behind the project (Quixotic Projects founders Josh Fontaine, Carina Soto Velasquez, and Adam Tsou) that tacos and tostadas would never appeal to French tastes, they said, "Look at all the Tex-Mex chains and packaged burrito mixes! They're ready for someone to expose them to the real thing." And they were right. They focused on authenticity and quality and shunned any and all caricatures of Mexican culture. "Nothing was dumbed down," says Fontaine, an East Coaster who grew up eating Mexican food. And for those who question the value of eating Mexican food in Paris, Fontaine insists that Candelaria, now a veritable institution, wasn't created for tourists. It was created for Parisians.

For other chefs, their ventures filled gaps in the market. Chef Yoni Saada was accustomed to spending his summers during childhood in the South of France, where the Pan-bagnat sandwich—composed of *pain de campagne*, or white bread, and the fixings of a traditional Salade

niçoise—was a symbolic lunchtime staple (it originated in Nice). After he finished cooking school, he spent two years working in Aix-en-Provence and made frequent trips to Chez Michel in Cassis to eat the best Pan-bagnat in the region (until, sadly, the institution shuttered). Once he settled in Paris, he went on the hunt for a sandwich that would approximate its quality and high nostalgia quotient but found nothing of note. Bagnard, then, is Saada's homage to his childhood street-food favorite, using top-shelf ingredients. The DNA of the concept, says Saada, can be found in the carefully selected ingredients (tuna, anchovies, and sardines by Ortiz; olives and olive oil by the small producer Kalios; fresh lettuce and vegetables; and bread especially conceived for the sandwich) and a rollicking space that feels like a cross between laid-back southern France and lively Tel Aviv, Saada's home away from home.

"The Lulu is the original Niçois Pan-bagnat save for one difference: Our bread is made from semi–whole wheat flour, olive oil, and Guérande sea salt versus the traditional bread, which is usually white," says Saada. "White bread is too crumbly, so in order for the whole sandwich not to break apart once all the ingredients are in, it's extremely thick. To me, it felt like you were eating only bread! My recipe was created to strike the right balance." The bread is supplied by Émile & Jules, artisanal bakers located in Grosrouvre, on the edge of the Rambouillet forest about an hour outside of Paris. The rationale behind Saada's business is simple: "Street food shouldn't be seen as low quality just because it's affordable. My credo? Eat well for little."

With more international influence and greater exposure to other cultures, expectations have changed. Is there a place for the checkered-tableclothed tables, steak frites, and wicker chairs? Absolutely. Are those shifting desires an intimation of the end of, on the other end of the spectrum, the high gastronomic temples vying for Michelin praise? *Pas du tout.* There is, in fact, room for more than two food categories, and in the time since Kristin Frederick rolled into town touting the merits of good old-fashioned burgers, the dining categories have effectively blurred.

Even the elite stratum of the culinary world became curious, weaving more "low-brow" elements into their cooking as a nod to a new epoch where fast-and-good bites appeal to all. It's why at chef Gregory Marchand's Frenchie or Jean-François Piège's Clover or Braden Perkins's Verjus, you may find dishes that incorporate condiments, spices, and ingredients that were once largely considered less noble and refined. To wit: ketchup, barbecue sauce, kimchi, curry, and bacon. At Ellsworth, the second restaurant from Braden Perkins and Laura Adrian, diners rave about the potato skins topped

---

OPPOSITE As soon as hot dogs made their way onto menus around town, Coralie Jouhier and Daqui Gomis, a young vegan couple, knew that there was opportunity to adapt them for vegetarians and vegans. They opened Le Tricycle and their concept began just as it sounds—a tricycle food cart that would roll into events and street-food festivals. In 2015, they took it a step further and opened a brick-and-mortar restaurant on rue du Paradis in a hip corner of the 10th arrondissement with a menu dedicated to various vegetarian and vegan hot dogs, soups, salads, and desserts, playing up flavors native to the French islands, such as Martinique, where Jouhier used to live (think: plantains). They offer a flavorful departure from what most Parisians assume to be true about vegetarian and vegan fare— that it is bland and uninteresting—and have successfully won over vegetarians and carnivores alike.

"Pierre doesn't just cook for us, he feeds us. There's a huge difference."

—WENDY LYN, FOOD WRITER AND TOUR GUIDE

"The Lulu," the original Niçois Pan-bagnat with bread made from semi–whole wheat flour, olive oil, and Guérande sea salt instead of the traditional bread, which is usually white.

with melted Tomme cheese, paprika, and crunchy chicken skin or corn dogs stuffed with house-made rabbit sausage. Philippe Excoffier, the former longtime chef for the American ambassador in Paris, created a lobster and avocado burger for the embassy's international staff after observing the ever-shifting tastes among Parisians. It's now a permanent fixture of his menu at his namesake bistro in the 7th arrondissement. That many awarded, gastronomic chefs have opened quality fast-food concepts and even more accessible wine bars was a powerful rejoinder to their buttoned-up training. Tradition, technique, and heart remain at the source of all this food. It's merely the form that has changed.

LA CUISINE HEALTHY

I arrived in Paris like many American twentysomethings: curious to eat everything but extremely diet conscious. I was a chronic exerciser and felt the need to stay active even more when I realized how frequently I was giving in to temptation—chocolate, bread, and pastries in copious quantities, sometimes twice daily.

But in ten years, my food values have softened. I attribute that to life with a Frenchman who rules nothing out but consumes everything *en modération*. And as the bon vivant chocolatier Jacques Genin reminded me as we were headfirst into bottomless mugs of his decadent hot chocolate, "Life is just too damn short, *ma puce*. When things are made well, there's no reason for regret."

While I don't give a hard-line refusal to many things, I do stay away from processed foods and anything that doesn't bring pleasure and joy (another of M. Genin's abiding principles). In doing so, I've made more room for umami joys like *demi-sel* butter, luscious dark chocolate, well-cooked fish and meat, and quality coffee. More than ever, Parisians are operating under the same philosophy, focusing their attention more and more on *where* and *how* their food is sourced. *Green, cuisine healthy, détox, bio, sans gluten, veggie*—these food buzzwords have become fixtures of the local vernacular, coaxed along by investigative reports on television, essays in women's lifestyle magazines, and food publications that cover health-conscious trends from abroad, including the movements led by influential personalities like Gwyneth Paltrow and her website Goop. There exists an idealized notion that the French diet is naturally and culturally sounder than that of the rest of the world and that French women, in particular, do not gain weight (and therefore, shouldn't need to embrace any of these clean-eating words). The reality is that one in ten people are obese and 40 percent are overweight.[14] At various points since I've lived and worked in Paris, I have known French women who smoked cigarettes and chain-chugged diet soda to silence their appetites, skipped meals, and adhered to detoxing cures whenever they overindulged. *Minceur* (slimness) tips and tricks have been propagated in French women's magazines since long before food fads and restrictive lifestyle diets gained popularity, which indicated to me early on that the message around *French Women Don't Get Fat* was mostly myth.

The upside to a greater concern over the types of food consumed and where it comes from is greater openness to and interest in meals less reliant on meat. The days of vegetarianism (or worse,

OPPOSITE A basket of purple radishes at L'Épicerie Végétale, a produce shop with extraordinary fruits and vegetables grown around Paris.

Q&A

THOMAS ABRAMOWICZ, THE BEAST

A FRENCHMAN WHO DOES Texas barbecue as good as, if not better than, the Americans? It's true! For the four years that Thomas Abramowicz worked in New York City, he lived with a roommate who hailed from Fort Worth, Texas, who exposed him to the storied tradition of barbecue, which had nary a presence in France. As he approached thirty with professional uncertainty and a pressing itch for change, the culture around barbecue looked more and more appealing. And in what is becoming a common tale of shifting from corporate to craft, he left his stable job in marketing within the LVMH group to bring barbecue to Paris—with all the right equipment, top-shelf meats, and a passion that soars.

What made you so sure that Parisians would be ready for barbecue?

We are meat eaters here in France, so in that respect, I knew it would be a fit. It's just that nobody knew this way of cooking. The idea had been marinating in my head for seven years, and when I realized that no one had attempted to do barbecue in the city during that time, I knew I needed to do it. I was also confident that Parisians would be ready for it because they like quality meats. The way of thinking

OPPOSITE Thomas Abramowicz, founder of The Beast, the capital's first and best Texas barbecue restaurant.

is to eat less but better. Climb up the ladders of the production chain and you can easily trace the ingredients back to the farmer in two seconds because everything is labeled and transparent. And, the quality speaks for itself!

How did you make the transition into barbecue after realizing the corporate track was no longer for you?

I first came back to Paris and thought about my next move. I'd need to do a whole lot of research if I was going to do it right. It all sort of began with the book *The Prophets of Smoked Meat* by Daniel Vaughn, the barbecue columnist for *Texas Monthly*. I happened to meet him at an event just weeks after buying his book and explained what I wanted to do in Paris. I asked for his advice and he introduced me to Wayne Mueller, the owner of Louie Mueller Barbecue, at the Big Apple Barbecue Block Party. Wayne offered to train me, so three months later, I was in Tyler, Texas, to learn the basics with his team. He didn't have anything to gain from our partnership but he was kind enough to welcome me into his kitchen, and I learned everything I know today. He is very much my mentor.

How easy was it to source the equipment and ingredients for The Beast?

While I was in Texas, I went to this little tiny town called Mesquite in the suburbs of

Dallas. That happens to be where J&R, the best commercial manufacturer for barbecue smokers, has its headquarters. They're like the Rolls-Royce of smokers! I knew that if I wanted to do it right, I needed the right equipment. So I spent ten days in their factory working on the smoking unit to learn how to operate it, smoking briskets for the first time in my life, on my own. I then had a smoker custom-built for me (wood only); it took three months to produce and three months to ship to Paris. For ingredients, I basically did a Tour de France to visit farmers and butchers across the country to find the right cuts for the perfect marbling. I knew I wouldn't have much trouble finding excellent pork and poultry, but we don't have brisket in France so that was tougher. Most of the farmers I met didn't even know what it was! That's when I realized I couldn't source it in France. The meats are too lean, which are perfect for grilling but not for twenty hours of smoking. Instead, I work with a butcher who imports Black Angus from the US, the same brand as Franklin, which is the mecca of barbecue in Austin.

In what ways did you incorporate French elements into the business?

I may not be an American citizen but my heart is still there. I wanted The Beast to have the double culture I feel I have. Even though we do traditional Texas barbecue, which means we only do dry rubs (the barbecue sauce is homemade, but it's served on the side, never

covering the meats like with Memphis or Kansas City barbecue), I mostly work with craftsmen from France. The oak tables are made by hand by a carpenter in Montreuil, and the table legs are vintage and typical of French bistros. We only serve craft beers from France (save for the collaboration between a craft brewery in the north of France and Jester King, one of the best microbreweries in Austin), and our beer on tap is made in Montreuil especially for us by the Franco-American duo behind the local brewery Deck & Donohue. My wines are French and natural, produced with respect for the environment. We also challenge ourselves by doing barbecue twists on French recipes as weekly specials: bourbon-soaked magret de canard, smoked gratin Dauphinois, and duck confit Parmentier.

So was it as challenging to open your business in France as the myth suggests?

Before, I'd say the French didn't have the means or the courage to pursue certain projects. Now, when they see someone succeeding, it makes them want to do it too. It's hard; we have a lot of taxes and regulation barriers, but it's possible. And you need good examples to motivate you. I saw the team from [the cocktail bar] Le Mary Celeste booming and they made me believe I could do it. And I'm thankful for that because they showed me that you can succeed in France when you're dedicated to your job and do things with passion.

OPPOSITE The best of Texas barbecue in Paris at The Beast, featuring the Texas trifecta: brisket, beef ribs, and beef sausage with excellent sides and craft beer.

"I teach the foundations of Texas barbecue with the hopes that my trainees will carry on the tradition. But it's up to them to make it their own. Thomas has adapted the style into a French setting superbly and successfully. I couldn't be prouder!"

—WAYNE MUELLER, OWNER OF JAMES BEARD AWARD–WINNING LOUIE MUELLER BARBECUE

veganism) eliciting a groan and an eye roll among the French appear to be gone. Now, bookstore shelves are lined with beautifully designed and enticing reads about healthier lifestyles, beginning with vegetables and ending with ancient grains.

Access to information, trends, studies, and ways of living in other countries has deeply informed Parisian habits. You can't change their almost genetic predisposition to carbing, but Parisians are open to new things, once they see they can be done well. Does that mean they don't fall prey to trendy diets and fads? Absolutely not. They've latched onto the same juicing, organic, and natural movements that have been sprouting the world over. The difference between the way in which Parisians now approach veggie-centric diets and the way most Americans do is that they come from an intrinsically more balanced background with food. It's less radical (cut out everything!), more sound (give it a try; learn something new).

But those are more recent factors. Veggie-vegan-juice-based eating gained momentum in Paris, in fact, long before the media labeled it a new food category and certainly before it was considered fashionable. Sol Semilla, an organic vegan canteen a stone's throw from the Canal Saint-Martin, opened its doors in 2007 touting the benefits of grains, beans, and superfoods to overall health. When I first stumbled upon it shortly after moving to Paris, I remember asking my husband why there weren't more places like it. "It's for hippies! This isn't California," he told me. And while I laughed, I knew that was the general attitude at the time (flash-forward ten years later, and it was *he* who reserved Sol Semilla for a dinner date with friends). Whether for ethical, wellness, or economic reasons, meatless, nutrient-rich, and plant-heavy diets were considered marginal, a preoccupation of health quacks who didn't know what they were missing by eschewing bacon.

It was thanks to New Yorker Marc Grossman, who opened Bob's Juice Bar, that Parisians would begin their fascination with clean living. Grossman, a filmmaker married to a Frenchwoman, was living on the rue Lucien-Sampaix in the 10th arrondissement long before it began gentrifying. It was a combination of expat nostalgia and impulse that led him to put aside the film he was writing and start his own business. "I didn't have any real cooking or restaurant experience. This whole thing started as just a general thought," he told me over lunch at Bob's Bake Shop. "There was a lack of health food and a lack of juice bars specifically. And I felt that would be appealing and unlike anything the city had seen. And then, one day, I discovered the space directly across the street from my apartment was for rent." A week later, he signed the contract and got to work.

With filtered and mixed juices, salads, homemade bagel sandwiches, matcha cookies, and muffins, his tiny juice bar remains a neighborhood institution and the project that kick-started a whole new career. Bob's Kitchen, a pescetarian canteen in the 3rd arrondissement, followed suit with a larger kitchen space that allowed him and his French business partner Amaury De Veyrac to produce more variety—futomaki, veggie stews, nutrient-rich salads, teas, and, of course, juices. With sit-down service and more seating, Bob's Kitchen quickly amassed a loyal following of locals and fashionable out-of-towners (a handful of celebrities and fashion industry personalities have been known to drop by for a bite) and business hasn't slowed since.

Boutique yam'Tcha

MICHELIN-STARRED CHEF Adeline Grattard is best known for her spontaneous and instinctive Franco-Chinese cuisine at yam'Tcha, a beloved tasting table that she has run with her husband Chiwah Chan since 2009. Here, she blends techniques and flavors from both cultures' culinary traditions with a distinct predilection for the wok, her tool of choice. At her tea salon and steamed-bun offshoot, simply called Boutique yam'Tcha, her team serves up buns *à la minute* in a variety of combinations: Basque pork, eggplant and Laguiole cheese, Amarena cherry, caramelized onion, or curry and Stilton.

Bob's Bake Shop
& Juice Bar

THE 10TH ARRONDISSEMENT pint-sized
shop started by Marc Grossman stoked
an interest in fresh and cold-pressed juices
that Parisians didn't even know they had.
Marc Grossman (pictured above) kneads the
dough for his New York–style bagels, made
fresh daily at Bob's Bake Shop. At right, daily
soups and sandwiches with well-sourced
ingredients and homemade breads, buns,
and bagels at Bob's Bake Shop.

Bob's Bake Shop, a deli-diner in the 18th arrondissement's Halle Pajol, an eco-sustainable structure in a rehabilitated section of the neighborhood, expanded both concepts and added a catering arm to the business. Soups, salads, make-your-own sandwiches, juices, craft coffee, craft beer, and some of the city's best Anglo-inspired cakes and tarts make up the menu that draws people in from all corners of town. And while Parisians have pegged his establishments as *healthy* joints, he insists that's an improper classification. "We have healthy options, that's true, but we've always had cookies and muffins. The French just want to put everything in a clear-cut box!"

Pushing vegetable-driven eating around the same time was Rose Bakery, an English organic canteen with outposts in London, Paris, New York City, and Seoul. For years, it was the only place to get a big, fat plate of vegetables, seasonal salads, and organic cakes. It laid the blueprint for health-minded eateries that would launch years later—Nanashi, Café Pinson, Le Potager du Marais, Soul Kitchen, Le Tricycle, and La Guinguette d'Angèle. Slowly, meatless cuisine has become not only more common but also widely accepted. Some restaurants have opted to introduce it gradually, like at Dune in the 11th arrondissement, which began by making the Tuesday menu entirely vegan. And if you dine at Alain Ducasse au Plaza Athénée, you'll see that grains and vegetables have usurped the space on the plate once reserved for meat.

Health food or not, Grossman's small juice bar and the spate of Anglo-inspired canteens and juiceries that followed were instrumental in shifting the local perception of imported concepts. That and the fact that they emerged as various food scares and scandals were forcing people to question the probity of their food purveyors. A sharpened distrust of big agribusiness led the public to think long and hard about what they put into their bodies, food author and blogger Clotilde Dusoulier notes. "I think it has finally dawned on people, and I would say it's a fairly recent realization, that French big food does not have the consumers' best interest at heart." So people started paying attention and asking more questions. A rise in co-ops like La Ruche Qui Dit Oui!, which directly connects consumers and farmers, who are tasked with bringing their produce to various points of sale across town, are further signs, she says, that the shape of the demand is shifting. "A certain layer of society is willing to make efforts and expend energy to obtain really high-quality ingredients," and that's likely to continue.

LE SANS-GLUTEN AND LE CHOUX KALE

What seemed to the rest of the world to be an obsession born and bred in America has found disciples across the Atlantic. That's right, *sans gluten* is a buzzword on heavy rotation, and for good reason. A handful of gluten-free bakeries and eateries have convinced locals that forgoing gluten doesn't have to mean the end of indulgence. More importantly, they are godsends for gluten-intolerant travelers who can now happily partake in the Parisian pastry experience.

The bakery Helmut Newcake and the restaurant Noglu got locals talking about gluten, partly because both owners suffer from celiac disease, but it was Chambelland bakery and canteen that secured *le sans gluten* a permanent place in the Parisian food lexicon. Behind the rows of glistening tarts and hefty breads is baker-biologist Thomas Teffri-Chambelland and a few French firsts: the first organic *and* gluten-free bakery and the first to use rice flour sourced from the baker's own mill in the Alpes-de-Haute-Provence. A decade of recipe experimentation certainly paid off as lines snake around the corner for *Chambellines*, narrow loaves in sweet or savory varieties, and a medley of seasonal desserts, made fresh daily. Teffri-Chambelland's grainy breads have even found their way onto the tables of Alain Ducasse au Plaza Athénée. Gluten or no gluten, I go weekly because their breads and cakes are well-made and delicious.

Then came the arrival of kale. The healthy leafy green has historically existed in France but fell into neglect following World War II due to its association with wartime deprivation. It wasn't until the American expat Kristen Beddard, author of *Bonjour Kale: A Memoir of Paris, Love, and Recipes* and the creator of the Kale Project, went to great lengths to raise awareness of it that it came back into favor and found a new market.

A lifelong kale consumer, Beddard was baffled by its absence at French farmers' markets when she moved to Paris in 2011 and quickly began toying with the idea of advocating for it in Paris. She naturally leaned on its qualities as a superfood, the common positioning in America, and set off to create a website that would highlight its health benefits, the ways in which it could be used in cooking, and, once she managed to convince farmers to grow it, where to find it across the capital. A quick chat with a French friend would point her in a new direction. "The concept of a superfood means nothings to us, he told me, because we don't think of food in that way. So that was key in helping me shape the way I talked about kale from then on," Beddard says. *Bringing the healthiest vegetable to Paris* wasn't the right messaging because the French already eat a variety of vegetables; they don't need the healthiest of them all. They get the nutrients they need from lettuce, peppers, beets, spinach, and more. "Americans position everything in terms of how something can save us, and the French don't think that way."

Instead, the discourse around kale became *le légume oublié*, the forgotten vegetable, and Beddard's contribution was that she was bringing something back to their culture that already existed. That resonated more broadly and not only with local media. Food industry folk, from well-known produce vendors like Joël Thiébault to award-winning chefs like Alain Passard, were excited to grow and cook it, and soon, healthy fast food joints and institutions like Ladurée were angling for her keen insights and farmer contacts. Today, it isn't unusual to find kale at most open-air markets and on fine restaurant menus.

The trend in lighter and fresher food in a neo-bistro setting trickled into fast-casual spots, where varied vegetables, including the *légumes oubliés*, have taken pride of place on menus. Raw, roasted, braised, and steamed, parsnips, sunchokes, and kale are more sought after than ever before, including at select Auchan and Monoprix supermarkets (outside Paris as well), open-air markets, and the new generation of gourmet greengrocers à la Dean & DeLuca, like La Maison Plisson, Causses, L'Épicerie Végétale, and Papa Sapiens. Eating these foods is as much a lifestyle choice as a health consideration, but the positive outcome is a population that makes more informed choices, a shift that isn't for naught.

Maison Plisson

PARIS'S ANSWER TO DEAN & DELUCA—half gourmet food emporium, half bakery-restaurant, open daily. Delphine Plisson left the world of fashion to follow her appetite. In this case, it was an appetite for fresh produce, artisanal products, and the people who produce them. Inspired by New York's Dean & DeLuca, she sought to create a similar culinary emporium for Paris, a mix of greengrocer and café with a selection of exclusively artisanal items that reduce waste (and none of the brands you might find in a supermarket). Inside, you'll find some three thousand products, sweet and savory, 80 percent of which are French, and leading food artisans at the helm of cheese, meat, and produce counters. The café menu is overseen by one of the city's top chefs, Bruno Doucet, and the luscious baked goods are from the talented team at Liberté, Benoît Castel's Canal Saint-Martin bakery. And to satisfy the expectation for transparent sourcing, the name and a short biography of each artisan is displayed alongside their products, a human touch that has also popped up at other gourmet grocers like Papa Sapiens and Causses.

The Green Guardians at
L'Épicerie Végétale

> "When things are good and beautiful,
> that's where the magic happens."
>
> —ZOÉ KOVACS, CO-FOUNDER OF L'ÉPICERIE VÉGÉTALE

BEFORE THIS BOHEMIAN produce Eden set up shop, the rue de la Fontaine au Roi was merely a means of cutting over from avenue Parmentier to the rue Saint-Maur—a desolate road with few redeeming qualities. Since 2015, L'Épicerie Végétale has not only brought color and life to the street but also fostered a deeper sense of community in the neighborhood. Parisians from across the city stand rapt before crates brimming with beautiful fruits and vegetables sourced primarily from Île-de-France (the Paris region) producers and come for rare varieties of products previously unknown (like green Sicilian Satsuma). Even local chefs have begun sourcing their ingredients here. With their homespun, rustic veggie den, owners Zoé Kovacs and Guillaume Servet have upended the idea of vegetables and veggie-driven eating as a trend; it's life, nature, back to the land. As evidenced by the flood of customers filling the store, the habit of frequenting markets and small producers has been revived beautifully.

Their insouciant and hyperactive disposition (think: a madcap Lucille Ball duo) makes me think of young children who spend hours gathering seashells and other detritus from the sea to share with their families, excitedly shouting, "Look what I found!" There is innocence to their love for their adopted trade, a love that emerged out of intense saturation with meaningless consumerism. As trained photographers, they regularly worked on photo shoots for global consumer brands. It certainly paid the bills but left them feeling empty. In their free time, they volunteered at a greengrocer in the 10th arrondissement, helping the owner make trips to visit farmers in the region. It's because of this experience that they realized they were meant to suss out the best of the Île-de-France bounty.

OPPOSITE Zoé Kovacs and Guillaume Servet, the duo behind the beautiful produce and flower eden, L'Épicerie Végétale. Their shop was one of several that brought new life to a sleepy, ill-trafficked street in the 11th arrondissement.

IN SEARCH OF BETTER BREAD

And then there's bread, the très sacrosanct staple that has undergone its own mini revolution. It should come as no surprise that bread is a cultural symbol inextricably connected to mealtime: tartines with butter and jam at breakfast, baguette sandwiches or wedges of pain de campagne with lunch, and hearty loaves for dinner to accompany the inevitable slice (or plate) of cheese. And yet what may surprise you is that, up until the neo-bistro boom, much of what occupied prime real estate on restaurant tables was insipid, hard-verging-on-stale, and uninspired. Even as early as 1983, longtime expatriate and journalist Patricia Wells wrote in the *New York Times* that the baguette (to call out the most iconic French favorite) was undergoing a period of reevaluation after declining in quality. "The French are well aware that the bread that's revered around the world is not what it used to be…. Bakers are in a hurry, they're not concerned about quality and, often, neither are their customers. In fact, one Paris baker admitted that he mixed in day-old frozen baguettes with fresh ones and didn't see any need to inform customers. (It's legal to freeze bread, as long as consumers are informed.)"[15]

And that's only one of several, surprisingly legal tricks that bakers employed to cut production time. Bread production as a whole has suffered greatly from industrialization, mechanization, and the use of additives and frozen dough. Even bakeries considered *artisan*, which means their bread is kneaded, shaped, and baked on the premises, may still be using low-quality flours. Since the majority of restaurants procured (and largely still procure) their bread from neighborhood bakeries, the impact was widespread.

Then there are the ways in which bread has been served in restaurants—almost always as a complimentary item in the dining experience. Save for a short-lived attempt in the early 2000s by a handful of restaurant owners to charge for bread, there has been little incentive to offer anything special, particularly when quality rhymes with costly.

Further minimizing its role at the table are lifestyle shifts like increasingly busy work schedules that lead to eating on the go or skipping meals and carbohydrate-shunning diets that have vilified bread. Only 10 percent of the French population consumes bread at each meal for a total of 130 grams per day, five times less than in 1900.[16] Bread has to compete with presliced packaged bread

---

OPPOSITE Basking in the virtuous glow of a gluten-free and almost entirely plant-based diet, Angèle Ferreux-Maeght smiles brightly for the curious Parisians who drop by La Guinguette d'Angèle, her adorable sliver of a "detox" counter, to pick up their lunch provisions. Her stints in San Francisco (notably at an organic produce stand in the Ferry Building) and Australia, both universal hubs of green living, inspired her path toward naturopathy. Back in Paris, she got her start catering fashion shows and events where the most common request was "vegan and gluten-free" nibbles. It was a tall order at first, given that most Parisians were only just beginning to understand vegetarianism and veganism. Now with a bestselling book behind her, *Délicieusement Green*, she says the interest goes well beyond trend. "Those who try out this sort of eating truly feel a difference: more energy and improved wellness overall. Its message is simple and will continue long after me: Eat healthy, with a conscious mind, and full of joie de vivre!"

from the supermarket and individually wrapped processed cakes and brioches, which gained steam as the quality of bread declined. Pitted against growing dietary concerns like gluten allergies or the idea that bread inherently causes weight gain, the industry has had even greater challenges to overcome.

L'Observatoire du Pain (the Bread Observatory), the bakers' lobby, has made it their mission to promote bread and the craft of bread making in France as a cultural pillar that bridges generations. If they sound familiar it may be because you caught wind of their heavily advertised campaign from 2013, "*Coucou, tu as pris le pain?*" ("Hi there, did you pick up the bread?"), a slogan inspired by the California Milk Processor Board's "Got Milk?" promotion. The campaign was meant to pull on heartstrings as much as it was meant to educate about bread's nutritional properties and artisanal production: What could be more thoughtful than picking up fresh bread from the bakery on the way home from work? The lobby emphasized bread's social value.

Their posters and branding were everywhere for the better part of a year, but did it really have a tangible impact on consumption habits? The jury's out. I'd wager that what really helped raise awareness around artisanal practices and improve the quality of the bread served in restaurants was the same thing driving broader changes in food—a desire for transparency and passionate people in the kitchen.

With the restaurant refresh in Paris came a new role for bread. The national staple moved from the sidelines of the meal to become an equally important companion to any dish. Chefs who opted not to make their own (usually sourdough loaves) called on the help of a small but impressive brigade of artisanal bakers like Lionel Poilâne, Jean-Luc Poujauran, Thierry Breton (chef-restaurateur), Dominique Saibron, Gontran Cherrier, Émile and Jules Winocour, Thomas Teffri-Chambelland (of the gluten-free maison Chambelland), Rodolphe Landemaine, and Christophe Vasseur, whose rustic flatbread (the Pain des Amis) graces a wide spectrum of tables from the triple-Michelin-starred Alain Ducasse restaurants in the Plaza Athénée and Le Meurice luxury hotels to Holybelly, the coffee and brunch institution.

Vasseur's arrival into the baking world wasn't preordained. In fact, he had a successful career in fashion sales before he reached saturation and redirected his focus to pursue a labor-intensive, childhood dream that would hold greater meaning in his life: becoming an *artisan boulanger*. "The turning point for me was during a presentation of a new collection of fashion accessories before a group of buyers from a department store. I wanted to say to them 'come with me, let's get a coffee at the corner café and talk about the important things that can help change our world!' These products I'm selling are unimportant. They wear their name perfectly: They're just accessories." At thirty, he traded his suit and tie for an apron and ambitiously opened Du Pain et Des Idées in the 10th arrondissement, one block from the Canal Saint-Martin. He didn't just become any baker but rather one of the city's leading talents, recognized in 2008 as the best baker in the city by the gourmet magazine *Gault & Millau*. Reconnecting with time-honored (and century-old) baking methods and traditions has, in fact, become the new modern, and Vasseur is unrelenting when it comes to

---

OPPOSITE Christophe Vasseur's artisanal bakery Du Pain et des Idées in the 10th arrondissement.

respecting the industry's roots. In a bakery (and protected monument) dating back to 1889, he works almost exclusively with sourdough for his breads and devotes much of his time to producing baguettes with naturally strong flavor (it takes him seven hours to make them, versus two hours in most bakeries).

If the lines that snake around the corner of his shop every day are any indication, Vasseur's efforts have struck a chord, and not only with locals; visitors excitedly cross the city for a taste of his extraordinary puff pastries like the chocolate-pistachio escargot (my favorite) or the *chausson aux pommes*, as well as his signature breads. In all the years I've lived in Paris, I've never once seen the shop empty, no matter the circumstances, and that's a real testament to the quality of his products. "I'm touched by my bakery's popularity. I never could have imagined that it would make people so happy! But I suppose that's what happens when we do the work we're passionate about."

LOOKING FORWARD

Health food, street food, the emergence of foreign chefs, and a greater emphasis on artisanal cooking and baking methods reveal how much the food scene truly is evolving. At the inaugural Taste of Paris event held in May 2015 underneath the warmth of the glass canopy of the Grand Palais, Alain Ducasse—a household name well beyond France—jettisoned any and all outdated attitudes about what cuisine in Paris is when he said, "French cuisine has never been this diverse, varied, and extraordinarily or magnificently represented by chefs from so many generations, old and new." We may not have an unobstructed view of how things will play out in the city's dining future, but the wheels of change are indeed in motion.

/

OPPOSITE Jane Drotter's Yard is the neighborhood bistro par excellence and a personal favorite in the 11th arrondissement.

PARISIAN PERSPECTIVE

ELODIE FAGAN, 30

FOOD AND TECH WRITER AND PUBLICIST FOR *LE RECHO*, REFUGEE FOOD TRUCK

Do you feel like Paris is changing?

Definitely, but it is much slower than in other big cities, probably due to the fact that we're risk-averse people (look at all that security we have, from the health care system to our unemployment policies) and tend to look to the past a lot. But young French people have never traveled as much as they do now, and they are starting to look for novelty. Along with international influences in food, design, fashion, came a wave of foreigners who decided to give the capital some edge with concepts seen in Brooklyn, Berlin, Melbourne, and beyond. It created a natural competition for new, exciting places and raised the standards significantly. Look at the food scene: There's been a huge renewal of Paris's most emblematic cuisine, that of the bistro. With that came the rise of city guides [online itineraries geared toward locals and tourists alike], which created a culture of "destinations." I call it the MyLittleParis.com effect, where everyone is always looking for the brand new tapas bar, cocktail joint, or trendy spot. People have a list of *destinations* to see and visit. It may sound very common, but French people are creatures of habit. They don't usually go out of their way to try new things; they stick to what's familiar. So this reflects a big change in attitude and behavior!

Why is it such an exciting time to live and visit Paris now?

We're finally getting both exciting new ideas and a very high level of execution. Although we haven't always been good at innovating (when you look at the past fifteen years, most trends came from Scandinavia, America, even Belgium), we're extremely talented at interpreting and we're very critical of the execution. We make things our own.

You love exploring the food scene. What do you think has changed the most?

We've become more curious and demanding. Historically, we've had a reputation as having very high standards. Somehow along the way, we lost touch with that. It became a privilege for a certain elite. Until somewhat recently, most brasseries and restaurants were serving ready-made food, and you couldn't just walk into any brasserie expecting a decent entrecôte frites. The only solid food was to be found in high-end restaurants. But since we've opened to the world a little more, we've accepted the idea that a great dining experience should be available for any kind of budget.

the new
COFFEE

"Coffee is a lot more than just a drink;
it's something happening."

—GERTRUDE STEIN

I picked up a coffee habit in Paris much in the way that many young, impressionable study abroad students pick up smoking—it was a question of exposure and environment. Shortly after arriving in Paris in 2006, I began dating a Frenchman (now my husband of eight years) who formally introduced me to the city's hallowed café culture. Our early dates revolved around the café as a third space—a place to see and be seen and, most importantly for our budding romance, an ideal location to loaf for hours getting to know each other.

At the time, my palate for coffee was limited to only a few references. They spanned the quality scale from Folger's drip coffee on one end to Philadelphia's La Colombe, a nationally renowned specialty coffee roaster with several shops in town (and now in Chicago, New York, and Washington, DC), on the other. Whenever our schedules aligned, my friend and Temple University classmate and I would head to La Colombe's Rittenhouse Square café, where we would nurse cappuccinos for hours and chat about school or our ambitions to travel, among generations of coffee lovers. Absent the formal café culture of Paris, the American coffee shop was the best source of comforting community I could access.

Then with little affection for the taste of coffee, I relied on milk-based drinks and a few spoonfuls of sugar to mask the flavor. Once in Paris, where espresso is the leading drink of choice, I knew I'd need to change my habits. If throwing back a shot or two meant that I was one step closer to living life like a Parisian, I was certainly game to try. To be sure, this required dutiful observation, and to kick off my future as a serious coffee consumer, I followed my husband's lead. A double espresso, no sugar, with a glass of water was the most frequent request. Occasionally, he'd opt for an *allongé*, a long black coffee, to jumpstart the day.

Wherever we went across town, the coffee was strong and in steady supply but appallingly unpleasant. It was bitter and harsh and ravaged the palate with one sip. Given my modest knowledge of the drink then, I assumed this was the intended reaction. Switching to milky *café crème* was hardly an improvement: Almost all brasseries or corner cafés use shelf-stable UHT milk, named for the "ultra-high temperature" process to produce it, not fresh milk, whose taste and texture most Americans are accustomed to. As for the ashy coffee taste, I quickly learned that the French were reared on beans from the robusta plant, an affordable but low-quality variety that proliferates in Western Africa and is most commonly used by cafés and brasseries across the city. The taste was, in fact, little more than an accessory to the shared experience. And just like that, my fantasy of Parisian café life proved a delusion.

PREVIOUS SPREAD Coffee beans measured out and ready to use at Honor Café.

Honor Café, the city's first outdoor specialty coffee shop, doesn't merely preach to the converted coffee "geeks" but welcomes a true diversity of clients, from mothers with their children, older couples, entrepreneurs, office workers, and tourists who come for a fresh lunch and a beautifully prepared coffee.

A Coffee Lover's Guide

For flat white fans, head to **HONOR CAFÉ**, where the English-Australian owners turn out expert cups with latte art that's sure to impress the most discerning.

To mix high-quality breakfast and lunch fare with your coffee (and sit-down service), nobody does it better than **HOLYBELLY** (but arrive just before it opens to avoid lines).

For simple soups, salads, and sandwiches made fresh daily to go along with your coffee, your options are legion—**TEN BELLES, CAFÉ OBERKAMPF, CAFÉ LOUSTIC, CAFÉ LOMI, COUTUME, KB CAFÉ, HONOR, LA FONTAINE DE BELLEVILLE** and **THE BROKEN ARM**. It's up to you to decide which neighborhood you are most keen to explore.

Sip and shop at **THE BROKEN ARM**, a fashion and accessories concept store—coffee shop hybrid located across from the Square du Temple, or **CAFÉ SMÖRGÅS**, the Swedish coffee shop annex to the homewares shop **LA TRÉSORERIE**.

Learn about the nuanced tastes and aromas of coffee by attending a coffee cupping at **BELLEVILLE BRÛLERIE, TERRES DE CAFÉ**, or **THE BEANS ON FIRE** (then pick up a bag of freshly roasted coffee to take home with you).

See a complete list of The New Paris *specialty coffee shops in the guide on page 256.*

For a country whose values are closely tied to provenance, pedigree, and *dégustation*—the idea of tasting and savoring—and whose culinary contributions have been recognized by UNESCO on the Intangible Cultural Heritage list, I found it baffling that coffee escaped the same level of precision, care, and source of comestible pride. Where was the reverence for craftsmanship? Didn't they know that what they were drinking was vile? How did coffee slip through the cracks? Faced with such broad indifference, I was determined to understand more. I began frequenting the city's leading specialty shops, learning from their best baristas and roasters, from Chris Nielson and Tom Clark to David Flynn and Aleaume Paturle, and taking the steps to brew at home. In the process, I developed a fond appreciation for specialty coffee and became, like an ever-increasing number of travelers, a coffee tourist, willing to go to great lengths to get my hands on the best brew possible, no matter where I am.

But to understand why coffee has become a major topic of fascination in recent years, I need to offer a brief explanation of the product's maligned past in Paris.

CAFÉ CULTURE VS. COFFEE CULTURE

First, it is important to make the distinction between two entirely different concepts: the centuries-old Parisian café culture and its much younger coffee culture.

Parisians are inveterate café-goers today because of a tradition born in the seventeenth century, which saw a boom of cafés sprout across Europe. In Parisian lore, that culture began at Café Procope in 1686, opened by Italian immigrant Francesco Procopio dei Coltelli. The egalitarian social activity that emerged from it was a veritable revolution in customs and behaviors. The value of such spaces was in connecting with others, particularly people of varying socioeconomic backgrounds. During World War II, that meant connecting with others over the shared trauma of wartime. As W. Scott Haine explains in his book *The World of the Paris Café*, the café became a safe, comforting haven during periods of unrest—a hotbed for conversation, philosophical thought, writing, and sharing beliefs publicly. Though they weren't accepted spaces for the bourgeoisie at the time, elite figures like de Beauvoir and Sartre rejected "respectable domestic spaces of the bourgeoisie such as private salons, gardens, and offices" to be engaged in what he calls "cauldrons of conversation and thought"[17] at places like Café de Flore (opened in 1890). The café as a space bridged the gap between public and private life, leisure and work, individual and family, and perhaps most importantly at the time, it was a launchpad for political ferment (which, as you can imagine, made those in power very anxious).

In both pre- and postwar Paris, the value and cultural significance of the café as a social space extended far beyond food or drink. In fact, what people were drinking or how good it was warranted nary a consideration. The role of coffee as a suitable alternative to alcohol was first seen as a medical salve for the elite and then later as a social accessory in the ritual of gathering. What

---

OPPOSITE Coffee lovers linger at the Terres de Café flagship for cuppings, equipment, or to lounge on one of their swinging chairs.

beguiled the literary set at the time is part of what appeals to the modern traveler today—"the elaborate decor…multi-colored bottles, mirrors, and, in some cases, ornamentation framing the counter. The bar's radiance, magic, and mystery appeared to many observers to be the secular equivalent of a church altar,'"[18] writes Haine. Three hundred years later, that social tradition persists at relic cafés like Café de Flore, Les Deux Magots, and La Coupole, with coffee as lousy as it was at inception. Still, the café space is key to understanding the idealized Parisian experience and the mythology around it.

By the 1950s, the concept of the Italian coffee bar and the modern espresso machine thrived and made their way west to New York, sparking a local coffeehouse craze. "Such coffee shops gave birth, as one nostalgic customer put it, to a 'generation that, for the price of an espresso, could imagine itself in the Europe that few of its members had ever seen,'"[19] wrote Mark Pendergrast of the allure of the European café model in *Uncommon Grounds: The History of Coffee and How It Transformed Our World*. Those early introductions to café life were powerful and went on to inform salient cultural tropes that came alive in postcards, photographs, and film scenes. We are repeatedly shown wicker café chairs neatly lined in serried ranks, gaggles of Parisians sipping their coffee over intense conversation or reading the newspaper, scribbling in journals or simply observing the movement around them, and these scenes perpetuate the romanticized view of café life. But nowhere does the drink itself become part of the fantasy.

Those who have little experience with specialty coffee may not actually be offended by what is served in cafés. In fact, in response to my cheers of joy that quality coffee was finally finding a home in Paris, a Francophile friend in the States who makes regular trips to Paris said the dismal espresso shots were part of the quintessential café experience she looked forward to upon each trip. Another friend who lived in Paris for several months with her husband and considers herself a coffee geek admitted to feeding the myth. "I was projecting what I wanted to see, what I wanted the café experience to be. Of course a coffee seated at one of those iconic cafés was going to be good!" As unfortunate as I find this, and that such cafés don't hold themselves to higher quality standards, I get it. Just like I understand that there is something mildly charming in the brazenness of Parisian waiters. Why else would we subject ourselves to the sass?

For French people, coffee is traditionally consumed not for its taste but for the jolt and ritual it provides. At the end of a meal, it serves to clean the palate and aid digestion. It's the companion to a smoke break, occupying one hand while the cigarette occupies the other. It's an accessory to social exchange, rarely the focus.

ROBUSTA: A BIT OF HISTORY

So cultural context aside, why has the coffee been so lousy? As I mentioned in the beginning of this chapter, that can partially be attributed to France's history of importing robusta beans, harvested in their colonies in West Africa, where the plant proliferates. The coffee plant grows in low-elevation areas, requires minimal attention, is more disease-resistant, and is considerably less expensive than those that produce Arabica beans, the more precious alternative you may know,

Old meets new at Folks and Sparrows Café.

which require higher altitudes (between 2,000 and 6,500 feet or 600 to 2,000 meters), a temperate climate, and extra care. Arabica is known for the complexity and subtlety of its flavors.

Using robusta beans wouldn't necessarily be a problem if the final product in the cup wasn't so poor. All the words I used to describe my first espresso—bitter, harsh, ashy—are typically used to describe robusta. Unfortunately, due to its abundance and high commercial value, robusta is what makes its way into the commodity product[20] consumed by the majority of people all over the globe: instant coffee.

Having imported the beans from the colonies since the late seventeenth century, exposure greatly conditioned the French palate (prior to deregulation in the 1950s—the end of coffee quotas imposed on inhabitants during the German occupation limiting the ability to import Arabica from countries other than France's former colonies—robusta made up 80 percent of French coffee imports; today it's about 50 percent).[21] The acrid, burnt taste wasn't a bother because, well, no one knew any better. It's a bit like comparing industrial peanut butter packed with sugar and additives with a spoonful of the natural stuff (I speak from experience): The taste and experience are so vastly different, it's only normal to prefer the familiar. What's more, individual experience and memory are tied to such products that guide our preferences. Convincing die-hard Skippy fans to adapt to the wholesome alternative, oil separation and all, takes time. And the same can be said for the process by which specialty coffee believers have tried to educate the French on what they're drinking.

But when assessing the quality of coffee, it isn't just harvested beans that must be taken into consideration but also processing, roasting, grinding, and brewing. Coffee is a *fresh* product and each stage of the journey, from plant to cup, greatly impacts the final taste.

CAFÉ FACILE

Then there is the issue of how the average Parisian café sources and prepares its coffee. Coffee is generally sourced from bulk roasters whose beans are of poor quality and over-roasted[22] but priced to entice the café owner looking to make high margins on each cup. It also makes for an easy business choice when deals with such companies come with machinery, drink ware, and other accessories free of charge, allowing the café owner to be operational quickly and without great financial burden. It's a turnkey business with one major caveat: The café owner gets locked into serving *only* what the company provides (it's an issue in the beer world as well, which you'll read about in Chapter Four, see page 152). Behind the bar, the problem is a glaring lack of care. Machines are infrequently cleaned, the beans are old and stale, and the baristas improperly trained. Multiply this scenario by the number of cafés across the city and you have a pandemic of bad coffee.

But much in the way that bistronomy and street food have bred intrepid leaders campaigning for change, so too has the specialty coffee "revolution" in Paris. Like I said, the notion of terroir—that taste is inextricably connected to a region's climate, geography, and even the composition of its soil—is a cornerstone of French culinary culture, and that means the French have a fine-tuned

"I always try to keep an amateur eye when I work, to never lose sight of what made me fall in love with coffee in the first place."

—MIHAELA IORDACHE, BARISTA AND ROASTER AT BELLEVILLE BRÛLERIE

Coffee cups at Café Loustic.

"I think I was looking to fall into something. I had dropped my law studies and was open to whatever would come my way. I just knew it had to be manual *and* intellectually stimulating. Coffee fit the bill perfectly."

—ALBANE THÉRY, COFFEE CONSULTANT

The slow method:
filter coffee.

sense for the nuances in what they are consuming. "In wine, you have two hundred aromatic notes, whereas coffee has eight hundred," said Joris Pfaff, owner of Cafés Pfaff family roaster (established in 1930) in the Yvelines department west of Paris, when I met with him during the research for this book. "It's a very complex product, so understanding how to discern between origins is important." Knowing this, the pioneers of the coffee movement in Paris believed the French palate to be sophisticated and developed enough to appreciate the subtleties and flavor profiles inherent to coffee. All they'd need to do was taste and learn to believe it. The individuals mentioned in this chapter knew they would have to frame their messaging right and drive it home—that what they were roasting and serving was a terroir product of comparable quality to the wines, cheeses, produce, and other comestibles the French revere so highly.

BACK TO CRAFT: THE "SLOW COFFEE" MOVEMENT TODAY

That foreign influence in Paris has done wonders to spark a revival in the craft of coffee roasting and preparation speaks to the value placed on artisanal practices in many areas, an observably widespread phenomenon. This began with La Caféothèque, a coffee shop, roastery, and coffee school launched in 2005 by Gloria Montenegro, once the Guatemalan Ambassador to France. For years, it was the only option for those seeking a better cup of coffee. But what few realized was that the space was the culmination of years of dedicated research and tastings that took Montenegro to coffee regions around the world. Before she opened the coffee shop, she created the Académie de Caféologie, an academy of coffee tasters with whom she could share the vast knowledge she had acquired and introduce diverse profiles of regional varietals with samples she received from producers (interestingly, it's the old-world Café Procope, the city's first café, which served frown-worthy coffee, that played host to these monthly gatherings).

"The French palate is educated for tasting," Montenegro says, referring, of course, to wine. And that insight, combined with her contacts in the wine industry, led her to establish what she calls an "oenological protocol of coffee," a rating system comparable to that used in wine that would serve as the guidepost for the Académie's cuppings. That barometer not only helped curious Parisians appreciate the varying degrees of taste and quality inherent to coffee but also was presented to them in a language they already understood. Educating locals with the same terms and values they expect from wine and its terroir was an important step in a long journey to reassert the worth of quality coffee and the process of making it.

Today, La Caféothèque is a mainstay in the community, and the Académie continues with tastings and cultural events. "For us, baristering is still secondary to roasting," Montenegro's daughter Christina told me during one of my visits. "It's the producer, the land, and the region's biodiversity that makes the coffee. The barista has a responsibility, of course, but roasting is priority."

Though many of the movement's most talented figures got their start or met people who would lead them into coffee at La Caféothèque, it wasn't until years after Montenegro's arrival that anyone else tried their hand at bringing forth broader change. And most of coffee's impassioned leaders found their way in by chance.

Café Loustic

CHANNA GALHENAGE GOT HOOKED on coffee at the age of ten, when his mother bought him his first cappuccino. That set the course for a lifelong love of the bean. While living in London as an adult, he regularly frequented Bar Italia, a 1950s Italian-owned institution in Soho, and the century-old Algerian Coffee Stores, but upon moving to Paris in 2003, he felt the dearth of options. It wasn't until he came across a story in *Monocle* about Rob Berghmans, the owner of Caffènation roaster in Antwerp, and subsequently went to visit him at his shop, that he arrived at his epiphanic moment and began planning a career change. The idea of helping to build Paris's own specialty coffee culture provided the out he was looking for, and he's been a leader in the coffee scene ever since.

To bring his vision for Café Loustic to life, Galhenage worked with the blockbuster Parisian designer Dorothée Meilichzon (see page 249), named designer of the year by Maison & Objet in 2015. She helped him bridge the Parisian café culture and coffee culture with a beautiful design that looks and feels unlike anywhere else in Paris. That includes comfortable sofas handmade in Brittany, swivel tables to facilitate sharing, original brick and stone, a long bamboo bar, a reprint of 1950s Hermès wallpaper spanning the front room, and red and white floor tiles that recalled his love for Seville, Spain. "People imagine it's contemporary, occasionally likening it to Brooklyn, but it's actually French; Dorothée borrowed from 1950s–1960s French design!" says Galhenage.

Hippolyte Courty was a history teacher, food critic, wine agent, and all-around epicurean long before he found himself importing and roasting single origin[23] coffees at L'Arbre à Café, which he opened in 2009. In fact, prior to that, he had only a passing knowledge of the product and didn't think very highly of it as a drink. It wasn't until a publisher asked him to write a book about coffee that he experienced the gustatory awakening that led him headfirst into the industry. Specifically, the catalyst was coffee from the Fraijanes region of Guatemala, free of the metallic, burnt taste he and everyone else were so used to. And that set him on a journey to explore and study the entire process from harvesting to drying, fermentation, roasting, grinding, and methods of extraction. He was on a mission to share all the ways in which coffee could be enjoyed and demonstrate how well it fit within the culinary world he had emerged from, a discourse that endeared him to the likes of pastry king Pierre Hermé, who now uses grand cru coffee in his pastries rather than the common coffee extract alternative, and Michelin-starred chefs like Jean-François Piège, Alain Ducasse, and Anne-Sophie Pic, who has been known to incorporate his coffee into her dishes. Courty placed his bets on the restaurant business, convincing countless chefs to ditch the push-button Nespresso model for coffee on par with their rarefied cooking. It paid off: He has successfully carved out a distinct section of the industry for himself.

Christophe Servell of Terres de Café, one of the earliest to the scene, spent twenty years working in film before venturing into the world of wine and then into coffee. Already accustomed to making freshly ground coffee at home with a French press, he wanted to share the joy in that cup in a broad way. Transmitting the savoir faire in roasting and baristering was the base of the industry for the first several years he was in business. But since 2013, when the offering began to expand widely, he has seen more and more clients come in with a solid foundation about specialty coffee who regularly go across town to each roaster to taste what exists on the market. Today, Christophe insists on nurturing the relationship he has with producers. "They used to suffer while selling average quality beans. Now, with specialty they do better selling less and have the flexibility to pick and choose the roasters they sell to." The whole chain of the industry is transforming and that includes consumption habits.

Other Frenchmen like Aleaume Paturle of Café Lomi, Antoine Nétien of Coutume Café, Nicolas Piégay of KB Caféshop, Thomas Lehoux of Belleville Brûlerie, Nicolas Alary of Holybelly, and Nicolas Clerc of Télescope were exposed to quality coffee in their travels to countries where the specialty coffee culture was dominant—primarily the United States and Australia.

When specialty coffee first made waves in the French media it was frequently referred to as *la tendance australienne*, which left many of us wondering: Why was coffee so much better there? That Australians are represented in outsize proportions in the coffee scene is an outcome of their history. The former tea culture might thank both the American servicemen based in

---

OPPOSITE Coffee beans freshly roasted from Café Lomi, one of the few new-wave microroasters located in the city.

Australia during World War II who introduced them to pure coffee (versus coffee mixed with chicory) and the waves of Italian immigrants who came to Australia in the late 1950s, bringing with them a strong espresso and coffee shop culture, which went on to gain serious ground in the 1970s, for their reputation as a coffee mecca. Their early coffee shops were modern, well designed, and intimate—true community hubs where milky espresso drinks like cappuccinos and the massively exported flat white usurped instant and drip coffee. With time, antipodean roasters became more interested in sourcing the best beans possible from single estates or small batch producers and offered coffee lovers a sophisticated spectrum of flavors and tastes. Alternative brewing methods like filter, Syphon (vacuum coffee maker), AeroPress, Chemex, and cold brew also rose to popularity and are de rigueur in specialty shops around the world. The primary difference in the way Australians consume coffee (and tea) versus Americans or Europeans is that it is commonly drunk with a meal and has always been considered equally as important as the food. That style greatly inspired Nicolas Alary and Sarah Mouchot of Holybelly, the city's preeminent coffee shop–restaurant hybrid (see page 113). Today, the mecca of third-wave coffee[24] serves as the training ground for amateur coffee aficionados and aspiring baristas with a standard that soars far beyond what is produced anywhere else in the world.

Nicolas Piégay has strong memories of going to roasters with his parents when he was a kid to pick up beans for the week—a French habit of buying beans, good or bad, directly from a neighborhood roaster (*brûlerie*) that predated the rise of instant coffee and capsules purchased from the supermarket—but he didn't truly discover the merits of good coffee until he went to Australia in 2007 with the idea of starting up a French gourmet grocer. When his business idea didn't take off as planned, he worked in an organic shop that served specialty coffee. There, he observed two key characteristics of the Australian coffee scene that underscored its cultural importance: milk-based drinks were most popular, and there was always a dedicated person preparing the coffee. Consumers "expect their coffees to be made by specially trained baristas, not just anyone pressing a button on the coffee machine."[25] Back in Paris and inspired by his experiences down under, he worked toward opening his own coffee shop. Trying to get a space and secure a bank loan were major roadblocks in a time when the concept was virtually unprecedented. Smacked with refusals from bankers who didn't understand his vision, passion was the only thing keeping him going. It would take two years for him to make it happen, but KB Café opened its doors in 2010 in the neighborhood south of Pigalle in the 9th arrondissement—before the area's "cool" quotient reached epic proportions. There was a big learning curve in the beginning; the French couldn't imagine that the quality matched the asking price. "It's psychological," Piégay told me. "Quality coffee isn't meant to be a mass product. It's too much of a time and cost investment for it to be for everyone. But getting clients past the price was tough at first."

Nicolas Clerc was a photographer before opening Télescope in 2012. In fact, he was shooting a coffee story for *T: The New York Times Style Magazine* in 2010—a story by Oliver Strand that

---

OPPOSITE One of the must-order drinks at Télescope Café, a filter coffee.

"The biggest change from when I first got started is that clients tend to come in now with a solid base knowledge and ask questions about origins, not the drinks themselves."

—NICOLAS CLERC, OWNER OF TÉLESCOPE

Café Lomi

AT THE TURN OF THE NINETEENTH century, there were nearly 1,000 coffee roasters (or brûleries) in Paris. Gradually, the rise of supermarket convenience shopping and instant coffee put most of them out of business, and today, there are only a handful left. Café Lomi is one of only a few new wave micro-roasters located in the city, alongside L'Arbre à Café, Coutume, Belleville Brûlerie, and The Beans on Fire (Terres de Café is currently roasted in Strasbourg, and Hexagone coffee is roasted in Brittany where roaster Stéphane Cataldi is based).

Café Lomi is located about 650 feet (200 m) from the Goutte d'Or, an ethnically diverse, working class neighborhood once (laughably) labeled a "no-go zone" by Fox News. The mayor of the 18th arrondissement allowed them to rent the space for roasting and training provided they also create a coffee shop to foster community in the neighborhood. Many young designers, entrepreneurs, and artists live nearby and have helped build a collaborative environment. Social housing occupies the space just above the café.

questioned why coffee had been so bad in Paris—and unwittingly had his first crash course in artisanal coffee. Years later, after creating a loyal client base at his 2nd arrondissement coffee shop, sustainable consumption and extraction is foremost in Clerc's coffee philosophy. "My work in coffee has evolved not only in terms of the setting but the recipe and the extraction." He aims to tease out the maximum that he can from the coffee in terms of flavors. "It's responsible consumption! It's like eating an apple but cutting away all the skin, where the flavor is." When I asked him what he felt the biggest change has been in the industry, he spoke of the knowledge the clients are equipped with today. "I like getting Australians and Nordics in who have been drinking coffee like this for fifteen or twenty years and come in with an opinion. The more people know, the more they can sense the nuances and specificities in what we do, and that pushes all of us forward."

Aleaume Paturle got his start in specialty coffee in San Diego in 2002 and brought a robust skill set back to Paris, where he first opened Alto, a coffee cart (2005–2010) that was often stationed in front of the Galeries Lafayette department store. In 2007, he was named Best Barista in France and saw restaurateurs come out of the woodwork to carry his coffee. The market was readying itself for a full-fledged movement. He launched Café Lomi after selling Alto and found himself not only a larger space to roast but an experienced partner: Paul Arnephy (see opposite), an Australian who worked for him at Alto, who exudes a tremendous passion for the product and a natural ability to communicate about it when he trains. "He brought his affinity for light, acidic roasts, and we made it more French," says Paturle. "We don't want to replicate styles from Australia but rather adapt them to French tastes." As for the way coffee has boomed in a big way in the last two to three years specifically, he attributes it to a changing consumer climate. "We don't know anything anymore. We're stressed when we consume because we're rarely sure where anything is coming from." The rise in traceability and transparency as guideposts to consumption is indeed a phenomenon that goes beyond food and has supported the rise of specialty coffee in Paris.

So was it easy to persuade French people to adapt their habits and give more thought to what's in their cup? Hardly. Tom Clark, the Australian half of Coutume (micro-roaster and coffee shop), says that education was essential to getting things moving in Paris. He and partner Antoine Nétien spent a lot of energy organizing free coffee tastings and spending quality time with customers to transmit their passion and knowledge for the drink. "We felt we had to grow the revolution from the roots up, and in that way, each interaction was key to contributing to a wider movement. Transmitting the passion is the easy part—it's just a case of sharing stories and know-how [about] specialty coffee," but the drink needed to first get into consumers' hands.

Initially, Parisians were taken aback by specialty coffee. Since it didn't hew to what they were reared on, their first experience wasn't always enjoyable. On top of that, they lacked the vocabulary to articulate *why* they didn't like it. This is a point echoed by English-Australian couple Angelle Boucher and Daniel Warburton of Honor, the city's first outdoor specialty coffee corner. "Coffee explains itself only if you have a working framework, but most of our clients don't. So we help establish their expectations. We tell them what flavors they might taste and what to pay attention to with that first sip." What's more, their coffee is served in a glass cup rather than a traditional

It's not only about the coffee at Honor. Owners Angelle Boucher Warburton and her husband Daniel Warburton (pictured) feature cakes from local bakers, including Broken Biscuits, a bakery run by an English-Irish duo of pastry chefs.

Q&A

DAVID FLYNN & THOMAS LEHOUX, BELLEVILLE BRÛLERIE AND LA FONTAINE DE BELLEVILLE

BEFORE AMERICAN EXPAT David Flynn and Thomas Lehoux joined forces in 2013 to open their own roastery in the 19th arrondissement, they were making coffee—David in the United States at Murky Coffee, then at Le Bal Café and Télescope in Paris; Thomas in Sydney at the Little Marionette followed by, in Paris, La Caféothèque and Ten Belles, the Canal Saint-Martin coffee institution. Together they formed Frog Fight, a friendly barista smackdown (think coffee cuppings and latte art competitions), which began as a way to galvanize interest around coffee and continues to reaffirm the credibility of the industry to a newly serious coffee-loving public. With Belleville Brûlerie, they cast their net wider to influence tastes with their own recipes.

How did you find your way into coffee and why did it appeal to you?

(LEHOUX) You fall into coffee by chance, I think. You try it out, see if you like it, and then you dive in completely. What has always interested me about the industry is that you're always learning new things, new drying methods, new processes of fermentation, roasting, or extraction. There is always so much to develop and plenty of people to convince that

OPPOSITE Belleville Brûlerie founders David Flynn and Thomas Lehoux.

the work we're doing is valuable. I don't really have any hobbies, so I invested all my energy into learning and developing the role of the barista.

(FLYNN) I needed a job while I was in college! And it went from there.

Many people imagine elaborate latte art when they think of specialty coffee, but from the beginning you both have dedicated your efforts to promote filter coffee. Why is that?

(FLYNN) In the United States, specialty coffee really rode in on the back of the espresso machine. People already knew what filtered coffee was; it's what they drank out of their big mugs every day. You certainly weren't going to convince them of the amazingness of your juicy and fruity drip coffee. No, the way you did it was, you gave them an amazing cappuccino or a chocolaty espresso that they had never tried, except maybe on vacation. But people didn't have any preconceived notions about espresso, so there you found a way in. They know it's coffee, but they don't really know how it's supposed to taste. In thinking about it in terms of France, we realized that people know how espresso tastes; it's in their culture. So we approached it in reverse and really started pushing filter coffee.

In a way, it was an easy sell because people were so shocked that you would ask them to pay for a *jus de chaussette* (sock juice, the common nickname for watery filter coffee) that they're like, "Well, if they're asking me to pay for it, it must be good." And there's the fact that the *allongé* is already very popular, which is basically a long espresso with water. Filter coffee really fits into that mold. You can sit and sip for a while; it's not just a shot at the bar. One of the things that Thomas and I did at Ten Belles and Télescope, respectively, was encourage people to give filter a try anytime they'd ask for an allongé. And almost everyone would taste it and be like, "This is great!" Like sommeliers, we guided people through that taste experience, which really helped legitimize our roles as experts they could feel comfortable deferring to.

How has specialty coffee in Paris changed since you got into the business? Do Parisians better understand why it's important to care about what's in their cup?
(LEHOUX) I think that Paris (and France overall) is an interesting terrain because there is endless potential. I think the important thing to keep in mind is that everyone, including the French, would like to drink better coffee, but they must first know that better coffee exists. The United States, Australia, Scandinavian countries, and the UK are not better adapted to understand it; however, they have had access to quality coffee for much longer. For the moment, specialty coffee is only known and consumed by a small portion of the worldwide population. We, the French, are a bit behind, that's true. As the chef Hélène Darroze has said, "The strength of our gastronomic traditions and the weight of our habits often prevent us from being at the forefront of trends." So the focus for all of us has been changing the habits from bitter black coffee consumed quickly at the bar to slow coffee with real flavor.

(FLYNN) It's been really fascinating to see all of the different clients that come through here on Saturdays, when we open to the public. We've got everyone from your average coffee shop client all the way up to seventy-year-old women who come weekly to buy their coffee. They say, "I'm so excited there's a *brûlerie* in the neighborhood again!" They still grind their own coffee and make it in a French press or an Italian coffee machine, just like they did before instant coffee took over. They come to us because the alternative is a coffee shop, whose codes and customs are unfamiliar and maybe even daunting to them. It's like, "A brûlerie? Oh yeah, this is where I go to get my fresh coffee. Got it." That's also why I think the specialty coffee movement has staying power. At the end of the day, people like things that taste good.

Start the day right at Ten Belles. Breakfast bedfellows like homemade pastries, granola, and yogurt should be paired with a filter or an expertly prepared flat white.

Shakespeare and Company Café

THERE ARE A FEW SPECIAL places in Paris that need little introduction—the Louvre, Notre Dame, the Eiffel Tower, a handful of parks, and, I'd argue, the literary institution Shakespeare and Company. But I'll give you a little background anyway. When it was owned by American expat Sylvia Beach in the 1920s and 1930s, it was a magnet for the period's literary greats, from Hemingway to Fitzgerald to Joyce. It shuttered during the Nazi occupation and only reopened in 1951, when George Whitman, another American, took over the space. Under Whitman's charge, the bookshop continued to be a draw for writers (Langston Hughes, Anaïs Nin, James Baldwin) who came to work, hang out, and eventually present their work. When he passed, his daughter Sylvia took the reins and has grown the business ever since. That one bookshop with such legacy has

been so fervently protected and cared for is a testament to Sylvia's love for the space—what it symbolizes within her family and for so many readers and writers around the world. In 2015, she honored her father's wishes and took over the adjacent property to open the official Shakespeare and Company Café, with specialty coffee by Café Lomi and a literary-leaning nibbles menu created by Bob's Bake Shop (see page 66). While it has preserved quite a number of original features—retro floor tiles on one side blend into the new concrete floor on the other, the exposed stone was brushed and cleaned, and the garage door from the previous space has been repurposed to enclose the bathroom—the space feels fresh and modern. Sylvia said, "It felt right to bring it into the future a bit, but the past is very much still here."

demitasse so that clients can see what they're drinking. Boucher said, "We have one chance of painting a customer's experience with specialty coffee, so it's up to us to make it as special as possible." Part of that experience is feeding the growing demand for meaningful exchanges—telling stories around their coffee and communicating their passion.

Take, for example, their cold brew, which provides an opportunity to teach about the process of cold extraction. They explain that it is brewed for fifteen hours overnight using a blend[26] from a single farm in Burundi and offers a unique taste experience because the coffee has never been heated. "Americans are so good at creating trends that novelty alone attracts people. In Paris, it's not quite so easy, so storytelling helps," explains Warburton.

While education is important, the strategy has changed for some micro-roasters and coffee shop owners. Paturle and Clerc believe that education in quality happens today through tasting and allowing the product to speak for itself. But that's partially because consumers are more and more knowledgeable. "We shouldn't need to explain," says Paturle, "unless the client inquires directly about method or origins."

But we mustn't forget that while progress has been made, something I have observed simply by spending much of my time socializing and working in these establishments, the specialty coffee culture remains marginal, a bubble that's mushrooming but has yet to reach its full potential. Most actors on the coffee stage want to see the democratization of specialty coffee, much in the way we have seen pedigreed ingredients and accessible fresh food democratize dining. But the cultural shifts influencing food consumption and dining habits didn't happen overnight, and they won't in coffee either. "I still get clients who come in and say, 'I'd like a café, s'il vous plaît' to which they reply 'un café normal' when they are invariably asked what *kind* they'd like. They don't specify an espresso, a noisette, or a filter coffee. They treat coffee as if there is only one type. The challenge is getting people to understand that coffee is dynamic and using different brewing methods will lend different results. Just as there are nuances in wine and people specify their preferences (even down to the region or the vineyard), coffee has its own. Those are important distinctions to make," says Chris Nielson, one of the most experienced coffee professionals in Paris.

Now, the hurdle isn't opening new coffee shops or convincing coffee aficionados that they should care about what's in the cup and the narrative around it, it's the *average* coffee drinker who does so blindly, without realizing the systems being supported by consuming an indifferent cup at the corner café, the office coffee machine, or the instant mass-produced everyday sludge sold in supermarkets. But for that to change, the infrastructure needs to evolve further. Greater value must be placed on the barista profession (in Australia, it's a handsomely paid, respected career taken very seriously); baristas must be paid better and given room for growth. Many coffee shop owners are championing the barista as a *sommelier du café*, a métier that demands skill and experience, and are working toward giving them long-term perspective. "We need to give baristas greater opportunity. I'm working on training my baristas to become managers of my shops or to help me open new ones in Paris or elsewhere in France," says Servell, of Terres de Café. Then, the demand must be made for better coffee at corner bistros and brasseries, since these are the places that can foster broad change.

Paturle says he wants to see clean machines, well-sourced beans, and trained baristas at every corner joint. He may not have to wait much longer. "More and more conventional brasseries are calling us to work with them." This shift was echoed by Servell, who has observed that restaurateurs are taking the time to tour the city's leading roasters and taste their products, without even stopping at the big box equivalents like Cafés Richard and Lavazza. Change is definitely afoot.

Coffee has become a collegial milieu that exhorts upstarts to make their own vision a reality. This isn't the *c'est impossible* town it once was, where every new concept demanded a Herculean effort to see the light of day. Now, it's a place of tremendous possibility, particularly for those who want to see new and inventive coffee concepts emerge. What began as a subculture of coffee purists has grown into a veritable movement, with influencers fanning out beyond the eastern hub where most shops are concentrated. "I think specialty coffee has often been branded as an 'outside' thing, with coffee shops in the city criticized for only being visited by expats. But at Hexagone, you really do see the local neighborhood—that is to say, true Parisians—embracing what they are doing," says my friend Anna Brones, author of *Paris Coffee Revolution*, about Hexagone Café, whose name is a nod to the geometric shape often used to refer to the country and which opened in the 14th arrondissement in a highly residential neighborhood. But despite tremendous growth in the last four to five years, Paris is far from being a saturated market. As Nielson said to me while I was writing a coffee story for the *New York Times*, "The coffee movement hasn't truly 'made it' in Paris until there is a presence in every arrondissement." The city is definitely on its way there, making this an exciting time for coffee lovers.

Overall, the French have certainly made up for lost time. In 2015, Barista Champion of France Charlotte Malaval was the first French barista to compete in the World Barista Championships, where she placed sixth. Not bad for a people who didn't even know what a barista was until very recently. Not only is Paris buzzing among coffee lovers and professionals across Europe, it's also garnered the attention of coffee geeks farther afield. One afternoon at Honor Café, I chatted with a coffee shop owner who hailed from Melbourne. I couldn't help but engage him when I saw his eyes light up after taking the first sip of his flat white. "We've been so impressed with what we've tasted in Paris on this trip," he told me. "It's a pleasure to see and, to be honest, a relief for us Australians who can't imagine a day without the good stuff!" At this point, neither can I.

Beyond simple espresso bars, many of the new wave joints have launched broader concepts to distinguish themselves from the others. The Broken Arm, in the heart of the North Marais, is part concept store, part specialty coffee shop, with a sharp selection of clothing and accessories on

OPPOSITE Walk up the rue de Belleville, past a smattering of Chinese wholesale shops and restaurants, and you'll find Cream, a small coffee bar that serves excellent pour-overs, sandwiches, and a short but sharp selection of cakes, all made in-house. Given their Belleville location and past working under the tutelage of former Ten Belles lead and Belleville Brûlerie cofounder Thomas Lehoux, it's not surprising that owners Joe Elliott and Maxime Armand serve Belleville Brûlerie beans exclusively.

one side of the space and a café on the other, with quality coffee and a chef who cooks up fresh seasonal dishes for lunch. La Trésorerie, a home goods store, took a more Nordic approach with their adjacent eatery Café Smörgås, which serves filter coffee, fresh juices, and *smörgås*, a Swedish open-faced sandwich. And Holybelly, in the 10th arrondissement, has been the unchallenged leader of pairing good food with good coffee since opening in 2013.

That Aussie-style good-food-and-coffee ambition has continued with new businesses like Café Oberkampf, opened in 2015, where owner Guy Griffin offers a short but solid menu of sandwiches, soups, salads, seasonal toasts, and shakshuka alongside excellent coffee and a wonderful community spirit (because I spent so much time there, especially while writing this book, friends joked that it was the "downstairs" to my apartment), and Mokonuts, opened in 2016, which blends Lebanese-inflected market dishes and comforting baked goods with coffee from the roaster L'Arbre à Café and homemade teas. Beyond food, new coffee concepts are emerging as well. At Steel Cyclewear & Coffee Shop, cycling and coffee bonhomie come together perfectly, attracting cycling fanatics looking for gear and coffee fans who come to hang out in their specialty coffee corner. And for bookish types, there is the Shakespeare and Company Café, a more modern coffee annex to the iconic bookstore next door (see page 106).

A BRIGHT FUTURE

As for the next stage, we've already seen the first intimation of what might become the future of coffee in the capital. The Beans on Fire, a collaborative roastery launched by two Colombians, Andrés Hoyos-Gomez and Maria Hernandez, was the industry's answer to shared office space and has allowed Nicolas Piégay of KB Caféshop, among other professionals and aspiring roasters, to start roasting his own beans. It was the next logical step in his journey to mastering coffee production. For Hoyos-Gomez and Hernandez, the concept of a shared roaster that welcomed both established coffee shops looking to develop their own signature and individuals looking to learn more about roasting as a profession was unique to the market. It's a passion-fueled hub for learning, sharing, tasting, and training unlike anything the city has seen before. Finally, the coffee future in Paris is bright.

OPPOSITE In the spring of 2016, the team behind Belleville Brûlerie opened La Fontaine de Belleville, a longstanding neighborhood café that they did very little to—a fresh coat of paint, some custom tabletops, and lighting—but the bones remained the same. The menu and ambience, however, went a long way to bridge the Parisian café culture and the burgeoning specialty coffee scene—affordable craft beer on tap, homemade croque monsieur, classic cocktails, and *good* filter coffee.

Holybelly,

Where Good Coffee Meets Good Food

*"France has not been a nation of entrepreneurs
but it's possible to succeed, and
we're the generation with the energy to do it."*

—NICOLAS ALARY, CO-OWNER OF HOLYBELLY

HOLYBELLY WAS THE LONE RANGER in the realm of mixing good coffee and good food when they opened in 2013 and have been the ne plus ultra in brunching ever since. I knew there was something different about Holybelly before the café-restaurant even opened its doors. Back in 2013, I discovered Nicolas Alary's work as a photographer for *Kinfolk Magazine* through mutual friends and quickly began following him on Twitter, where his profile led me to his "Behind the Bar" blog (now called Holyblog), a forum to document his journey with Sarah Mouchot, his partner in life and business, into the restaurant world—their first foray into entrepreneurialism. Alary chronicled everything from the birth of their idea to the grand opening, with play-by-play specifics of all the administrative hurdles, financial challenges (and the emotions that result from them), and construction delays in between. It was the most honest and surprising account of starting a business I had ever seen written online from a French person. Publicizing personal matters, especially those related to finances, is generally considered untoward, but they spared no detail. "When we were putting together our business plan, we were looking for help through the process but had trouble finding any. It was our way of having a trace of our own progress and creating a resource for others,"[27] Alary told me.

You would think, as I did, that it should be easy enough to offer quality food and quality coffee under the same roof, especially in a city of such culinary might and sensitivity to taste. But even now, several years after Holybelly first opened, no other establishment has been able to replicate or even approximate their simple but unequivocally good approach to both. And that's true on all fronts: food, beverage, service, and design.

The primacy of hospitality has been a hallmark to their business ethos from the start, one that challenged long-held models of indifference in Parisian service. To that they owe their experiences as expats in Vancouver and later in Melbourne. "We left France partly because there was no way to harness our own energy. Paris was slow and heavy . . . and nothing was changing," explains Alary. "I realized just how much Paris was suffering on the coffee and affordable food front when I saw firsthand how good it was elsewhere." In

OPPOSITE Sarah Mouchot and Nicolas Alary, founders of Holybelly.

the time that they lived outside of France—with Alary perfecting the art of specialty coffee at Market Lane in Melbourne and Mouchot gaining serious kitchen experience at Duchess of Spotswood—things in Paris were creeping forward. When they returned to France in 2012, they sensed there was change in the air. "There was finally good coffee and interesting food but hardly anywhere to get both (and by food, I mean actual meals, not muffins and coffee shop nibbles, with a proper kitchen on the premises)." The timing proved to be right for their idea, and they tackled the project with a more North American approach to risk taking. "France breeds 'safe' workers, rarely go-getters. Entrepreneurial motivation must be within you already, because the state certainly isn't going to nurture it!" Despite some built-in barriers and a challenging start-up system to navigate, they felt they owed it to themselves to bring to life a space they knew the city would welcome.

Holybelly, as they initially imagined it, was relatively modest. A laid-back atmosphere to unite good specialty coffee and fresh, seasonal food, much like the innumerable "brekkie" joints they frequented in Melbourne. Breakfast and brunch means eggs three different ways, a smattering of rotating sides, house-made granola, or sweet and savory pancakes (among the best I've had *anywhere*). During the week, a savory lunch menu guided by the seasons whose inspirations can't be easily defined. Some dishes are Anglo, some are French, some are Mexican (white fish brandade, lentil dhal, split pea and ham hock soup, or *paleron de boeuf*)—it's all about what the duo wants to eat themselves.

"Eggs and sides first thing in the morning was a hard sell for Parisians initially because it wasn't part of the breakfast tradition (which is mostly toast, pastries, and coffee) but now they've gotten into it. It's been exciting to see them open up!" beamed Mouchot. They quickly learned they had tapped into something unique in Paris when they became a magnet for both coffee aficionados and breakfast lovers within weeks of opening. Besides movie premieres and burger trucks, I had never seen Parisians queue enthusiastically for anything, and the queues for breakfast midmorning, even on a weekday, were long. People turned up as much for the prepossessing interior—original floor tiling and exposed brick, leather banquettes and reclaimed wood tables, a stunning skylight strung with twinkle lights, plants that make it feel like you are dining in a garden, and an open kitchen with bar seats to watch Mouchot and her sous-chefs work—as for the "best brunch in Paris" and proper service.

Three years later and as busy as ever, the couple's greatest strengths have been an amalgam of factors, including their exposure to the Australian brekkie culture of high-quality coffee and full, savory breakfast pastries. They came back to France, observed a gap, and jumped headfirst into unfamiliar territory. They are natural storytellers and community builders, making diners feel like guests in their home and their staff invaluable members of the family (and all it takes is one look at the menu, peppered with anecdotes and pop-cultural quips, to get a sense of their character). But key to their success is their physical presence—Alary in the front of house and behind the coffee bar, Mouchot as head chef in the kitchen—that ensures the restaurant embodies the values they established in the beginning and will have longevity. "We're lucky that we're a duo and have complementary visions. We each have a specialization and can maintain the quality." In each flat "Walter" white, a reference to the leading character in the critically acclaimed television series *Breaking Bad* and a weekend special, is a singular energy that has roused not only the 10th arrondissement but also the city at large.

OPPOSITE Poached eggs and sides, coffee, and pancakes at Holybelly.

"In September 2014, I had meatballs on the menu. They were served in a red wine sauce with smoked sheep's milk cheese and late-summer tomatoes. A client came up to me after the meal to say that they were just like her Italian grandmother prepared them. Feedback like that is all the fuel we need to continue!"

—SARAH MOUCHOT, CO-OWNER / CHEF OF HOLYBELLY

the new
SWEETS

"The Fine Arts are five in number: Painting, Music, Poetry, Sculpture, and Architecture—whereof the principal branch is Confectionery."

—MARIE-ANTOINE CARÊME, EARLY NINETEENTH-CENTURY CHEF

I spent the better part of my childhood thinking about and seeking out desserts. It began with rich, oversize cheese Danishes for breakfast, fetched during morning outings with my father during languid summers by the beach at the only worthy bakery in town; perfectly crisp and chewy chocolate chip cookies as an after school pick-me-up; and peanut butter–filled chocolate cups whenever I could get my hands on them, before my affections veered entirely French.

When I moved to Paris, my first and favorite food memories—those that would lay the groundwork for my future preoccupations as a food and travel writer—were those conferred by the flavors and textures in French pastry, a nostalgic comfort despite their novelty to me. I began modestly with flaky viennoiseries (breakfast pastries like croissants, *pain au chocolat*, *chausson aux pommes*), tacked on plump and moist pistachio financiers, then moved onto *tarte au citron*, cream puffs (*choux*), and the divine Saint-Honoré before settling into a loyal love affair with the éclair, the bestselling pastry in France,[28] and my Proustian madeleine. My explorations through pastry mirrored my personal evolutions as an adult in Paris—my tastes became more sophisticated and discerning with every passing year.

Through the lens of the éclair, that meant that not just any would do. While I loved their simple composition, I found the classic oblong choux (a puff pastry also used to make profiteroles, chouquettes, and the Saint-Honoré) available at corner bakeries too decadent and the universal favorite flavors—chocolate, caramel, coffee—rarely inspiring. Luckily, the éclair underwent an impressive revival (more on that in this chapter), halving in size and diversifying; rainbow-hued, exotic flavors, and grand cru chocolates rose to the forefront. I reached for the luscious dark chocolate éclair at Carl Marletti (regularly ranked among the top five pâtisseries in the city by *Le Figaro* newspaper), the raspberry passion fruit or lemon yuzu from L'Éclair de Génie, and intense coffee with a thin, milk chocolate shell by Philippe Conticini, formerly of La Pâtisserie des Rêves. And with the changing seasons came new flavor opportunities and reasons to indulge.

That's part of what has changed. You can hardly scan a street without clamping your eyes on treats of all colors, shapes, and sizes that glisten in shop windows, beckoning impressionable *gourmandes* like me. Proud of their heritage, bakeries brandish signs on their windows affirming their credentials—"In Paris since 1870," some might read. These are the corner pastry shops of our imaginations. However, not all of them are particularly well designed or modern, and that includes their confections. The owners of my corner bakery repainted their façade six years ago but left the interior unchanged; it looks exactly the same as it must have in the 1980s when it first opened for

---

PREVIOUS SPREAD Olivier Ménard, co-owner of Une Glace à Paris, getting ready to dig into his favorite flavors *du moment*.

"Pastry has become autonomous and exists independently from cooking. Finally, it's no longer an add-on—it's the focus in and out of restaurants."

—PHILIPPE CONTICINI

Le Phil'goût by Phillippe Conticini for Fou de Pâtisserie boutique: a pastry composed of a crispy hazelnut crust, red berries, lime and vanilla mousse, and a touch of *fleur de sel*.

"It's important that tradition remains the base of what we do, but it shouldn't be a burden or weigh us down. Technique should be a tool at the service of taste."

—HUGUES POUGET, CHEF PÂTISSIER AND OWNER OF HUGO & VICTOR

Seasonal tartes at Hugo & Victor.

business. The pastries are heavy, cloyingly sweet, and visually imperfect, and as much as I enjoy their multigrain loaves, I'd wager their desserts are mailed-in: reheated or assembled on-site from ingredients sourced from wholesalers. As the public becomes better informed about these tactics, the more they lean on the specialized artisans they can trust—those with one sole shop where everything is rolled, shaped, baked, glazed, and assembled *sur place* or those running high-end mini-pastry chains with firm standards of quality.

TRADITIONAL PASTRIES GET A MAKEOVER

These are no longer the days of only buying cakes and pastries in the boulangerie-pâtisserie, one-stop shops for bread *and* pastries (which usually excel at one or the other, rarely both), nor of finding artistic pastry exclusively in luxury hotels.

Though it may be tempting to dismiss all the sweet marvels across town as mere *desserts*, that would be reductive and overlook their role as cultural touchstones—their creators part of the lifeblood of the nation. Whereas in America sweets are invariably tied to excess, health, and morality—we use words like *sinfully* delicious or *guilty* pleasure to describe their consumption—the French approach them as joys that don't need to be confined to special occasions or celebrations.[29] They are entwined in a balanced, everyday lifestyle and in times of recession or uncertainty, they are even more important—an affordable luxury that lifts the spirits.

Of course, it certainly helps that in the time I've lived in Paris there has been a dramatic shift in the sweets themselves. They are smaller, lighter, more seasonal, and more experimental with flavor combinations. To understand in simple terms how the pastry and confection industries have changed in the last ten to twenty years, I went straight to an authority: Pierre Hermé.

"Before, pâtisserie was about the form. Today, it's all about taste," M. Hermé told me during our chat. That may seem like a modest distinction, but that shift in focus revolutionized the industry. He certainly had a hand in making it happen too. Practically born to become a pastry chef—the fourth generation in his family to pursue the trade—Hermé is the best-known exemplar of the ultra-creative, hyper-driven French pastry chef, revered by insatiable sugar lovers around the world. Twenty years ago, at a time when high-quality sweets only existed at palace hotels (a title given to a select group of luxury hotels in France), gourmet caterers, and chocolate shops, he transformed pastry into an accessible luxury. In 1988, when working for Fauchon, the haute-pastry mecca, he introduced collections, like those in fashion. It was a way, he told me, of infusing creativity into the pantheon of classics that followed the "rule book" to the point of being staid and uninspired (right down to the macaron, which he elevated to a work of, now ubiquitous, art).

With ingredients sourced with the same rigor as in cooking, he went on to invent new recipes and breathe life into old ones, adding a singular flair to each. In her book *Paris Sweets*, the inimitable Dorie Greenspan described her longtime friend's special gift: "I remember walking through Fauchon's kitchens with Pierre and tasting as we went along. What was most memorable—and what I later came to realize was Pierre's hallmark—was that each time I tasted something I thought I knew well, it tasted slightly different from the classic, and that slight difference made it even better."[30]

Jacques Genin

JACQUES GENIN'S almost gratuitous
Paris-Brest is award-winning for a reason.
The traditional recipe is a wheel of choux
pastry sliced in half, filled with hazelnut praline
cream, and topped with a crispy crust of
slivered almonds and powdered sugar. As
my friend Meg Zimbeck said during a Paris-
Brest tasting panel I was part of, Genin's
interpretation has an unparalleled "purity
of nut flavor and incredible balance."

Jacques Genin is perhaps best known
for his exquisite chocolates in experimental
flavors and his buttery-soft caramels but a
special mention must go to the pâtes de
fruits (shown above), the only ones I'll eat.
Why? The sweetness comes entirely from
the natural sugars in the fruits themselves,
producing a candy that's refreshing and
bursting with fruit (or vegetable) flavor.

"It's up to us as pastry chefs and chocolatiers to drive the right message about our profession, to encourage people to stop consuming garbage, and refuse to let big businesses take over our lives more than they already have."

—PASTRY CHEF JACQUES GENIN WITH SOPHIE VIDAL, HIS COPILOT AT HIS NAMESAKE PASTRY AND CHOCOLATE SHOP

At thirty-one years old, Jonathan Blot has a successful plated dessert bar called Acide in the up-and-coming Batignolles neighborhood in the 17th arrondissement. Blot started out nearly ten years ago focusing on macarons, producing nearly two thousand per day. But boredom set in quickly. "Customers can't get enough of them, but as a pastry chef who has gone through extensive training, it was frustrating not to be able to express my full range of skills and creativity. The macaron is versatile in its flavor combinations but obviously limited in its form," he said. Instead, he shifted his focus to a wider roster of French pastry that balances sweet and sour (hence the name Acide!), a touch he insists adds a refreshing finish that won't leave the mouth weighed down by sugar.

Things started to change while Hermé was at Fauchon and even more so when he was at the helm of Ladurée, where he not only revived the classics but made them eminently more accessible to all. "Pierre Hermé is entirely responsible for making French pastry what it is today. He brought modernity, technique, expertise, and shook up the old model," gushed Jacques Genin, my favorite of the city's esteemed chocolatiers,[31] "that respect is owed to him."

You might say this was the very beginning of newfound recognition for bakers and pastry chefs all around. And it was about time. Venturing into the world of manual labor, even of the most delicious variety, was traditionally seen as a last resort vocation for those who did poorly in school or, worse, weren't intelligent enough. The noble paths to pursue in life have been those requiring intellect, time, and focused study in preparatory classes, university, and business schools with an expectation that students have a clear and calculated vision of where they want to go in life at an inordinately young age. But as a result of pioneers like Hermé, Philippe Conticini, Christophe Adam, Patrick Roger, Jacques Genin, and countless others venerated in magazines and on television, their trade is finally being acknowledged as the challenging, creative, *métier de passion* it truly is.

This recognition has also trickled into fine dining restaurant kitchens, where the hierarchy of importance has traditionally placed pastry chefs and candy makers at the bottom of the ladder: chef de cuisine, boulanger, pâtissier, and *confiseur* (candy maker). "The pastry chef never had a say in anything," noted chocolatier-pâtissier Jacques Genin. "Now they're not only given more creative freedom; they're in the spotlight as much as any chef." He would know—before opening his namesake boutique and tea salon in the North Marais (a gorgeous, seventeenth-century building that was once Yves Saint Laurent's couture atelier), he was a virtual unknown, holed up in a private laboratory in the 15th arrondissement where he prepared revelatory chocolates with the help of his right-hand gal Sophie Vidal, that he sold exclusively to top restaurants, including those in high-end hotels (which he still supplies today).

With his shop, which opened in 2008, he ushered in a new era of French pastry, chocolates, and candies. Driving it, of course, was a religious obsession with quality, freshness, and the quest for excellence. "I had to be a bit crazy to take a space like this as the market was crashing and undergo two years of renovations," says Genin. "But that's how I function." On top of that, he wasn't widely known. Still, he came onto the scene full throttle with pillowy flavored caramels (reinvented so they won't stick to your teeth!), jellied fruits and vegetables, bold chocolates (tonka bean, Sichuan peppercorn, mint, bergamot, grapefruit, and caper), sleek metallic confection cases that broke with usual packaging codes, and reinvented traditional pastries like the *tarte au citron* and the Paris-Brest (created in honor of the Paris-Brest cycling race) that would go on to win him awards. He is intense and demanding, qualities that have earned him something of a reputation. But it's hard to fault his method when his creations so closely approximate perfection.

In fact, if there is one common thread uniting my all-star favorites—Jacques Genin, Nicolas Cloiseau (La Maison du Chocolat), Claire Damon (Des Gâteaux et du Pain, see page 137), and Cédric Grolet (Le Meurice Hôtel)—it is a laser-like focus on detail, right down to rigorous sourcing. "We seek the best ingredients out there because we refuse to accept mediocrity as an option. Doing what we do is like loving someone: It takes effort and daily attention," Genin reminded me. Watching them work with their teams, whether to cream butter, roll out dough, or put the finishing touches on their latest masterpieces with swift, fluid, and almost poetic movements, is akin to watching an artist create a chef d'oeuvre or observing a prima ballerina demonstrate her skill through movement. I have never been a great fan of art or museums, but I get my artistic fix through chocolatiers and pâtissiers and the emotions they convey with each morsel. At the heart of each intricately prepared cake, tart, or chocolate square is an unshakable respect for the craft, and that's something you can taste.

Ethics are also driving what chefs produce and how the public consumes. Emmanuel Ryon, a Meilleur Ouvrier de France (ice cream specialty, see page 149), World Pastry Champion (1999), and half of the duo behind the stellar ice cream shop Une Glace à Paris, remarked that "clients are willing to pay more for quality today, which wasn't the case ten or fifteen years ago," and are genuinely more curious than ever before, interested in knowing about ingredients and excited to experiment with edgy or unexpected flavors.

The evolutions in the industry are reflections of our competing desires as a population. We hold on to nostalgic comforts, the classics we expect to be there for us at each visit, like the *tarte au citron*, the éclair *au chocolat*, the Paris-Brest. But as products of the attention economy, we also expect and demand constant novelty to seduce us. During Bac Sucré week 2015, when the rue du Bac's strip of star pâtisseries and chocolateries banded together to celebrate their craft with limited-edition products, tastings, and events for children, I visited Philippe Conticini's former shop, La Pâtisserie des Rêves, once a cult favorite, and overheard a Parisian client interrogating the poor sales girl about their lack of new flavors. "But it's the season! I was told there would be summer flavors in June!" she barked. What was amusing to both me and the shop girl was that there was novelty right under her nose: two summer ice cream flavors and the Bac Sucré Miam box, a package of treats for the occasion. And in almost the same breath she went on to lament a discontinued product. It would have been inappropriate had it not been so laughably absurd.

Despite feeling the pressure to innovate for consumers, almost every chef I spoke to expressed a more personal pressure—a self-imposed challenge to create with new, rare ingredients or reinvent the shape, form, and texture of signature desserts, as Nicolas Cloiseau, Jonathan Blot, and Carl Marletti, among the others in this chapter, have done so masterfully. Because today, it isn't enough to have talent or to replicate a recipe. Those who excel express their entire artistic being—their character, their emotions—through what they produce. That, Philippe Conticini says, is the only way to profoundly reach people with who they are as chefs. Don't be misled by the long history of the trade. Pâtisserie as a profession and as an art is living the early stages of its very own renaissance.

OPPOSITE It's nearly impossible to elect a favorite from Carl Marletti's svelte namesake bakery in the Latin Quarter, but he's perhaps best known for his *fraisier* (strawberry shortcake), named the city's best in 2014 by *Le Figaro*, and his tarte au citron. I've fallen for his Lily Valley, a violet twist on the Saint-Honoré named for his wife, a florist. And how could you resist sampling all of his classics? After all, as Marletti says, "When it comes to cuisine, you can eat well in so many countries now. But France is still the beating heart of pastry."

Nicolas Cloiseau, a Meilleur Ouvrier de France in chocolate making and the head of creation at La Maison du Chocolat, a perennial favorite.

CHOCOLATE: AN EVERYDAY ART

Before even speaking to the changes in the Parisian chocolate world, it's important to remember that chocolate is so much more than chocolate. In each piece or bar of chocolate is an experience, an expression of profound emotion, a spark of magic, a fragment of the French chocolatier's soul. From there, it's easier to understand why so many of the chocolate world's lodestars perpetually push themselves to create new recipes, improve existing favorites, and build relationships with cocoa producers from around the world; it's to keep that joyful experience alive.

That being said, several changes have carried chocolate beyond the mini revolution that Robert Linxe touched off forty years ago with his refined, light, and luxuriously presented ganaches, pralines, and chocolates at La Maison du Chocolat. My favorite Belgian chocolatier Pierre Marcolini, one of the pioneers of the bean-to-bar movement with four shops in Paris, points to a greater spectrum of flavors and textures and greater ease of innovation within the industry. "Today, we're moving toward the cocoa bean's origins and highlighting its natural, vegetal notes. Chocolate consumers are more open to spicy, smoky, and oaky, which opens up new ground for us as chocolate makers," Marcolini explains. "And working with the bean throughout the whole process gives us greater creative range. With roasting, we can add other ingredients like coffee or spices that naturally flavor the bean."

While the emblematic ganache (chocolates with velvety, flavored centers made of high-quality cream, chocolate, and butter) has been the calling card of La Maison du Chocolat since its beginnings, head chocolatier and Meilleur Ouvrier de France Nicolas Cloiseau wouldn't dare leave the recipes untouched. Each year, he works to update the permanent collection of ganaches by searching for different varieties of fruit to improve the flavor and stay relevant—the hardest part of the job, he told me. For the chocolat-cassis ganache, he began working with a variety of black currant that is both sweet and floral, as in perfume. "I don't like to look at what others in the business are doing; I look to complementary crafts like fashion or fragrance for inspiration," says Cloiseau. And occasionally, science. In 2016, he helped launch L'Envol, a brand-new collection of his signature ganaches that he created after experimenting with French scientist Fabrice Riblet for four years. Together, they discovered that by treating air as its own ingredient and infusing it back into the ganache during production, the result yielded an ethereally light and airy texture; the flavors locked in and exploded with aromatic bubbles. It is truly something that must be tasted to be believed.

When it comes to varying the chocolate he uses, he doesn't base his selection solely on its country of origin. "Chocolate varies by its terroir, like wine and coffee. I choose based on its aromatic qualities." That became clear when I sat down with Cloiseau to preview his 2015 Holiday Delicacies collection of chocolates. He walked me through the flavors I would experience in each square—*le début*, *le milieu*, and *la fin de bouche*, a subtle succession of tastes. I closed my eyes and focused on each flavor that awakened in my mouth, little by little. In the cinnamon and fig ganache, in which both an infusion of the cinnamon leaf and the cinnamon bud are used in combination with slivers of moist figs to lend a more elegant flavor, I first sensed the cinnamon's subtle spice, followed by the warmth of the fig before a dark chocolate finish took hold. I repeated

Flavored truffles from La Maison du Chocolat, using all-natural colorants: yuzu with sancho pepper berry; black currant; and vanilla caramel dotted with fleur de sel.

the exercise when I tasted his Esprit Salé collection, a permanent set of five savory chocolates—Espelette pepper ganache with a touch of Guérande sea salt; black olive and olive oil pralines; full-bodied dark chocolate ganache with Guérande sea salt; hazelnut and cep mushroom praline (Cloiseau uses young ceps for their natural notes of hazelnut); and the most puzzling to my taste buds, caramelized onion ganache with figs. It was an intriguing sensorial experience meant to exist beyond the realm of the familiar.

Cloiseau first created savory chocolates as part of the Meilleur Ouvrier de France competition in 2007 (the challenge was to create apéritif chocolates; he went for pepper, foie gras, and fennel), but the idea stayed with him long after he took home the award. It wasn't until he felt he had a solid base as head pastry chef that he sensed it was time to take La Maison du Chocolat in new directions. "I knew I'd be bringing clients off the beaten path with this collection, so I reassured them with a signature recipe—the ganache with just a dash of sea salt."

In the same meeting with Cloiseau, I snagged an early look at his chef d'oeuvre for the holiday collection, an artistic piece produced in limited quantities, mostly to be admired. It's no exaggeration when I say that his Wreath of Wonder took my breath away when I first saw it lording over the counter in their boulevard de la Madeleine boutique. A rare marvel, the eleven-pound structure was composed of eighty-four holly leaves in dark chocolate perforated in four sizes, some with gold-leaf finishes. These were affixed to two chocolate disks embellished with gold-leaf coated mendiant nuts: a mix of almonds from Valencia, hazelnuts from Piedmont, pecans from Texas, and pistachios from Sicily. It was finished off by delicate, red dark chocolate ornaments and ribbons. Twelve wreaths were produced in total, each requiring four and a half days of assembly, and priced at a whopping sixteen hundred dollars. It was magnificent and too exquisite to eat, to be sure. But the holidays are one of the key moments of the year for Cloiseau and his team to explore the full breadth of their creativity, weaving art from chocolate's many forms.

Others have made names for themselves with variations on the theme of experimentation. Jean-Paul Hévin, a Meilleur Ouvrier de France and master chocolate maker, has gone beyond perfected basics to explore less expected associations, like chocolate and strong, fragrant cheeses (think: Reblochon or Époisses with cumin) while Patrick Roger, another esteemed Meilleur Ouvrier de France, has risen to become the most artistic of the chocolate visionaries in Paris, using it as a foundation for sculptures—orangutans and other animals, most notably—that draw crowds from the street (for the inauguration of the redesigned Rodin Museum in 2015, Roger created a large chocolate installation called *La Sculpture a du Goût*—a nod to Rodin's *Balzac*—which appeared in the museum's entrance).

But perhaps the biggest change of all is the fascination around chocolate. "Since 2012, chocolate has stirred up a whole lot of interest, including among those who aren't from the industry, like Alain Ducasse," Cloiseau told me. Alain Ducasse is often called the Godfather of French cuisine, and for good reason: The multi-Michelin-starred chef has opened restaurants across the globe, runs a popular cooking school in Paris, has authored dozens of cookbooks, and has become a brand unto himself in his illustrious twenty-five-year career. That he added a bean-to-bar chocolate manufacturer, the city's first, to his list of credentials speaks to his unflagging ambition and ever-widening reach. The idea for Ducasse's chocolate venture emerged from a conversation he had with his head corporate pastry chef, Nicolas Berger. Unwilling to settle for just opening yet another chocolate shop in a saturated market, he insisted on working with Berger to make chocolate from scratch, with a focus on releasing the distinct nuances of each bean to create an intense product that speaks to the most discerning of chocolate lovers.

While Paris has no shortage of renowned chocolatiers, until Ducasse, no French chocolate maker produced their chocolate from scratch[32] given the complexity of the process, which requires expensive, highly specialized machines and the savoir faire to operate them. And that's saying nothing of the keen sense for sourcing the beans, which is equally important and incredibly time-consuming, something Belgian chocolatier Pierre Marcolini knows firsthand: He has been focused on bean-to-bar production for fourteen years. Housed in a former auto garage a short walk from Place de la Bastille, the Ducasse chocolate factory features a glass-paneled laboratory where the public can watch Berger and his team in action from a beautiful boutique brimming with single-origin bars and assortments of individual chocolates. You might say Berger is Paris's very own Willy Wonka.

Chocolate has evolved from a product produced and consumed for special occasions to an everyday item. But not just any chocolate will do. "Buy an industrial chocolate bar from the supermarket and you'll feel the need to consume the whole thing to reach the flavor or feeling you're looking for," Jacques Genin told me as he handed me a sachet of chocolate-caper praline sticks, his latest creation, to try. "With artisanal, high-quality chocolate, that same feeling can be had with one or two squares." In many ways, that alone encompasses the shift for consumers.

Michelin-starred chef Cyril Lignac, whose pastry shop La Pâtisserie has made its mark on the 11th arrondissement, launched a chocolate-focused outpost in 2016—his personal contribution among the phalanx of chefs working to preserve French savoir faire in chocolate making. Lignac devised La Chocolaterie as an alternative to the jewelry-box preciousness of most chocolate shops. "Everything here is meant to be accessible," Lignac told me the day before it opened to the public. "People can come drink our homemade hot chocolate, share a pastry, read the paper, and stay awhile comfortably. It's designed to be an everyday café for chocolate lovers." And after they do so, they can take home one of his many beautifully wrapped chocolate and candy bars. It's the chocolate bar you want to break into during afternoon tea or at the end of a meal absent of more elaborate desserts.

Today, the refrain is "eat better but eat less." And yes, better might sometimes mean more expensive. But by investing in the chocolatier's craft, you are investing in their staff, their relationship with the cocoa bean producers, and the future of the industry as a whole. I'll break off a square to that.

OPPOSITE La Chocolaterie, Cyril Lignac's homage to chocolate bars and chocolate desserts in a space meant for lingering.

Bringing the Pascade to Paris

STOP ANY PARISIAN ON the street and ask them where they last had an excellent *pascade* and you're likely to be met with a quizzical, "*Quoi?*" The pascade is essentially a crêpe soufflé, a dish "of the people" from the Aveyron region, traditionally consumed among friends and family on the Sunday after Easter (it falls into the category of crêpes and galettes, which also have religious origins). It is virtually unknown outside of the region. There is only one chef who has made it his signature. Chef Alexandre Bourdas not only grew up eating them but also developed a romantic fondness for them as he became a chef. When he opened his Michelin-starred restaurant SaQuaNa in Honfleur, Normandy, he wanted to incorporate it into the menu as an amuse-bouche, largely as a way to make the two-star experience less stuffy. As he describes it, it's a dish made for sharing and sparks exchange. "At some point, you need to decide who breaks into it first!" he says, and indeed, it was served as an icebreaker for the dinner. His interpretation of the pascade, called l'Originelle (truffle oil, chives, and a touch of sugar) blends luxury and terroir. But the possibilities to take the specialty a step further were endless, so he expanded the concept and brought it to Paris.

At his canteen in the 2nd arrondissement, aptly called Pascade, he focuses entirely on different iterations of the pascade as containers for veritable meals. On the savory front, you might have asparagus maki, Rougail de Saucisse (roasted sausage, chili, tomato, and grapefruit dressing), and chicken yassa. But my favorite part of the Pascade meal is the sweet finish.

Bourdas has also partnered with other high-profile chefs like David Toutain, Gregory Marchand of Frenchie, and chocolatier Pierre Marcolini, who have each developed a pascade recipe that was available on the menu for an entire month.

OPPOSITE Alexandre Bourdas's sweet pascade *Oh les figues, Oh les figues!* It's an ode to figs, featuring citrus fruit, a touch of rum, and mint for a refreshing finish.

Q&A

CLAIRE DAMON, DES GÂTEAUX ET DU PAIN

YOU MIGHT SAY Claire Damon is fixated on fruit. The high-profile pastry chef, schooled in elite pastry kitchens from Fauchon and Pierre Hermé to the Plaza Athénée under Christophe Michalak, launches only one chocolate-based dessert a year but is known for her tartes, millefeuilles, and other classically shaped French pastries gussied up with seasonal fruit and unique flavor combinations. She was also the first woman to open her own haute pâtisserie in Paris at the age of twenty-nine and remains one of the few. Her steely confidence masks feelings of vulnerability and frustration—for too long, in such male-dominated industries as cuisine and pastry, female talents have been relegated to the shadows. Still, she soldiers on and crafts what she strongly believes is an inventive and focused array of sweets that best reflects her personality. Evidently, they reflect mine as well, because Des Gâteaux et du Pain is, by far, my go-to pastry redoubt.

It isn't hyperbolic to say that you are obsessed with fruit. Why and how does it inspire your work?

I grew up on an orchard, so the connection with nature has always been very important to

me. I started by researching fruit producers because Rungis [a wholesale food market] didn't offer what I was looking for. Over time, I enjoyed working with [fruit] more and more. Only later did I truly understand the importance of plants and botanicals in my work; they have become my primary source of inspiration.

I choose the fruits I work with judiciously, only from the best producers. We then work with them in complete respect for our artistic vision. Fruits are an exceptionally rare, raw resource that have become a luxury. They have also become my signature. Monochromatic colors emerge from respecting the seasons, and it's another aspect of my work that I think is important—the link between color, taste, and feeling. It's not about head-turning colors but taste and seasonality.

What has changed the most in the pastry industry in recent years?

On the positive side, the consumer is more demanding. They expect better ingredients and have a fascination with pastry that goes beyond "that's pretty!" They're asking themselves questions about what they take home, and that's important. On the pastry side, there's a wave of people who are entering the industry after a career change and don't necessarily have the depth of training they need to be operational. Pastry requires time, in learning and executing, but today, no one seems to have the time for anything. We *must* find the time.

You've been cutting the sugar content in your pastries since long before it was a health fad. Why?

We measure the maturity of each fruit and its natural density of sugar to make adjustments in added sweetness. I don't lower sugar content because it's trendy; I do it to tease out and enhance the flavorful, pure note of the fruit I'm working with. It's like fashion and art—when it's good and beautiful, there is very little that needs to be done to it.

Which recipe are you most proud of?

There are several, each inspired by something personal. Le Lipstick pastry [a round, almond-crust tarte filled and coated with seasonal fruit] came about after a regular customer told me that I looked happier on days that I wore lipstick to work. I couldn't get it out of mind, so I ran with it! It gets updated throughout the year with seasonal fruit. Le Kashmir—a soft, round cake with notes of saffron, dates, and orange—is one of my signatures, inspired by my favorite Led Zeppelin song. And more recently I created Les Petits Bâteaux after observing the handcrafted wooden sailboats in the duck pond in the Luxembourg Gardens that have been rented out to children for ninety years. The shape of the pastry recalls the sails of the boats, and I update the flavors, like glazed chestnut, almond cream, and passion fruit on a shortbread crust, with every season. Seeing it instantly transports me to the gardens!

An abundance of mango: This shortbread tarte at Des Gâteaux et du Pain is garnished with a mango cream, light chiboust cream made with Tahitian vanilla, and a compote of fresh mango.

SINGLE-PRODUCT SHOPS

So what comes after creating new recipes and riffing on old ones? Specialization. And not just focusing on one genre of pastry like chocolate tartes or choux-based desserts but winnowing the selection to one, sole pastry. The much-loved macaron played an important role in paving the way for shops taking such an approach. Specialists like Pierre Hermé, and later the duo at Pain de Sucre and Jonathan Blot at Acide, showed sweet-lovers that, simple in form though it may be, the macaron had endless flavor possibilities and was a vehicle for creativity. Olive oil, vanilla, and slices of green olives; foie gras and chocolate; white truffle and hazelnut—the combinations are sometimes curious but always intriguing.

More recently, however, it was Christophe Adam, éclair master of Fauchon fame, who led the charge of single-product shops with L'Éclair de Génie, his wonderland of rainbow éclairs in raspberry passion fruit, lemon yuzu, Madagascar vanilla, pecan, or mascarpone salted caramel— a wide palette of flavors few had expected. Those who knew Adam's work for Fauchon might not have been surprised when he narrowed his focus—during his fifteen-year tenure there, he experimented wildly and developed more than a hundred original éclair recipes for which the pâtisserie is still known. In his own shop, he plays up the humble oblong pastry as a work of art that's suitable for *gourmandes* of all ages thanks to its size. Low-mess quotient aside, its appeal is both its simplicity and the exacting precision required to master it. Building on this insight, places like Popelini, La Maison du Chou, and Profiterole Chérie developed recipes entirely around the cream puff, which uses the same pastry base as the éclair. Colorful, flavorful, and eminently giftable, all three choux-loving shops have infused new vigor into old favorites.

Meringues have also gotten their space to shine. Lille pâtissier Frédéric Vaucamps brought his shop, Aux Merveilleux de Fred, to Paris, where he opened several outposts, on both banks of the river. Credited with popularizing the century-old Merveilleux[33] recipe, an ethereally light, layered meringue mound coated with sweet whipped cream and enveloped in a variety of coatings from chocolate flakes to caramelized hazelnuts that originated in his native Northern France, Vaucamps prepares them in exactly the same fashion as when he first began churning them out in 1982, extending the flavor offering ever so slightly in recent years. When I asked him why he chose to devote his attention exclusively to this pastry, he said he wasn't looking to create a concept, though it certainly appeared that way to newcomers. "Focusing on one thing allows us to be competitive as pastry chefs. I used to have a regular bakery, and le Merveilleux always outsold my other pastries." So not only was it a smart business move to listen to his clients but it also allowed him to dedicate his attention to perfecting the pastry, thereby establishing him as *the* reference.

In each of their locations, Vaucamps's shops have a similar design esthetic—a discreet wooden storefront, counters, and display cases in Rojo Alicante marble, a bohemian crystal chandelier that

OPPOSITE If éclairs have renewed appeal today it's entirely thanks to the creative mind of Christophe Adam, the former head pastry chef at Fauchon who invented more than a hundred original éclair recipes. Despite the rainbow palette of flavors you'll find at L'Éclair de Génie at any given time, Adam says his tastes remain classic: "There's no question: The salted caramel is my favorite!"

lords over the open kitchen, beige marble floor tiling with tiny black cabochons, and murals and frescoes inspired by eighteenth-century art. To immerse the uninitiated into the pastry's storied tradition, all Merveilleux are prepared, ingredient by ingredient, in front of customers. The modern twist lies in the recipe itself, which is far less rich than the original.

As a business, single-product shops make sense. "With a poor economy, many of us asked ourselves how we could make profitable what is effectively a *métier de passion*," Jonathan Blot told me, adding that he made a similar consideration to focus on macarons exclusively when he first opened his shop. "Not only that, but people are looking for the best, so we have a resurgence of specialists. Experts in éclairs, in madeleines, in meringues—it reassures customers." Reassuring and accessible for the customer, this approach is also beneficial to the baker, who can more easily control production.

But for sisters Fiona Leluc and Fatina Faye, the single-product format fit their nostalgic fondness for the sablé, a sweet shortbread biscuit as tied to the French identity as the chocolate chip cookie is to Americans' (and it has major social currency—they may be gifts at Christmas, an offering for teatime with friends or family, or an afternoon snack for school children). Delicate, melt-in-your-mouth sea-salt sablés take pride of place in their two-year-old neo-retro pâtisserie called Bontemps (where every light fixture, cake tray, and dish was antiqued by the sisters themselves), in the form of bite-size sandwich cookies filled with flavored creams like gianduja, orange flower, lemon, coffee, passion fruit, bergamot, chocolate–tonka bean, and Madagascar vanilla, all made fresh daily; full cakes elegantly shaped like hearts or flowers; and a variety of hearty tartes whose influences run Anglo-Saxon—pecan, banana-caramel flambé.[34] "We don't just work with ingredients or flavors considered traditionally French, because we love peanut, banana, mango—we listen to our cravings!" Leluc explained before going on to say that regardless of what's inside, the sablé is the feel-good comfort she baked after long, hard days as a financial advisor, her former career. "I traded one male-dominated field for another! But Fatina and I are doing what we love with the recipes that make us happy."

To be sure, they don't only make themselves happy. Whether it's the Motown tunes setting the tone in the shop, Faye's warm smile as guests enter, or simply the luscious treats themselves, which feel like a comforting hug, the Bontemps style has found a loyal audience. The adjunct to the mayor of the 3rd arrondissement, whose office sits squarely across the street, came into the shop one day while I was eating my way through their entire selection of mini sablés. She expressed how proud she was of what the women had created and contributed to the neighborhood: "Their shop is my antidepressant!" she told me. And mine.

OPPOSITE You might say the cream puffs at Popelini dethroned the king-of-cute-macaron. At least they did for Parisians, who are endlessly beguiled by the seasonal varieties Lauren Koumetz dreams up for her trio of boutiques. Among the flavors that regularly find their way into the pastry case: coffee, Madagascar vanilla, rose with confit raspberries, lemon, praline, salted caramel, pistachio with confit morello cherries, and a chou du jour, which is always a sure bet.

Bontemps Pâtisserie

THERE IS LITTLE MORE REDOLENT of French childhood than the sablé, a buttery shortbread cookie baked to perfection and given the spotlight it deserves at Bontemps, a family-run bakery in the North Marais. Head pastry chef Fiona Leluc (at left, with her sister Fatina Faye) left the world of finance to pursue baking. The shop's short-order success was an unmistakable sign that she had made the right decision. Fiona and her co-chefs make everything from scratch daily, from the shortbread dough to the lemon curds and fruit fillings.

The little shortbread joys at Bontemps Pâtisserie, filled with fresh fillings from coffee ganache to banana cream to passion fruit.

"Why did I focus on just profiteroles? . . . I love that they correspond perfectly to the savoir faire of a pastry chef *and* that of an ice cream maker. You need to know how to make the puff pastry, which is very simple but must be perfect. You also have to be able to make the filling, composed of cream and ice cream, and the topping. It's a pastry that really brings together multiple areas of expertise, and on top of that, I added the element of making it *à la minute*, in front of the client in my shop. Above all, profiteroles had fallen out of favor so I wanted to give people a reason to seek them out again."

—PHILIPPE URRACA, OWNER OF PROFITEROLE CHÉRIE AND A MEILLEUR OUVRIER DE FRANCE

THE JAPANESE TOUCH

Cooking isn't the only area in which Japanese chefs have been making their mark in Paris (see page 41). Among the small group of Japanese pastry chefs seducing Parisians with their unique renditions of French pastries, Sadaharu Aoki (pâtissier and chocolatier) and the young Mori Yoshida are the most famous. Already something of a star in Japan, Aoki is known in Paris as the first to fuse Japanese ingredients like yuzu, matcha, black sesame, and adzuki beans with classic recipes. The traditional Opéra cake becomes the Bamboo, Aoki's bestselling twist, composed of alternating layers of joconde biscuit, chocolate ganache, and matcha buttercream. The traditional éclair gets a black sesame makeover, and even the macaron gets its own edgy combo—wasabi-horseradish. Yoshida, on the other hand, remains loyal to French savoir faire, updating recipes in their form and with seasonal ingredients (his *chaussons aux pommes* are out of this world) in his 7th arrondissement boulangerie-pâtisserie, opened in 2013.

Of the Japanese admiration for French pastry making and the country's Meilleur Ouvrier de France program specifically, Philippe Urraca says it is best explained by the comparisons with Japanese samurai training that they both evoke. "I've had Japanese people tell me that a Meilleur Ouvrier de France is someone who suffers to do good and please others; someone who suffers for excellence and to push the boundaries of their creativity." For the Japanese, France *is* pastry. And it almost goes without saying that the best place to learn and shine as foreign talent is in Paris.

EVOLVING THE CRAFT

Rare ingredients, new forms, exotic flavors—it's difficult to say where pastry will go in the years and decades to come but one thing is certain: The people behind the trade can innovate for the future knowing that their work is revered and repected by a much broader set of the population than ever before.

OPPOSITE Just call Phillippe Urraca the king of profiteroles, shown opposite in lemon meringue and crème de marrons.

"There was a long period of weak products—no balance, no texture, and experimentation only for the sake of experimenting. In addition to having access to better products, pastry chefs are traveling more themselves and pulling inspiration from varieties of flavors in places like Asia and Latin America."

—EMMANUEL RYON, CO-OWNER OF UNE GLACE À PARIS

Meilleur Ouvrier de France (M.O.F.), the Olympic Title for Craftsmen

AT THE END OF THE documentary *Kings of Pastry*, Philippe Urraca, the master of ceremonies and the president of the Meilleurs Ouvriers de France (Best Craftsmen of France) pastry competition, steps up before sixteen finalists, all standing solemnly behind him, and their loved ones. With tears in his eyes, he inhales deeply and expresses how difficult it was for the jury to make a decision given such a high-caliber cohort of pastry craftsmen. This came at the end of a grueling, three-day time-trial competition in Lyon where finalists concocted exquisite desserts, pastries, and edible sculptures so intricate you couldn't help but sit rapt in front of the screen as they toiled over them to perfection. Having seen the finalists labor over their creations and power through mishaps, Urraca was visibly moved; it recalled his own experiences in the competition. "It's tremendously difficult to tell these pastry chefs that they weren't good enough this time but they shouldn't give up; they should compete again," Urraca says. "I went through that; it's tough."

Founded in 1924 to elevate the country's level of craft and reinforce the importance of manual work, the Meilleur Ouvrier de France program (often shortened to M.O.F.) encompasses more than two hundred artisanal trades, from pastry and chocolate to woodworking and floral design. Pastry and chocolate are said to be among the most challenging but are also some of the most publicized. "The pastry competition is difficult because it covers so much: Finalists don't only work with pâtisserie but are asked to work with chocolate, sugar, and produce plated [restaurant-style] desserts!" says Urraca.

Preparing for the exam isn't unlike training to compete in the Olympics—it demands rigor, indefatigable drive, and a considerable investment of time and energy. On average, participants work tirelessly for two years leading up to the preliminary competition and that is in addition to their day jobs as bakers, pastry chefs, instructors, or business owners. The diligence and focus required to prepare puts considerable strain on family and social life, leading some to swear off the pursuit if they don't become laureates on the first try. No level of celebrity can help a participant's chances, as this is, at its very core, a test of pure talent and a reflection of the trade's storied heritage. The blue, white, and red collar is a gauge of quality, excellence, dexterity, and skill that stays with its wearer for life; every day the prestigious title must be honored. And when no finalist meets the expectations of the jury, no prize is awarded. Unprecedented, it was the case in the Meilleur Ouvrier de France Chocolate competition in 2015.

A heritage program though it may be, the pastry competition has evolved since Urraca became president to ensure the finalists are tested for their ability to create for today's tastes. "It was on cruise control for a long time, but I came in and modernized some aspects of the competition. In 2015, we had the finalists prepare reception cakes that would be transported to a hotel and then displayed. It was the first time we were allowed to do this—in transporting them, there was great risk for the creations themselves, but it meant so much to the chefs to see their work in the spotlight." And even after more than ninety years since the competition's inception, the prestige that a Meilleur Ouvrier de France award bestows helps bolster new business ventures. Emmanuel Ryon, co-owner of Une Glace à Paris, speaks to the reassurance in quality and excellence conferred by the collar and the sign in front of his shop. "I hesitated putting it up, unsure it would really speak to people, but it worked in our favor. Local clients came to tell us how thrilled they were to have an artisan in the neighborhood!"

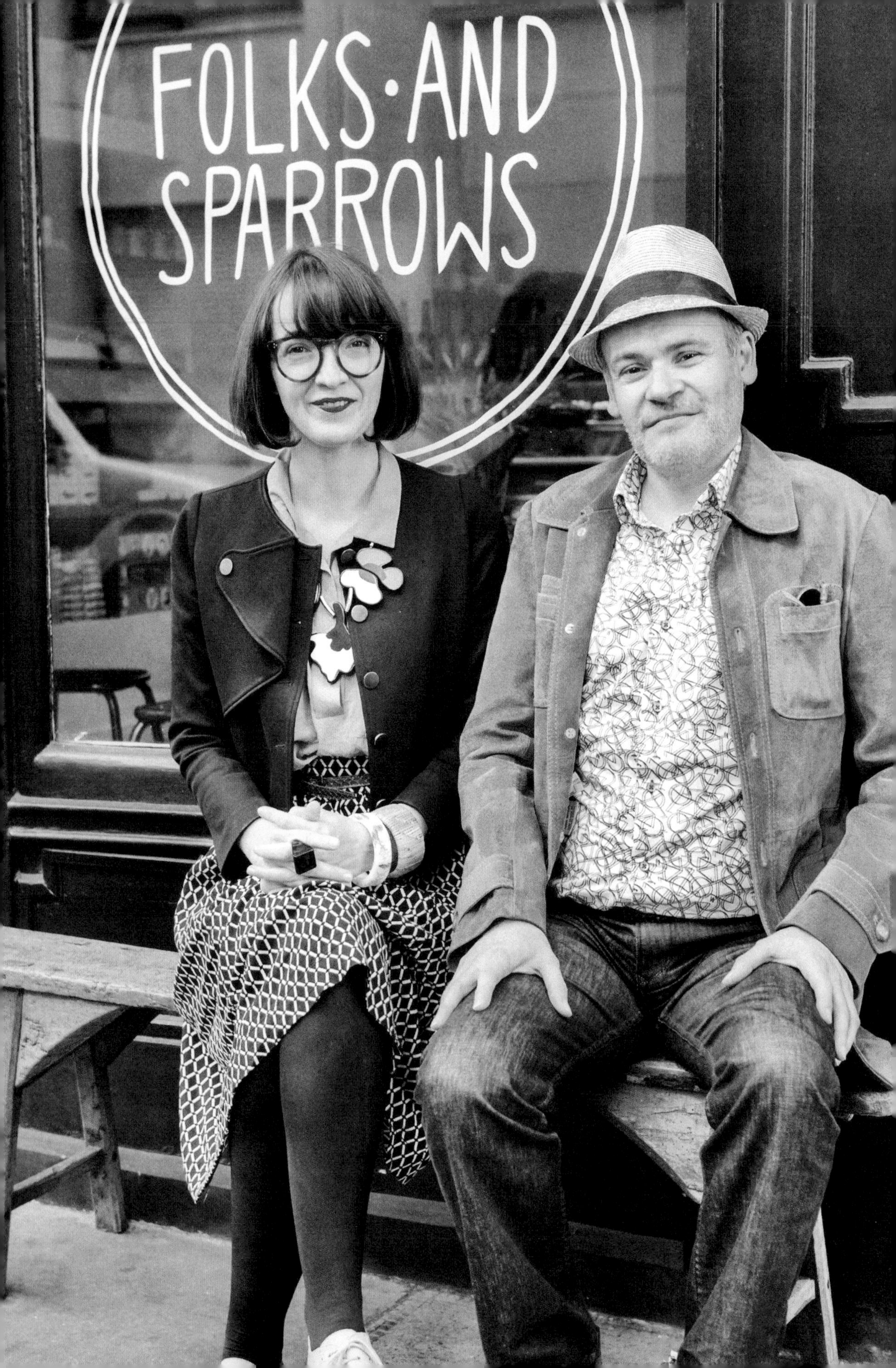
FOLKS·AND
SPARROWS

PARISIAN PERSPECTIVE

LAURENCE GUILLOUD, 34, AND FABRICE LE DANTEC, 45
JOURNALIST AND PHOTOGRAPHER, CREATORS OF *L'INSTANT PARISIEN* MAGAZINE

You are both originally from Lyon. What attracted to you Paris and how does it inspire your work?

We were attracted to Paris and settled down here because of its *je ne sais quoi*, that singular something that still escapes definition. Maybe it was partly for its intellectual and artistic heritage that is still quite present. But the city wasn't meant to be a history book; it's a saga with new characters, unexpected turns, and theatrics. If we consider the city as a television series, we unconsciously agree to participate in writing its future seasons. It's our collective challenge and responsibility to make sure that fascinating and exciting things continue to develop!

People are saying there is something in the air in Paris, something new and different. Do you feel it?

In Paris, we have found an energy that we were often missing in Lyon. Paris is also a very mixed place, and we've never met people from so many walks of life. The world converges in Paris, and that diversity generates an inspiring and creative dynamic.

So many young people are flocking to Paris and opening up businesses. What's behind this wave?

Indeed, it's a surprising phenomenon! Our encounters for *L'Instant Parisien* have shown us that there is truly an enthusiastic spike in young people dropping everything to create something of their own. The economic travails our country has faced have made people realize to what extent it is vital to find meaning in their work. It reminds us that to blossom, we must take control of our professional lives, take chances, innovate. Everyone knows Paris, and France in general, doesn't have a very entrepreneurial spirit, but all of that is starting to change at a dizzying speed.

Old vs. new Paris: Can they coexist?

When we think of historic Paris, we think of the 1950s and 1960s, the bohemian era filled with novelists, poets, and thinkers. There is still a section of "Old Paris" that resists uniformity, in neighborhoods such as Ménilmontant and Belleville, which pulse with energy. So let's be optimistic: Yes, they can coexist! And they must. The Paris that moves and changes (and changes itself) is only just beginning to reveal itself.

the new LIBATIONS

"Show me how you drink and
I'll tell you who you are."

—ÉMILE PEYNAUD, FRENCH WINE OENOLOGIST,
ALSO KNOWN AS "THE FOREFATHER OF MODERN OENOLOGY"

As drinkers go, I was very much a tenderfoot when I arrived in Paris at age twenty. My college years were more studious than they were adventurous (although I like to think that moving abroad wholly made up for the lack of partying) so my tastes were entirely informed by the drinks I tried in Paris.

To finish off the first meal he cooked for me, my husband served me a glass of vin jaune from Bergerac, a cloying white wine that I initially adored because, well, it was sweet and I knew little else. My first experience with Parisian cocktails was unmemorable save for the fact that the bar that played host to my introduction was called Le Kitch and featured garlands and Christmas lights all year round. The barman was heavy-handed, turning a mojito (the de rigueur drink of choice at the time) into a gateway to immediate inebriation.

As for beer, I was a neophyte at best. Leffe, Kronenbourg, Budweiser, and Heineken were my only working framework, and I knew I didn't like those. I associated beer with a partying lifestyle that didn't resonate with me—wild nights under the bleachers or at a friend's house when their parents weren't home, uncontrolled spring breaks, and rowdy football gatherings. The perception of the drink as cheap and less refined than wine or spirits, a feeling I would later learn was widely shared by the French, led me to reject it altogether.

That said, entering prime adulthood in Paris as craft cocktails, beer, and natural wine ascended and earned all manner of popular acclaim felt like a blessing. It meant I could explore new tastes and flavors without bias. I had no expectations and everything to learn. And in interviewing some of the individuals leading the movement, I learned not only how impressive the city's growth has been in these areas but also how much these libations can enhance a meal.

PREVIOUS SPREAD Unlike most of the city's craft cocktail joints, which play up a clandestine, sultry lounge vibe, Café Moderne's decidedly French space was preserved in spirit and decor by Ahmed "Mido" Yahi and his partners: old métro seats, old bistro tables, original tiling, and a long, wooden bar, etc. Their space, a former couscous restaurant of the same name, has natural cachet and inspired Mido immediately. OPPOSITE Owners Joseph Akhavan (pictured) and Samantha Sanford named their bar, Mabel, as a cheeky nod to Mabel Walker Willebrandt, the US Assistant Attorney General tasked with enforcing Prohibition policy during the 1920s, though she was personally opposed to Prohibition.

GRAND PIGALLE

CRAFT COCKTAILS

To say that cocktails are a new phenomenon in Paris is to overlook a culture of distilling liquors dating back to the 1800s, one that gained greater traction more than one hundred years later during American prohibition, when newly unemployed bartenders came to Europe in droves and landed in some of the continent's best hotel bars. Then, there is the importance of two iconic bars that popularized the American-English cocktail tradition in the 1920s—Harry's New York Bar and the Bar Hemingway at the Ritz Paris, renowned in equal parts for its creative cocktails, its literary and artistic clientele, and its star barman, Colin Peter Field, who revived the bar in 1994 after it went dormant in the mid-seventies. The Englishman and longtime expat in Paris has been called the "LeBron James of liquor, the Matisse of martinis, the Yves Saint Laurent of gimlets,"[35] but he is, above all, instrumental to Paris's presence on the cocktail map. It is a result of his skill and advocacy of bartending that the Ministry of Education began offering a formal degree in 2011— a Meilleur Ouvrier de France program for barmen—meant to bolster the profession.

However, to trace the democratization of craft cocktails as drinks accessible to all, we have to look to 2007 and focus on a trio of bon vivants with a vision—a vision whose impact reverberated widely and rapidly, ushering in a scene that was once relegated to luxury hotels and executed poorly by no-name bars. Romée de Goriainoff, Olivier Bon, and Pierre-Charles Cros of the Experimental Group (EG) were a bellwether to Paris nightlife and the first to move cocktails beyond their traditional codes in hotel bars with their first and most famous bar, the Experimental Cocktail Club. They offered prohibition-era tipples, using top-shelf ingredients and liquors that Parisians wouldn't find in their local supermarket or corner store (no more Absolut! no more Jack Daniels!) and concentrated their efforts entirely on taste. Hard spirits, more popular at the turn of the century, became the foundation for their cocktails.

They weren't interested in replicating classic martinis, mojitos, and cosmos (although they wouldn't refuse to make them if customers insisted). Instead, they pulled from what they learned, tasted, and experienced in Montreal, New York, and London, each with established cocktail cultures, in the early 2000s as young, impressionable, and most importantly, curious students. They wanted an environment that spoke to their generation—less formal and stuffy, more approachable—and drinks made with good products and offered at price points they could afford (ten to fifteen euros). They sourced the best-quality spirits and fruit, made their own syrups and bitters, and worked with the right designer (Dorothée Meilichzon, see page 249) to create an

---

OPPOSITE What's the next logical step for the cocktail kings behind the Experimental Group? A B&B— bed and beverage—their nickname for their debut into the hospitality business with the Grand Pigalle boutique hotel in the 9th arrondissement (and a mere block from some of the city's best bars). Guests can order craft cocktails to be delivered to their rooms (should the house cocktail in the minibar not suffice) or spend their time rubbing elbows with the many locals who drop into the spacious lounge and café for lunch and afternoon meetings during the day, post-work aperitifs, and nightcaps. As with all of the EG's spaces, it's sexy, comfortable, and beautifully designed by Dorothée Meilichzon (think: a mix of 1920s Parisian glamour and understated Hollywood regency)—good times are guaranteed.

entirely new image of the cocktail bar. "Friends told us we were crazy, that Parisians didn't drink cocktails, they drink wine!" says Bon. But all of that changed within six months of opening their first bar, and they've never looked back.

From their contribution emerged an entirely new cultural cachet. Beyond a well-edited and masterfully executed menu, the Experimental boys knew how to create atmosphere. Their first space and those that have followed—Prescription Cocktail Club, La Compagnie des Vins Surnaturels, Beef Club, Fish Club, the Grand Pigalle Hôtel (their first foray into the broader world of hospitality), and Night Flight in the Hôtel Bachaumont—have a unique look and feel, with exacting standards of decor, and are big on mood with intimate lighting, laid-back tunes, and plush furnishings made for late-night lingering. "They brought a wave of fresh air to the city and [the Experimental Cocktail Club] opened on a dead side street off of the rue Montorgueil, which changed the neighborhood. And they gave us a modern cocktail culture: good drinks, quality spirits, fresh ingredients, and a fun environment," says Carina Soto Velasquez, the first employee and manager of the Experimental Cocktail Club.

They mastered their craft and have set their sights beyond French borders: the EG style can now be found in New York, London, and Ibiza, with more projects to follow. But perhaps their most enduring impact is the talent who graduated from their bars to launch their own unique spaces and concepts with a passion and creativity on par with that of the city's best chefs.

Velasquez is perhaps the most well-known Experimental Cocktail Club alum, having left to start a mini empire of her own with Americans Josh Fontaine and Adam Tsou. Their company, Quixotic Projects, is the force behind Candelaria, the city's first Mexican taqueria. With its unmarked cocktail den specializing in agave spirits, the restaurant-bar has consistently been recognized as a must-visit destination by Tales of the Cocktail and World's 50 Best Bars, which ranked it ninth in 2013, the highest showing for a French cocktail bar. They spun gold out of Candelaria's success and went on to open Glass in 2012, a rock 'n' roll cocktail bar in Pigalle inspired by the New York bars in which Fontaine and Tsou had worked years prior; then the seafood-and-cocktails small-plates restaurant Le Mary Celeste in 2013; and Hero in 2015, a Korean-inspired canteen with inventive cocktails near the once-seedy Strasbourg Saint-Denis neighborhood. More than cocktail creators, the three have proven themselves crafters of experience: Each of their locations has strong good-times vibes and an environment that keeps locals sidling up to the bar.

Velasquez told me that one advantage to launching in the wake of an economic crisis was that longevity depended on exhibiting creativity in spades, and Quixotic Projects certainly excelled in that area. Only the people with the strongest ideas and the gumption to fight for them would find success. "Hospitality, gastronomy, and bartending have been part of French culture for ages. Today, we're seeing a renaissance of artisanal professions that had been banalized for far too long," she remarked.

What's behind the movement? In her book *Paris Cocktails*, author Doni Belau sums it up beautifully. "Take the locavore movement, the artisanal quest, the DIY urge, and an ever-increasingly sophisticated palate. Combine that in a cocktail shaker with hundreds of specialized small-batch

Le Mary Celeste

THERE IS A TENDERNESS and finesse in the small plates at Le Mary Celeste that outclasses imitation bars that followed in its footsteps. It's not a scene, nor is it masquerading as something's it's not. It's a place for good food (and that includes a variety of oysters between September and April) and good drinks, be they cocktails, craft beer, or natural wine. You can often find the bartenders having as much fun shaking and stirring the drinks as the guests are drinking them. And what I love is how it transformed from another link in a chain of cocktail concepts into its own, sustainable presence on a quiet corner of the North Marais. Mixologists from around the world have been known to make guest bartending appearances, switching up the original menu and exposing regulars to different styles. For the beer contingent, there's no shortage of Deck & Donohue, Demory, and Brooklyn brews to go around.

Seen at right, the Quixotic Projects trio (and the brains behind Le Mary Celeste, Glass, and Hero): Josh Fontaine, Carina Soto Velasquez, and Adam Tsou.

Classic French spirits like Armagnac create the foundation for the cocktails at Le Syndicat.

A Bar for Everyone

CONTRIBUTED BY FOREST COLLINS

These days, it wouldn't be a stretch to call the City of Light the City of Liquor. With the resurgence in cocktail culture, there truly is a Paris bar for every kind of imbiber.

BACKPACKERS: Students and shoestring travelers will like the laid-back attitude and rowdy fun at the **RED HOUSE,** but they'll especially love the five-euro Negronis.

PARTY PEOPLE: A cool young crowd congregates at **GLASS** for late hours, loud music, and a dive-bar vibe, complete with a beer-and-shot combo alongside a tight cocktail list.

FRANCOPHILES: Lovers of all things French hit **LE SYNDICAT,** where barmen Frenchify classics or create modern cocktails using only homegrown spirits and ingredients.

COCKTAIL GEEKS: Discerning cocktillians slip through the unmarked door at **CANDELARIA** taqueria and into the hidden bar to sip on La Guêpe Verte, their modern classic featuring tequila infused with hot pepper, mixed with lime and agave, and garnished with a cucumber slice.

FOODIES: Modern gastronomes stop by **PASDELOUP** to try their always evolving cocktail and food pairing options, like a melt-in-your-mouth chevon sandwich served with a cachaça-based cocktail created exclusively for (and sold only with) the pairing.

SINGLES: Solo drinkers head to **OBER MAMMA** for a spritz during *aperitivo* hour, when the bar is so busy that they can't help but rub elbows with someone fun and friendly.

SOPHISTICATED COUPLES: Lovers looking for luxury, romance, and mood lighting canoodle in the cozy corners of the bar at the 9th arrondissement's boutique hotel **MAISON SOUQUET,** a former pleasure house.

FOREST COLLINS *is the creator of the website* 52 Martinis, *a guide to the best cocktail bars in Paris, and founder of the Chamber, a private pop-up cocktail club. For more ideas on where to drink see page 257.*

products made in France, garnish with passion and artistry, and you've got the Parisian craft bar movement."[36] And it makes sense. After all, the movement wasn't created in a vacuum; it came on the heels of a food movement that flipped dining and consuming on its head. "In France, we're lucky to have all the best products (it's one of our biggest strengths!) and it allows us to be super creative. And because we make our own syrups, we can talk to clients knowledgeably about what's really in each drink," Café Moderne's owner and award-winning head barman Ahmed "Mido" Yahi, a self-taught mixologist who learned by letting his palate guide the way, told me over drinks in his bar. "Today, you can offer a tarragon-ginger syrup or a foie gras cocktail and guests won't think it's weird because flavor experimentation is more widely accepted, in both food and drink. Bars are basically like restaurants at this point; they use extremely fresh products." Even better, he's excited by the idea that today's adolescents will grow up into an existing cocktail culture that is celebrated. "I already get fathers who come in with their eighteen-year-old sons for meatballs and cocktails; it's awesome. Family bonding certainly isn't something you're likely to see in a nightclub!"

More than ever, Parisians are more curious and willing to try new things, with a little guidance from the experts. "With Candelaria's South American spirit, we, of course, incorporated tequila and mezcal in particular, neither of which had a market in Paris before we opened. Now, we sell more Del Maguey than anyone else in continental Europe," Fontaine says. Because of that openness, there are fewer limits for the barman. Amaury Guyot of the whiskey-centric bar Sherry Butt and Dersou (see page 44), for example, tailors his drinks to his partner Taku Sekine's dishes, many of which rotate daily according to the ingredients available from small purveyors.

When it comes to educating the cocktail-curious, a few people and places have made their mark on the industry, including Joseph Akhavan. As part of the team that opened Mama Shelter, the first of the Starck-designed boutique hotels, in 2008, and then as key recipe developer at La Conserverie, Joseph was part of the craft cocktail movement's first wave in Paris. But he's earned high marks in more recent years for his rum den and grilled cheese bar Mabel, located in the Silicon Sentier, the 2nd arrondissement's tech hub, which he runs with his partner, Samantha Sanford. "We wanted to break the codes of rum bars, which are usually tropical or tiki themed. We take it somewhere different," Akhavan told me as he prepared a drink for me to try. And it was certainly easy to do with a toolbox of more than 120 references and an intense passion for the product. Their goal was to make clients see rum as a more noble product, one that could be as interesting and versatile as any other spirit, especially in cocktails. "Rum has often been associated with 'cheap' brands and still is, perhaps because of what you can find in supermarkets or at clubs. When you have a bad experience with a spirit, you rarely go back to it." And as a result, Akhavan and Sanford offer *Routes des Rhums*, a menu option where guests can try three different rums from the same region and taste their complexities firsthand. As part of the anti-rum contingent for most of my adult life, I can speak from experience that Akhavan has a talent, not merely for persuasion ("you can't say you don't like it if you don't try it") but for targeting his recommendations. He knows his product, he understands the subtleties in flavor that emerge from his drinks, and he rises to the challenge of concocting a drink that will please even the most amateur of palates.

The development in the cocktail scene that I've been most excited about, though, is the return of products sourced closer to home. Globalization has made access to products from all over the world much easier, and that's particularly true in the bar world. To fight the uniformity in offerings, bartenders have begun looking inward to tell stories with their drinks.

Leading the way in the revivalist category is Sullivan Doh, a young mixologist and Ferrandi graduate who gained experience at two of the city's best bars—Prescription Cocktail Club and Sherry Butt—who took his penchant for Cognac, Armagnac, and Calvados and ran with it in a big way at Le Syndicat. His focus? All French spirits. "The market was full of cocktail bars when Romain Le Mouëllic, my business partner, approached me about opening my own bar. I knew it was going to take a strong, sustainable concept," he told me. Featuring everything from absinthe, Pineau des Charentes, and vermouth to Picon and Suze on their menus, bartenders like Doh are raising their glasses to once-forgotten spirits. "The whole world knows or at least has heard of French alcohols and liqueurs and associates them with savoir faire and quality. And yet they're not at all popular in France," said Doh, who was inducted with his partner into the Compagnie des Mousquetaires d'Armagnac (Armagnac Musketeers), a prestigious club whose members do their utmost to promote Armagnac.

That's especially true for Cognac, *the* French luxury spirit par excellence, which is consumed largely beyond the region where it is produced. According to the Bureau National Interprofessionnel du Cognac,[37] nearly 98 percent of the country's Cognac production is exported outside of France, primarily to the United States, the UK, and Asia. Knowing this, Doh and his partner wanted to galvanize Parisian drinkers around French heritage products. Their mission is even woven into their name: Le Syndicat: Organisation de Défense des Spiritueux Français. French spirits, they insist, are steeped in history and reflect the identity of France and its regions. Faced with the influx of foreign concepts, shops, and products, it's becoming even more important to preserve and honor what the country does best. And the wider cocktail audience took notice: In under a year, Le Syndicat was nominated for Best New International Bar in the Spirited Awards (given by Tales of the Cocktail) and then one of six Bars to Visit in 2016 by *Spirits Business* magazine.

I asked Doh how he sees the changes in the industry, since the Experimental Group put craft back on the map, and he described the evolutions in waves. "The second wave began in 2011 with Candelaria, which brought something fresh and unique to the scene. Then followed Sherry Butt, Little Red Door, Dirty Dick, Glass, and a number of really excellent bars that pushed cocktails further via specialization in 2012." But 2014 saw the pivotal shift; a "tsunami," according to Doh. "So many bars opened, each as good as the one before it—Baton Rouge, A La Française, PasdeLoup, Lulu White, CopperBay. Cocktails aren't about trend anymore; they're a way to express creativity and innovation. They've set the standard for what will come next."

Affordable craft cocktails may have been slow to sprout in Paris, but the individuals driving the scene today have drastically changed the city's nightlife and have more than lived up to the city's reputation as a top-tier cocktail destination.

Le Syndicat

ARMAGNAC IS ONE OF the many classic French spirits that owner-mixologist Sullivan Doh (pictured above) seeks to introduce to a younger drinking public at Le Syndicat.

"Initially, we wanted to move away from the speakeasy format because it had become so common in Paris, but it fit with the space that we found on rue du Faubourg-Saint-Denis," says Doh. The neighborhood felt right for them because it's so mixed—working class with a newly trendy tilt that appeals to a young, curious generation of gastronomes. But the bar itself is easy to miss: The building looks abandoned, the façade is a patchwork of concert posters and advertisements, and

there is a noticeable lack of formal signage. But inside, it's intimate industrial-chic with a design by Cut Architectures. The most well-lit section of the space is rightly on the bar itself, with the spotlight squarely on an astounding selection of French spirits and Doh's cocktail-making stage.

Two of their signature drinks include the Laurier d'Apollon, with homemade ginger syrup, fresh lemon juice, apricot liqueur, Blanche de Normandie (apple brandy), and bay-leaf mousse; and the Smoking Car, a twist on the Sidecar with orange flower, fresh lemon juice, dry curaçao, and VSOP Cognac, served in a flask smoked with bitter orange peel.

"Today, when people talk about cocktail capitals, they mention New York, London, and Paris. In only a few years, we made up for the decades we lagged behind."

—AHMED "MIDO" YAHI, CO-OWNER AND HEAD MIXOLOGIST AT CAFÉ MODERNE

ABOVE Not long after opening Café Moderne, Mido started participating in competitions around the world as a means to get feedback on his work. In 2014, after creating about eighteen cocktails and demonstrating rituals of service, he was elected Best Barman of in France (World Class), and in 2015, after eight months of preparation, he ranked third in the world. Now, he gives master classes all over France and abroad. "We're a community, so when we compete we're not just representing our own bars and restaurants, we're representing the entire country," he said.

A (Legal) Parisian
— Distillery —

FIVE YEARS OF BATTLING
bureaucracy and a crowd-funding
campaign later, brothers Nicolas
and Sébastien Julhès, of the 10th
arrondissement's family-owned *épicerie*
of the same name, succeeded in opening
the first legal micro-distillery in Paris in
more than a century. They produce their
own gin, vodka, brandy, and a malt spirit
that will become Paris's first whiskey
after aging (about three years). Unlike
large distilleries, the duo is focused on
experimentation and collaborations with
like-minded artisans in varying fields.
And they're taking the concept of *Made
in Paris* to exciting new heights.

NATURAL WINE ON THE RISE

Similarly exciting developments have been felt in the world of wine with the rise in popularity of natural wine. When I told my friend Wendy that I wanted to talk about the topic, her eyes widened, her mouth morphed into a cracked smile, and she offered a simple, "Ha! Good luck!" If you're seeking an incontrovertible understanding of what natural wine is, like I was when I first started seeing the term brandished on bistro and wine bar menus across town, you're likely to be met with varying answers.

Like many things in Paris, food or otherwise, natural wine falls into the category of polarizing topics of discussion. On the one hand, you have enthusiasts that believe wholeheartedly in its virtues—made from grapes farmed organically, often biodynamically; non-corrective vinification practices like indigenous yeast, low or no addition of sulfites; and, in most cases, neither fining nor filtration—but critics are unconvinced of its taste and value. In eschewing additives, they argue, the results are too inconsistent or even *étrange* (strange), the word my conventional wine-drinking father-in-law used to describe the first glass of natural red he tried. Whether ideological, philosophical, or commercial judgments are at play in selecting natural wine, the bottom line is that wine should be about pleasure. Is one approach necessarily better than the other? It depends entirely on who you ask.

"A natural wine might be cloudy, spritzy, off-dry, and oxidized all at once," wine writer and *Not Drinking Poison in Paris* blogger Aaron Ayscough told me over a glass of wine at Vivant Cave one summer evening. "In the context of natural wine, these traits alone wouldn't prevent it from being considered a masterpiece. The trade-off for the freewheeling stylistic cornucopia of contemporary natural wine in Paris is that the wines tend to be more fragile, and their graces more fleeting, than conventional wine." A strong proponent of natural wine, Ayscough does his due diligence to taste conventional wines as a way of better understanding the nuances in those he typically drinks. "I do that to be able to know what is of quality in the natural wine, to know what's coming from the process, and what's coming from the terroir."

More draconian devotees insist that natural is the *only* acceptable wine and don't bother with conventional wines at all. For this set of drinkers, wine is meant to convey the terroir—the specifics of the soil, climate, environment, and emotional ties to the land—and any flaws are part of each bottle's unique story and should be respected. David Loyola, owner of Aux Deux Amis, a wine bar and after-hours chef hangout in the 11th arrondissement, believes that working with and offering natural wines means respecting the ground, the leaves, the grapes, and even the weeds. Pierre Jancou, sommelier and restaurateur, is a diehard advocate of *les vins vivants*

OPPOSITE Natural-wine bar, neo-bistro, neighborhood institution—Clown Bar was a historic bistro from 1902 and the former watering hole for the staff of the Cirque d'Hiver, the adjacent circus. The space was taken over by former Saturne talents, who proposed a market-driven menu of shareable small plates and natural wines offered by the glass. And while the interior has been refurbished, the most whimsical elements (and those with listed status) have been preserved beautifully: tiling on the wall behind the zinc bar featuring Sarreguemine clowns, who also adorn the painted glass ceiling.

(or, living wines, his preferred moniker for natural wines) and has been one of the most vocal champions of the movement in Paris, structuring the menus at the restaurants he has managed, like Racines, Vivant, and Heimat, around small, natural winemakers.

Like many others, Jancou's foray into natural wine began with a revelation at first sip. "I was drinking natural wine before I even knew anything about it! It became a trend for some, but for me it's a natural extension of the way I consume"—detached from industrial agribusiness. "It was more digestible. I also had a bit of a sulfite allergy, so conventional wines would go straight to my head." To drink, learn about, and serve non-interventionist wine, he believes, is a way of returning to the roots of winemaking. "At first, chemicals were added to correct mistakes or flaws related to the environment, but then it became a means to mask the fact that vintners were working with bad grapes," Jancou says matter-of-factly. It's like cultivating a garden—the better and healthier the grape, the greater the possibilities to make an extraordinary wine that is truly natural, free from an arsenal of additives. Disgusted by what agribusiness, pesticides, and other toxins are doing to us and the planet, he peddles a hardline ideology that resonates with some clients but falls on deaf ears for others. For the unconvinced, he doesn't push too hard and does his best to recommend a wine from the menu that will match their expectations. "We've been called beatniks and quacks since the 1980s. It's crazy how vehemently opposed some people are to the idea of natural wine!" While there is less vitriol directed to natural wine proponents today, their arguments are still often challenged.

Olivier Magny, co-owner of the O'Château wine bar and Les Caves du Louvre (a Parisian wine museum) and author of *Into Wine*, believes the hoopla around natural wine is part of a cult of purity the food and wine industries are experiencing today. "If you go back a few centuries, things like honey, herbs, or spices were very common additions to wine," he says. "What happened over the past few decades is that the science of oenology has made considerable leaps. We now understand how to make wine from a scientific standpoint. We understand the chemistry of winemaking: the action of yeasts, the role of temperatures, the specifics of oxygen control . . . . All that is very new." Natural wines, then, are the latest example of recent transformations in the world of wine.

"Sulfites have been used in winemaking for millennia. In antiquity, sulfur from volcanoes was well known for its antiseptic qualities. In winemaking, that translated to heating up sulfur resin to form pitch used in wine-storing amphorae. Using chemicals to make wine, to improve farming yields, or to preserve food is nothing new!" Magny added. The problem is with the term

---

OPPOSITE Camille Fourmont of Buvette, the most beloved little cave à manger on the east side of Paris, is trenchant about the marketization of natural wine. "The idea isn't to say that a bottle or glass is good simply because it's natural; this shouldn't be about trend. You must be able to discern what is good and what the flaws are in the wine that *shouldn't* be there. The conviction behind natural wine begins with the way it's made, then you consider taste. If it isn't good, I won't add it to my selection." Heed Fourmont's recommendations and try one of her more obscure wines, then pair it with one of her many unfussy but stunningly delicious small plates like fresh burrata with Sicilian olive oil from Cédric Casanova of La Tête dans les Olives, sardines with smoked salted butter and lemon chips, fresh hummus, or artisanal cheeses. The space is modest with only a few seats, so don't hesitate to take your bottle to go.

The Wine Lexicon

BIODYNAMICS: A holistic, organic farming movement that focuses on the health and preservation of the soil, a complete organism of its own, to make the plant stronger. The more esoteric side of the approach, relating farming and harvesting to the lunar and astrological calendars, was inspired by a series of lectures given by Austrian philosopher Rudolf Steiner in the 1920s. He believed that the subtle and invisible forces in nature influenced the health and wellness of all life.[38]

ORGANIC WINE: Refers to viticulture without the use of synthetic pesticides and often describes wine made from organically grown grapes and with limited or no sulfites.

NATURAL WINE OR VIN VIVANT: Though there isn't an official definition or regulatory norm, this term typically refers to vineyard *and* vinification practices. These wines are made from grapes farmed organically, often biodynamically, and with low or no addition of sulfites. In short: nothing should be added or removed during winemaking, though many disagree about the use of small amounts of sulfites during the bottling process.

Le Cave à Manger: Where Good Wine Meets Quality Eats

WHERE DO YOU GO TO drink good wine and nibble on high-quality small plates? The *cave à manger*, a cross between a wine bar and a tapas bar with a special liquor license that allows patrons to drink alcohol only if they order food. Wines are usually very reasonably priced and the snacks range from the ultrasimple—high-quality charcuterie, sardines, cheese, and Sicilian olives—to the more finessed—grilled octopus with grapefruit and fennel, line-caught fish of the day with Thai coriander, and chocolate and olive oil ganache for dessert. Good value aside, these laid-back eateries, like Frenchie Wine Bar, Clamato, Le 116, and L'Avant Comptoir, offer a great way to taste the cooking styles of chefs whose main restaurants might be challenging to book. For a broader list, flip to page 259.

Nibbles and natural wine at La Buvette in the 11th arrondissement.

natural, a misleading word to describe a process that isn't all that natural at all. "Without human intervention, we'd just have vinegar. Like many others, I support an approach less focused on chemicals, but when it comes to sulfites (SO_2), I much prefer pragmatism to ideology. Simply put: making a good wine with low SO_2 is very tricky. Remove sulfites and the odds of having wines with massive defects—oxidation, Brettanomyces, and volatile acidity—skyrockets."

See what I mean? The concept can't be neatly codified. But that more and more restaurants and wine bars are offering entire lists of natural varietals or incorporating them into a mixed selection is nonetheless an unmistakable sign that this is becoming more than a passing fancy. In fact, if Parisians are actively seeking out natural wines today, it's for the same reasons they've flocked to greengrocers stocked with kale and rare grains, vegan cafés, and market-driven restaurants: They want to have more control over what they're consuming.

Xavier Lacaud, the sommelier and manager of Clown Bar, an excellent neo-bistro and wine bar in the North Marais, told me that he tries to remind clients that choosing natural wine is about taste and well-being. "It's great to feed ourselves the right way, but if we're eating well, why wouldn't we try to drink better too? Finding your way into natural wine is simply an education of the palate," he says. It was a learned taste for him as well, but now he appreciates the real taste of fermented grape juice (what wine truly is!) and wants his clients to experience it for themselves. Like farm-to-table food, natural wine is fast becoming a realm to refine and explore one's palate.

If you are curious and want to try natural wines at home, the best place to start is by consulting the robust natural and biodynamic wine producers that many importers specialize in. In the United States, check out Louis/Dressner, Zev Rovine Selections, Selection Massale, Percy Selections, or Jenny and François Selections, and in the UK, Les Caves de Pyrene, Gergovie Wines, and Dynamic Vines.

CRAFT BEER

Six or seven years ago, it would have been unthinkable, laughable even, to call Paris a burgeoning craft beer capital. But the city of wine bars and cellars has experienced frothy change with a rising set of beer lovers who fostered a movement to revive the French brewing trade, with more variety and flavor than the standardized and tasteless drink the French have to come to associate with beer (think 1664, the French "Bud").

Few realize that grain-based beer is as old as Mesopotamia, predating wine, France's terroir product. Even fewer realize that a brewing tradition in Paris is nothing new either. As I mentioned on page 29, the word *brasserie* means "brewery" and refers to beer taverns set up by the Alsatian diaspora who fled to Paris after Alsace was annexed by Germany in 1870. Up until the twentieth century, these microbreweries multiplied following the World's Fairs of 1867 and 1878.[39] But these Parisian brasseries faced several challenges that would eventually halt their growth. Chief among them: a lack of space in the city to increase production and intense competition from German (mostly Bavarian), English, and French (small-town) low-fermentation breweries, which dominated the Parisian market. On top of that, they suffered from excise duties and a variety of

A wine shop by day, a *cave à manger* by night, La Cave à Michel is one of my favorite stops for a bite of whatever chef Romain Tischenko has concocted for the evening and a glass of natural wine suggested by the sommelier, Fabrice Mansouri, named *Omnivore*'s 2015 Sommelier of the Year. The bar and its big sister restaurant, Le Galopin, are largely untapped by tourists and offer a wonderful, laid-back local vibe in an up-and-coming neighborhood. "Those of us in wine and food have a political and social role. We improve people's daily lives. Our goal was never to drastically gentrify the neighborhood—we chose it because it's where we live!" explains Mansouri.

Where to Scope Out
the Natural Wine Subculture

CONTRIBUTED BY AARON AYSCOUGH

AS OF 2015, THE PRINCIPLES of natural wine have attained something close to ideological hegemony among Paris's young and ambitious chefs and restaurateurs. Almost no buzzy new restaurant opening occurs in east Paris without an accompanying natural wine list. But since such establishments can have the lifespans of fruit flies, it's worth highlighting the institutions—and the people who run them—whose influence in the natural wine scene has proved enduring.

CAFÉ DE LA NOUVELLE MAIRIE
The history of this left-bank institution is effectively the history of natural wine itself. Former owner Bernard Pontonnier, who occupied the premises from 1979 to 1985, was among the first Paris wine buyers to cultivate a selection of the natural wines just beginning to emerge from Beaujolais at the time. The café was closed from 1986 to 1994, only to reopen under the ownership of Nicolas Carmarans, a friend of Pontonnier. Carmarans left to become a natural winemaker in Aveyron in 2008, selling the café to his friends Benjamin Fourty and Corentin Bucillat. All three generations of owners still frequent the bar and bistro, which, with its deep wine list, stunning glass selections, and wide terrace, remains ground zero for natural wine in Paris.

LE BARATIN
Founded by Argentine-born chef Raquel Carena and her then-partner Olivier Camus in 1989, Le Baratin can safely be considered the inspiration behind Paris's contemporary natural-wine bistro renaissance. Chefs and restaurateurs citywide flock to Carena's bistro, perched on a side street in Belleville, for her masterfully prepared country cuisine and the vast, unlisted wine cellar of her new partner, Philippe Pinoteau, who stands baleful guard at the reservation book most nights. Both Camus and Pinoteau are credited as being among Paris's earliest and most influential supporters of natural wine.

LE VERRE VOLÉ
Let it be known loud and clear: Le Verre Volé, Cyril Bordarier's canal-side wine destination, is a restaurant and wine shop, not a wine bar. One can't just roll in and ask for a glass. Even trying to purchase bottles to go is challenging during mealtimes. What the establishment lacks in polish, it makes up for in value and influence: Bordarier was among the first to bring the *cave à manger* to Paris in 2000, and he remains its most successful practitioner. International wine tastemakers and the natives of the newly gentrified Canal Saint-Martin pack the place seven nights a week to dine on a winning mix of delicate, Asian-inflected small plates and more rustic country classics.

LA QUINCAVE
Frédéric Belcamp's Montparnasse wine shop and wine bar (est. 2003) is a rare outpost of jolly anarchy in a deeply conservative quartier. Mostly standing-room only, it attracts a loyal following of apéro-sippers and visiting winemakers, drawn by Belcamp's superlative selection of more than two hundred menu options at a given time, as well as his longstanding experience in the industry.

MA CAVE FLEURY
The wine bar of Champagne Fleury, the pioneering biodynamic champagne estate is warmly represented at Ma Cave by its delightful scion Morgane Fleury. Wedged amid the sex shops of the rue Saint-Denis, the bar is an unlikely spot for a romantic glass of bubbly, but that only ensures a crowd of regulars and aficionados, who come to enjoy the terrace and Morgane's well-priced selection of the wines of her fellow natural winemakers.

AARON AYSCOUGH *is the author of* Not Drinking Poison in Paris, *a blog about natural wine in Paris and France. A former sommelier for the Batali & Bastianich restaurant group, he has written about wine in Paris since 2009.*

other taxes, which made business operations costly. To try to circumvent high taxes, brewers used questionable methods like opening clandestine breweries, adding glucose syrup, molasses, or starch syrup to the wort, and producing highly concentrated beers then cutting them with water, among other techniques.[40] Despite being artisanal in terms of volumes produced, the use of poor ingredients led to tasteless, poor-quality beer (or, as my husband likes to call it, *la pisse!*).

Up until the end of the nineteenth century, there were about fifteen breweries located within the city limits, most located in the 14th arrondissement. By 1910, there were eight, each of which were large producers. They found stable success until World War II brought a whole new set of obstacles, from rationed ingredients to closures imposed by the Vichy regime. Flash-forward past a short-lived resurgence in the 1950s to the 1960s, when decline was sharp. Powerful corporations gobbled up the weaker, midsize breweries, whose value hinged upon their commercial networks and bars, and that decline continued for two decades. Just as the craft beer movement was germinating in the United States in the 1980s, where brewers moved away from tasteless lagers to hop-forward beers with bitter and fruity qualities,[41] the French capital's brewing history became a cultural footnote at best.

The inherent sophistication and craftsmanship associated with wine was in stark opposition to beer, which was relegated to "lesser" activities—parties, sporting events, canal-side picnics. But as a niche group of beer geeks and brewing amateurs caught wind of what was literally brewing in the American and English craft beer movements, the spirit of revival took hold. But there would be hurdles to overcome.

"Producing beer is expensive to begin with," says Mike Gilmore, the former head brewer of Frog Pubs in Paris and co-owner of Brew Unique, the city's first DIY brew center for consumers, which opened in 2015. Production tax is part of what hurt small brewers two centuries prior, but it isn't the only hurdle brewers needed to overcome in Paris. Beer tying, a centuries-old practice that has been illegal in the United States since 1890[42] and in England since 2014, presents another issue in securing distribution. Under the beer tie, breweries or large companies supply support equipment and even commercial space in exchange for loyalty, effectively locking bar owners into a contract to *exclusively* serve their beers. Given that start-up costs are steep, this is an attractive arrangement, that is until a landlord wishes to carry another label (from a craft brewer or large competitor) and serious problems arise. While craft beers from around the world have been able to find ample shelf space in specialty shops, most of the city's large cafés and brasseries—and their massive reach—are impenetrable due to tying. The other barrier to entry was awareness. Gilmore explains, "The French see beer in colors, but that's a limited lens to look through since there are thousands of different kinds of *blondes, blanches, brunes*…it's a hard mold to break for the general populace." But not impossible. After all, are all white and red wines created equal?

OPPOSITE Michael Kennedy, owner of the Paname Brewing Company (TOP LEFT). Craft beer expert Simon Thillou in his shop La Cave à Bulles (TOP RIGHT). If there is a locomotive to the bar side of the craft beer movement, it's La Fine Mousse (see also page 181). Founders (from left): Romain Thieffry, Laurent Cicurel, and Cyril Lalloum (BOTTOM).

What Is Considered Craft Beer?

A CRAFT BREWER, ACCORDING to the American Brewers Association, is small, independent, and traditional, producing six million barrels of beer or less per year (which means Samuel Adams can be categorized as a craft beer, a cause for debate among beer geeks and small brewers). While no official definition exists in France, breweries are generally considered artisanal if their production is between one thousand to ten thousand hectoliters per year (about eight hundred to eighty-five hundred barrels). Within the community, however, "craft" is often thought to be less about the process and more about the spirit and passion of brewing. Or as La Fine Mousse cofounder Cyril Lalloum put it to me, "For us, artisanal is the proximity of the brewer to his product." Though it may always be niche, the city's craft beer scene is primed for continued growth worthy of attention from the world's most discerning beer drinkers.

The beer pioneers in Paris today wouldn't have gotten very far without the support of a compelling group of bottle shops and bars across town willing to support their efforts. The beer renaissance's most influential advocate has been Simon Thillou, the city's foremost authority on all things craft beer, owner of the La Cave à Bulles specialty bottle shop, and co-owner of Brew Unique. He didn't seem all that surprised when I told him that I was a relatively new convert to beer, put off for years by its bitterness. Unlike sweetness, bitterness is a learned taste and not one that you acclimate to on the first sip. That has been part of the problem in persuading the French to give beer a real chance. Thillou was one of the exceptions, however. A taste of Belgian beer from Trappistes Rochefort was all it took to convince him of the drink's merits.

When Thillou opened his shop nine years ago, two-thirds of his stock was dedicated to French beers; the rest was a rotating roster of his favorites from around the world, including Belgium and the United States. He developed relationships with some of the small, little-known breweries across France to build his offering—a challenge given the limited options then. Today, producers come to him to be carried, and French beers remain his focus.

The first time I went to see Thillou in his shop, he introduced me to a beer from Daniel Thiriez, widely considered the founding father of the craft beer movement in France. Thiriez became known for his homemade yeast and a very dry, hoppy beer unlike anything the French had ever tasted before. Twenty years later and now internationally renowned in the beer community, Thiriez's namesake brewery has collaborated with American brewers like Jester King on special brews that expand his reach. Winner of the 2015 Omnivore Brewer of the Year (Brasseur de l'Année) award, Thiriez is perhaps the most referenced success story and has inspired many of the Parisian brewers.

In the footsteps of the United States, Canada, England, and Scandinavia, artisanal brewing is back in the capital with a focus that matches the population's ever-growing appetite for businesses and artisanal products predicated on heart, technique, and an unflagging commitment to taste over financial gain. "Like with most things here, there are two approaches—either you start with a full business plan and the intention of growing and attracting investors or you go about things in a more grassroots fashion, bootstrapping everything from operations to decor," noted my friend Jon Brand, a journalist working on a documentary about craft beer in Paris. "Many craft brewers here started out as home-brewing hobbyists who, after fruitless searches for good French beer, decided to scale up production and share their passion with more than just their friends." A return to centuries-old brewing roots though it may be, the movement in Paris isn't merely about recalling the past (which is a good thing, since beer's history in the capital hasn't always been worth venerating). It's about establishing a true image for Parisian beers in the eyes of the rest of the world and rewriting its narrative.

OPPOSITE Deck & Donohue on tap at La Fontaine de Belleville, a space that marries specialty coffee and Parisian café culture (which includes beer, wine, and spirit) to wonderful effect.

Parisian Brews: Paname Brewing Company

WITH ITS FIVE CRAFT BEERS produced on-site and a gorgeous veranda overlooking the banks of the Bassin de la Villette, a former port during the industrialization of waterways for trade in Paris and the largest artificial body of water in Paris, the Paname Brewing Company (PBC) has more than enough winning qualities to draw crowds. And they've come in droves since the brewpub opened in 2015, bringing even greater visibility not only to craft brewing but also to a section of the 19th arrondissement that has long been considered off the beaten path, even for locals. PBC sits alongside other cultural and leisure venues revitalizing the canal.

As for their beers: "Many Parisian brewers are working with purely local produce, trying to revive old French beer styles, while the others are working and experimenting with hops from all over the world. We have tried to take the best of both worlds: We use the best hops we can find depending on the beer style, but we try to take a big, flavored beer and give it an elegant finish à la Française," explains founder Michael Kennedy.

The beers are named after elements related to the area's history. "*Oeil de biche*," for example, is named after a tear-shaped tattoo that marked members of the Apaches, the infamous gang that ruled the streets of Paris (especially the 19th arrondissement) in the early twentieth century.

It isn't unusual to find locals having lunch at PBC or spending time with friends in the early evening over a table brimming with good quality beers. In the summer, the outdoor terrace succeeds in making Parisians feel like they just might be on holiday.

OPPOSITE When the sun comes out, Parisians will flock to the Bassin de la Villette and lounge along the docks or head to the Paname Brewing Company for delicious bar food and craft beer, made on the premises.

For some, like Yann Geffriaud of the microbrewery Outland, that narrative began by experimentation with home-brewing in New York City, where he worked as a schoolteacher. Back in France, he brewed in a garage and shared his experiments with friends. His exposure to the American craft beer community and its hoppy beers was key in his decision to make it his full-time focus in 2011. With an Americanized name and a product selection inspired predominantly by English and American styles (West Coast IPA, 'Merica IPA, Tasty Session IPA, English Brown, Oatmeal Stout), Outland has become a wonderful example of carrying the movement forward, growing slowly but steadily with an ever-growing presence in the city's beer bars.

Others have taken a far more French-centric approach to beer making. Thierry Roche of La Brasserie de La Goutte d'Or, the first microbrewery within the city limits at the start of the craft beer boom, produces beers in homage to the neighborhood where he brews and which are inspired by the Maghrebis and other African communities within it, incorporating different spices he sources locally. La Chapelle (chai wheat), Charbonnière (smoked), Château Rouge (amber/red ale), Myrha (pale ale—his first beer), to name a few, are named for areas or streets located within the 18th arrondissement's Goutte d'Or section, rarely frequented by tourists but bursting with life, vibrant colors, flavors, and diversity. My favorite addition to his offering was a tripel coffee beer called 3ter, made in collaboration with Parisian roasters Café Lomi (see page 98), an example of the craft worlds colliding masterfully.

And there are a host of others bringing greater attention and curiosity to the beer world with varied backgrounds, inspirations, and knowledge: Les Brasseurs du Grand Paris, a Franco-American gypsy-brewing venture with high-quality IPAs, porters, and American Pale Ales; Demory, a mythic label from 1827 revived in 2009 and brewed in Germany (for lack of space); Gallia, once Paris's largest brewery, revived in 2009 by two young Frenchmen with the help of the family that owned the original Old Gallia Brewery, started out brewing in the Czech Republic, where pilsner-style beer like the original Gallia is favored, but moved production to Pantin, just outside of Paris, in 2016; Deck & Donohue, a Franco-American brewery based in the Parisian suburb of Montreuil whose everyday beers (easily drinkable, thirst-quenching, not too high in alcohol) are available at more than fifty bars and restaurants in Paris (more about them on page 185); Parisis, brewed outside of Paris but with wide distribution, including supermarkets; BapBap, a newer label brewed in a seven-story converted storage facility in the 11th arrondissement; and the Paname Brewing Company, whose beers are produced in a building on the banks of the Bassin de la Villette and named after historical elements of the area.

OPPOSITE From the moment it opened in 2012, La Fine Mousse deservedly secured its positioning as the city's high temple of craft beer. They have an excellent, rotating selection of twenty craft beers on tap and a bottle collection of more than 150 different beers from Germany, Belgium, the United States, the Netherlands, Italy, Norway, and beyond. In keeping with their commitment to advocating broadly for the industry, the trio opened the first restaurant dedicated to beer and food pairings across the street from their bar and followed in 2015 with a book on the best of artisanal beer, *Le Meilleur de la Bière Artisanale*.

Parisian & Île de
— France Beers —

**A FEW TO LOOK FOR
ON YOUR NEXT VISIT:**

BapBap

Brasserie de la Vallée de Chevreuse

Crazy Hops

Deck & Donohue

Demory

Frog

Gallia

Les Brasseurs du Grand Paris

Outland

Paname Brewing Company

Parisis

"Parisian beer is made with intention.
There is a higher outreach–oriented
goal among craft brewers here. Make
good beer, share it, spread the word,
keep the passion alive."

—EMILY DILLING,
AUTHOR OF *THE PARIS MARKET COOKBOOK*

Beers by these brewers and the many others who continue to join the playing field are given pride of place at the city's leading taprooms and specialty bars like Le Supercoin, Brewberry, A la Bière Comme à la Bière, Les Trois 8, Express de Lyon, and La Fine Mousse, the epicenter of craft beer hubs.

While inroads have been made, the discourse around beer still needs some fine-tuning. Much like my own myopic view of beer, the French perspective still places wine on top as a cultural product (which you can observe front and center on most café and brasserie menus while beer sits alongside soft drinks and coffee). But the craft industry has become more and more vocal about the aromatic complexities in beer, which are more vast than those in wine. Part of that variation originates from hops, which "reflect a diversity of tastes and traditions that are part of an extraordinary evolution in beer—particularly in the United States where American-style lager once defined beer in much the same way Folgers defined coffee," writes Simran Sethi, author of *Bread, Wine, Chocolate: The Slow Loss of Foods We Love*.[43] When Brooklyn Brewery first entered the French market, they launched with their IPA but quickly found it wasn't selling. "Forcing people to try something their palates aren't accustomed to won't work," Nicolas Millet, marketing manager of House of Beer distribution told me at the first beer and food pairing event I attended in Paris, "especially when it isn't in the culture." Educating on what makes beer so complex and how it can be paired with food will be part of making the movement last. On the brewer side, longevity will come from learning how to grow and increase production. "The demand is stronger than the offer right now. Demand is good, but I'm lucky if I have enough to stock!" said Simon Thillou.

Though it is unlikely that beer will replace wine at the dinner table anytime soon, awareness is improving and opportunities to taste the best of what's coming out of the region are multiplying. "The way craft beer has managed to gain legitimacy has been through food, and not only at beer-focused spaces," says Kate Robinson, press relations manager for the Paris Beer Week organizing committee. "You see Parisian and regional beers at local burger and sandwich joints, cafés, gourmet grocers, and local food festivals." Between Brew Unique, Paris Beer Week approaching its fourth anniversary, and new attention from foreign beer labels that want to capitalize on a burgeoning new market, the world's beer lovers have reason to rejoice. The good stuff awaits in the city of wine.

OPPOSITE One of the owners of El Tast sporting a tee from Le Supercoin, another craft beer establishment in Paris.

Q&A

MIKE DONOHUE & THOMAS DECK, DECK & DONOHUE

MIKE DONOHUE AND THOMAS DECK became fast friends when they met at Georgetown University in 2002. Already an active home-brewer, Donohue quickly initiated Deck into a whole other world of beer. In 2005, they brewed their first beer and decided they'd one day open a brewery together. Donohue delved into brewing at 21st Amendment in San Francisco and Deck brewed at home as he worked in finance. After years of brewery visits, test brews, beer festivals, and training, both quit their jobs in 2013 to launch their own brewery in Montreuil, near Paris. Today, their beers are available at a number of beer shops, gourmet grocers, and more than fifty bars and restaurants in Paris alone, ushering in a new golden age of beer.

Mike, as an American reared in a culture of beer, how would you say the movement in Paris compares to that which has developed stateside?
It's difficult to compare the two since the movement in the United States is so broad and popular, while the movement here is so small and mostly niche, but it seems safe to say that there is now a small craft beer movement here. Looking at the first two Paris Beer Weeks alone, you can see the growth of breweries, bars, beer stores, and interest from the public.

We've also started to see the interest of larger, foreign breweries like BrewDog, Stone, and Green Flash that see France and Europe in general as areas for potential growth.

One strength here is the general appreciation of quality food among the French population, which should lend itself to choosing less industrial options for beer drinking. Another could be the relatively low legal hurdles to opening a brewery compared to those in the United States. Time will tell!

What would you say is the biggest difference between the way Parisians and Americans have traditionally consumed beers?
(DONOHUE) One thing for sure is how Parisians approach alcohol at mealtimes, where wine is preferred. Americans, on the other hand, seem to be less entrenched on the timing of when they consume a beer. Another difference is the size, as Parisians will typically order a half pint at a bar or café, while Americans tend to start with pints, perhaps because of how expensive beer can be here.

(DECK) Beers are considered thirst-quenchers, not a drink suitable for the dinner table. That said, French people know and drink beers from Northern France and Belgium, both regions

---

OPPOSITE Thomas Deck and Mike Donohue of Deck & Donohue.

with long traditions of beer-making. Belgian beers in particular are very yeast-forward versus hop-forward, so the American style of brewing (that we're seeing develop in Paris now) took longer to arrive here and find a market.

(DONOHUE) Then there's the way people refer to beer in general. Americans tend to talk about beer as ale, lager, and IPA. But most people we meet [in Paris] seem to believe that beer is limited to *blonde, blanche, ambrée,* or *brune*—its color—as it has traditionally been classified in France. So part of what we do is showcase a wide variety of beers to demonstrate the diversity that exists in the beer universe. Our hunch is that this can be interesting to consumers and open up new drinking contexts, including pairing with food, and appreciating beers for their different styles, ingredients, and brewing methods.

What is your approach to brewing?

(DONOHUE) We are really focused on drinkability and the idea that you can have two or three of the same beer without getting tired of it, which is sort of the opposite direction of many of the new breweries that seem to be trying to do the next crazy thing. We try to avoid gimmicks and focus on dry, balanced, and often hoppy beers.

(DECK) Our five core beers reflect what we personally enjoy drinking year-round, and we feel it's a good selection for getting people into beer. And we do our best to be as open as possible; we have public open house hours on Saturdays where our clients and curious beer drinkers can see our methods and process and taste test different beers. There's still a lot Parisians can learn about beer, and visiting us is a good place to start.

What's the most exciting development in the craft beer movement since you and Thomas launched D&D?

(DONOHUE) In Paris, I think the most exciting development has been the growth of access to craft beer for the consumer. With more beer shops, breweries, and beer events in the city, as well as more wine shops, gourmet shops, restaurants, and bars stocking craft beer, it's much easier to find the good stuff.

OPPOSITE A few of the local craft beers gaining popularity in Paris.

"The movement here is not about reviving Parisian beer, because it really wasn't very good, as far as taste is concerned; it's to implant the craft beer culture and give Parisians a variety of flavors and experiences."

—EDOUARD MINART, COFOUNDER OF BAPBAP BREWERY

Apéro hour at El Tast cave à bières.

Beer Pairings in Paris

CONTRIBUTED BY CAMILLE MALMQUIST

BEER AND FOOD HAVE a funny relationship in France. Unlike traditional beer cultures, such as those in Belgium, Germany, or the British Isles, France has mostly relegated beer drinking to low-class activities like sporting events, the morning café stops of garbage collectors, and informal parties; never would beer be the beverage of choice to accompany a fine meal. Even with the recent resurgence of craft beer in Paris, food options at specialty beer bars have remained, well, boring. Cheese and charcuterie boards are the standard, and while many of these may be of good quality, they pale in comparison to the menu offerings at the city's best wine bars (wine being an "acceptable" partner for fine food). Fortunately, this perception is shifting.

LA FINE MOUSSE, Paris's most venerated craft beer bar, led the charge in the summer of 2014, opening an ambitious double restaurant. On one side, they served multi-course gastronomic meals with beer pairings selected by a dedicated beer sommelier. The other side featured small plates in a wine bar–style atmosphere, all produced in a small kitchen helmed by a serious chef. The concept proved a bit too radical—whether too expensive or elaborate for the beer crowd or not taken seriously by the foodies is unclear—and in January 2015 they scaled back, adding taps to make the place feel more like an extension of the original bar, but still with an ambitious small-plates menu and suggested beer pairings.

Meanwhile, in autumn 2014, a great little place called LE TRIANGLE snuck onto the scene. The brainchild of a Québecois brewer, his French wife, and her chef brother, it is presumably Paris's first gastro-brewpub. They brew beer on-site and pour it alongside a rotating cast of high-quality guest beers from other craft breweries in Paris and beyond. The kitchen puts out high-caliber small plates—refined French classics like pig's trotters and seasonal delights such as pencil leeks on parsley root purée—that would be at home in any of the city's top wine bars, proving that beer and fine dining need no longer be mutually exclusive.

I would be remiss if I failed to mention THE GREEN GOOSE, an excellent Irish pub whose opening predates that of La Fine Mousse's restaurant by a few months. They serve what is best described as elevated pub food: scotch eggs, meat pies, and a renowned brunch, all lovingly made in-house. The menu suggests beer pairings from their impressive list of Irish craft beers.

Prior to these openings, if you wanted to drink good beer and eat dishes specifically designed to complement it, your options were limited to British pubs, a handful of pop-up events—largely initiated by Anglo-Saxons—or the few places serving traditional Belgian cuisine, though these leaned toward classic pub grub as opposed to fine dining. With Le Triangle and La Fine Mousse Restaurant leading the way, Parisians are beginning to catch on to the idea that beer is not only food-friendly, but that craft beer can, in fact, be a legitimate partner for chic, modern cuisine.

CAMILLE MALMQUIST *is a pastry chef and beer enthusiast who lived and worked in Paris for eight years.*

PARISIAN PERSPECTIVE

FRANCK ALEXANDRE, 46

OWNER, FOLKS AND SPARROWS CAFÉ

What motivated you to leave Paris many years ago?

I never felt like I belonged in Paris. When I left at the end of 1999, I felt like I was completely out of step with Parisian life—Paris was super classic at the time, not a great vibe, and not the kind of Internet culture like there is now, so young people weren't seeing what was happening elsewhere. We were totally *Franco-Français* [France-focused]. But that wasn't me; I had to leave.

My wife found a small apartment in pre-trendy Brooklyn and that's where we stayed. That's also where I found my way into hospitality. I needed a job, and Bar Tabac, a bustling French restaurant, had opened in Carroll Gardens and needed the help. I started as a waiter and then made my way up to general manager and then director. We were surrounded by Mexicans, Italians, and longtime New Yorkers in an area that was still maligned but managed to surf on Brooklyn's explosion (and the popularity of French establishments) and became one of the neighborhood's institutions. What's cool is that we participated in making Brooklyn a piece of what it is today.

Once you returned to Paris, what had changed the most?

I'm originally from the Canal Saint-Martin area, and when we returned to Paris, it was hardly recognizable. It was never a wealthy part of town by any means, but when we came back, it was changing and becoming one of the best examples of diversity in the city. I immediately noticed the boom of coffee shops on the east side of the city and was inspired by the communities they were creating. But overall, change is extremely slow in Paris. When we say that a neighborhood is exploding, it explodes over the course of ten years!

What feels most unique about Paris today?

There's something special that lingers over this city. We're going for drinks, having dinner, and going shopping in buildings with tremendous history. That juxtaposition of old and new creates a special feeling. Folks and Sparrows sits in a three-hundred-year-old building with a medieval cellar, which I think is an extra draw.

How does your experience in the States inform what you've built in Paris?

I became an adult and learned my trade there so it's deeply embedded into what I do here. If I didn't have that experience, I wouldn't have created this space. Others think of Brooklyn when they first visit Folks and Sparrows, but it's more like upstate New York! My tribe was and still is a group of Americans from the Catskills. In fact, some of my friends (bearded hippies like me) came to Paris to build the wood benches, shelves, and bars and create the menu lettering and illustrate the large sparrow on the wall behind the counter.

the new
SHOPPING & CRAFTS

"Pleasure in the job
puts perfection in the work."

—ARISTOTLE

The idea of shopping in Paris has long had a hold on the foreign imagination. Images of well-heeled boulevards lined with the most iconic names in fashion, quiet corners dotted with art dealers and antique treasure troves, and open-air markets brimming with exquisite produce, meats, cheeses, and even florals are as easy to summon to mind as baguettes and brioche. They aren't false, but the reality today is that independent French businesses jockey for space in a city now overrun by global chains and designers. The dominance of big manufacturing, mass market brands, and luxury labels is writ large, not only in the usual shopping districts like the Champs-Elysées and at the *grands magasins* (Le Bon Marché, Printemps, and Galeries Lafayette), but even on once-local streets where names like Givenchy, Moncler, and The Kooples have pushed out independently owned pharmacies, booksellers, hair salons, and a variety of other small businesses that give communities character. The same shops and labels you see in Paris also command prime shopping real estate in cities small and large from Los Angeles to Tokyo. There may be a certain appeal to shopping at an international brand in Paris, and people fall for all sorts of trinkets and minutiae in Paris (because "It's from *Paree!* It must be good!"), but it takes more digging to find one-of-a-kind creations or unique Parisian brands fraught with stories and made with heart.

The world of fashion is probably where this standardization has been felt the most. In contrast to American or English fashions, Parisian style is known for its timeless and classic looks. Rather than update their closets weekly or monthly, we're told that Parisian women maintain well-crafted essentials and invest in accent pieces like shoes, handbags, and jewelry, rotating their outfits each day. My mother-in-law is a good example of this. In the eleven years that I've known her, she has weaved in new sweaters, blazers, shoes, and jewelry only a handful of times, attributing greater value to well-made goods that are stylish and long-lasting. Fast, disposable fashions don't appeal to her nor

---

PREVIOUS SPREAD Morgane Sézalory, founder of Sézane, makes heels women can actually wear comfortably with any look, day or night. OPPOSITE Chantal Manoukian learned to make jewelry while working as a stylist for Isabel Marant and fell in love with the process of crafting with her own hands. But not crafting just anything—her whimsical jewelry collection is made from recycled goods and antiques for an overall look and feel that's vintage glamour with a touch of industrial flair. "The older the pieces are, the more I'm into it!" she told me when I visited her boutique-showroom, La Tonkinoise, which is scattered with repurposed watch bracelets, resin, glass, acetate, and other trinkets sourced from antique markets and trunk sales. Manoukian transforms neglected jewelry detritus—"vieux Paris"—into a totally new keepsake that's connected to fashion trends. Going off on her own was an answer to her line of self-questioning. "We all need meaning in our lives. I was asking myself, what is the value in my work?" And she found just the place to bring her old-but-new treasures to life, in the 11th arrondissement where she has lived for more than fifteen years.

to most French women of her generation. These are some of the same women who shop at luxury stores—they see their purchases as long-term legacy investments (and of course, a sign of prestige). Buy less, but buy better is the common thought, which will be easier on the wallet in the long run.

But the preponderance of high-street and lifestyle brands with homogenized styles and collections that are not only updated seasonally but throughout the season and as trends peak[44] has squashed the *less is more* ethos for younger generations and brought into question the value of the country's storied savoir faire.

Shoppers in France and beyond have been beaten over the head with the idea of consuming cheaply, quickly, and en masse. We traffic in sales and promotions without much thought, and we go through the motions of consuming and purging in a never-ending cycle. But the one-in-every-color mentality has reached saturation, and concerns around ethical manufacturing have moved to the forefront of consumer consideration. In the face of mindless consumerism and a dearth of traditional jobs, a countermovement has room to bubble to the surface, producing creative new labels and ambitious entrepreneurs. And that's largely what has happened in Paris.

Behind the impassioned stories of many of the upstarts featured in this chapter was a desire to be part of the movement that champions quality over quantity and to contribute something meaningful to the city. Some wanted to work with their hands and physically create; others wanted to make use of a unique vision, family tradition, or passion as a launchpad to work for themselves. No matter the impetus, getting started wasn't without its difficulties—at this point, the country's steep labor charges, taxes, and red tape are notorious. But it's not impossible. "The mentality in France is that if you don't have much money, you can't start a company. But it's not true," says Fabien Meaudre, founder of Le Baigneur organic skincare products for men, who worked in the corporate world before breaking out onto his own. What is true is that labor costs are often prohibitively expensive, which is why family-run operations have been so prevalent: There are no employees to pay.

"The city has really pushed *Made in Paris* and *Made in France* goods, which has helped us. And there *is* aid available as you're launching. But there is a lot of paperwork, which is a deterrent for some people. We looked at these complications as the price to pay to operate in our beautiful city!" Maxime Brenon told me about setting up his paper goods brand Papier Tigre with partners Julien Crespel and Agathe Demoulin. What's more, entrepreneurs can apply for commercial spaces owned by the city of Paris that have modest costs and no lease premiums. That's how textile designer Usha Bora could open the first retail space for her Franco-Indian lifestyle brand, Jamini. "The town hall of the 10th arrondissement was a driving factor in changing the face of retail and food in the neighborhood. Their teams are super involved and engaged in fostering community." In fact, the program, Vital'Quartier (initiated by the City of Paris in collaboration with the Chamber of Commerce), which allowed Bora to find a home for her brand, has been working since 2004 to take over vacant commercial spaces, push out wholesale textile shops (largely to

OPPOSITE Handcrafted necklaces from La Tonkinoise.

Handmade Crafts
for Men and Women with
Le Baigneur & Jamini

FABIEN MEAUDRE, FOUNDER of Le Baigneur, felt born to be independent and always knew that he'd one day create his own company. "I was interested in organic and sustainable products, specifically men's skincare and grooming. There are so few for men and even fewer that are organic. The organic boom in Paris confirmed my instincts that my concept would have a willing audience," he says.

He makes the soaps and products by hand in the production space he shares with craft brewer Deck & Donohue (see page 185) in Montreuil. His goal is to make the best product possible, guided by his personal beliefs and morals. For that reason, he refuses entirely to use plastics in packaging. The challenge with a business of this nature, he says, is staying true to his convictions. "It's tough to avoid plastics altogether, especially as you try to grow, but I look at it as a challenge. Not *everything* should be unbreakable and disposable. I want people to keep things longer and respect them more."

Usha Bora had similarly strong convictions, always knowing that her future should be in textiles. Over eighteen years in Paris, four of which were spent working for L'Oréal, *le mal du pays* (homesickness) kicked in. To reconnect with her native Assam, India, she began sourcing fabrics, embroideries, and weavings for major Parisian brands and designers like agnès b., Dior Kids, and Bonton. But to truly go back to her roots, she'd need to create something of her own. Jamini, her lifestyle and accessories brand that launched in 2010 (the first shop opened in 2014) is her contribution to the Parisian shopping scene, where tribal influences in goods have been limited. Bora's collection of hand-woven cushions, scarves, hand-block-printed quilts, womenswear, totes, and tree-free notebooks (made from elephant or rhino dung) combines Indian craftsmanship—she works with artisans in the foothills of Northeast India, Manipur, Bengal, and Orissa—and just the right dose of Parisian chic to appeal to a local audience. The most important element of the business was to promote the lesser-known arts and crafts from India, and she has done so beautifully. In 2015, she opened a second shop in the 9th arrondissement, the other emerging shopping quarter, just a short walk from Sept Cinq (see page 205). Looking back, Bora is glad she took the risk to pursue her own project. "Uncertainty pushes us to ask questions; questions most of us weren't asking ourselves even ten years ago," she says. "I know I did the right thing by listening to my gut!"

OPPOSITE Usha Bora, founder and designer of the Franco-Indian lifestyle brand Jamini (TOP). Men's grooming never looked so good. Le Baigneur is more than well-designed packaging; it's an organic skincare line made in Montreuil, just outside of Paris (BOTTOM).

Aubervilliers in the northeastern suburbs of Paris), and bring in artisans as a means of reviving key zones in the city, like Saint-Denis, Beaubourg-Temple, rue de Lancry, Gare de l'Est and Gare du Nord, and Belleville, where unoccupied spaces and a standardization of businesses were damaging the neighborhoods' social fabric and sense of community. "I applied for city-owned commercial space and got it—that meant one less thing to worry about as I was building my brand," Bora told me. And the initiative to support the preservation of local businesses and artisans will continue through 2021 with a second wave of the program.[45]

Successful, large French brands that have been exported internationally, like Maje, Sandro, and Comptoir des Cotonniers, still hold sway in the capital, but there is growing hunger for more independent shops and labels. Culture journalist Géraldine Dormoy told me she feels that consumers are more and more curious about *new* brands. "These young labels and companies really deserve praise, especially as it becomes more and more difficult to exist among such a plethora of offerings," Dormoy says. As consumers worldwide seek out experiences over products[46] (both of which are represented in equal measure in Paris), artisans, crafters, and upstarts are trying to tip the balance in favor of goods that offer not only an experience but also a narrative people can latch onto.

Within a five-block radius of my apartment, I have access to a handful of cheesemongers, fishmongers, bakers, butchers, locksmiths, cobblers, and a few independent booksellers that have withstood the arrival of no less than three supermarket chains and an ever-growing culture of online shopping. (Though they were late adopters, the French have embraced e-commerce consumption, ranking third in sales among European Union countries surveyed.[47] Convenience is cited as the number one reason for purchasing online versus in local shops.[48]) When I first moved into my neighborhood and found that I had many small merchants and grocers at my fingertips, I was excited to support the local community and hop between shops for my groceries—bread from one shop, cheese and eggs from another, and so forth, until my basket would overflow. I was a student with the luxury of time, then, and shared habits with the older women who ventured out with their caddies trailing behind them to pick up provisions for the day, conversing with neighborhood merchants and learning about their trade. To this day, despite a far busier schedule and a glut of convenience shops and mini supermarkets, I do the bulk of my shopping at local, independent shops—not only because I strongly believe they should be preserved but also because I've heard the stories of their struggles firsthand and felt the changing landscape. Between 2007 and 2011, *les commerces de proximité* (local shops), including *les commerçants de bouches* (small food businesses), bookstores, press kiosks, and paper shops were in decline; there was a 9.5 percent drop in the number of butchers, an 8.5 percent drop in dairy shops, and a 24.6 percent decline in press sales due to a lack of commercial space, while *superettes* (mini supermarkets), fast food establishments, and organic shops have continued to thrive.[49]

Fortunately, the success of the Vital'Quartier program has had a dramatic impact on the resurgence of small businesses, despite the natural tendency toward quick consumption and its guise of convenience. Now, as we're all inundated with tips on how to reconnect with a

Chic pieces from
Sézane, France's
first online-only
fashion label.

simpler lifestyle and awash with information about how our goods are sourced, produced, or packaged, consumption behaviors seem to be shifting. If the individuals creating brands and working with their hands are any indication, we're beginning to experience a slow but significant transformation in our value system.

The media has certainly helped this along. Aside from disconcerting investigative reports that have frightened people into making changes, they have put the spotlight on the people, places, and businesses helping to revive artisanal skills and promote manual ingenuity. For those venturing out on their own, the economic *crise* and an unsound job market provided the push they needed to take control of their own futures. On top of that, we live in a time where technology has widened the pool of options. People find themselves with greater flexibility in the types of careers they can pursue with less infrastructure required (thanks to shared production or working spaces) to start businesses and bring concepts to scale. Today's entrepreneurs turn their backs on lockstep professional trajectories even when it terrifies their loved ones. Fabien Meaudre of Le Baigneur says that his family thought he was floundering, unwilling to put forth the energy to go to business school. "Manual jobs are pursued by those who failed in school or are lazy—that's what people assume," he told me. "But enough of us persevered and believed in what we were doing, despite the critics. Craftsmanship was denigrated for so long, it isn't surprising that it would make a comeback."

Today's rising creative class challenges the cookie-cutter, one-size-fits-all model of big industry and is committed to producing goods that reflect both the consumer's individuality and their own passion. It isn't about reverting to atavistic products as much as it is about reviving the art of manual crafts and creation, which were already so tightly linked to France. "What I appreciate the most in this artisanal revival is that it's a form of resistance. The world is changing so quickly, but artisanal crafts nurture something ancestral and useful. They have their place in the world today, and I'm convinced they will in the future too," said Dormoy, who documents many of these artisans in her *L'Express* magazine column, Café Mode.

As DIY-ers, ambitious designers, and other creatives emerge, they open online boutiques and/or brick-and-mortar shops in neighborhoods, *not* within breathing room of the dense department store arteries of the city. Which means that the *boutique de quartier*—the neighborhood shop—is resurfacing all over the city and creating a new normal. In everything from foodstuffs to fashion, the question visitors should ask themselves shifts from "where are the best places to shop?" to "where can I find the most unique goods that I won't get anywhere else?"

I could have filled the pages of this book with stories and examples of artisans in wide-ranging fields who are finally finding a home and a spotlight for their work. I've focused, however, on those who have emerged as part of this movement's precipitous rise and have led the way for countless others.

OPPOSITE Beautiful fabrics and prints in a Sézane collection.

Fashion's New Wave

CONTRIBUTED BY ALICE CAVANAGH

"NEW" ISN'T NECESSARILY a word one would associate with Parisian fashion; "storied" and "established" are perhaps more apt. Fashion Mecca that this city is, we've seen little innovation from the major names, like Dior, Lanvin, and Balmain, in recent years. Big business, you could say, has gotten in the way of risk taking—the very foundation of creativity and trendsetting—and the names we've long lusted after no longer set the status quo. The real action in the city now takes place far away from the wide, luxury fashion boutique–lined boulevards of the 8th arrondissement, once a shopping stronghold, in the lively neighborhoods of the 10th, 11th, and 18th arrondissements. This is the stomping ground of the next generation of designers, like Demna Gvasalia of Vetements (and now also Balenciaga), Glenn Martens from Y/Project, Koché's Christelle Kocher, and the collective behind the streetwear brand Études Studio, who are flipping the stately Parisian industry on its head.

Rather than citing artistic, lofty inspirations, these creatives mine the everyday for their ideas: locales like the métro and even the supermarket, where the local inhabitants from these lively quartiers, from a mix of cultures and socioeconomic backgrounds, tend to mingle. As such, an industry once built on luxurious evening wear and "It-bags" has been replaced by couture-worthy streetwear that encompasses everything from ironic slogan tees and sweatshirts to other wardrobe essentials like bomber jackets and jeans. Even plastic market shopping bags aren't safe, as the likes of Gvasalia at Balenciaga refashion such pedestrian accessories into luxury leather shoppers.

Democratic influences aside, such unassuming garments are elevated by French savoir faire—the secret ingredient here lies with the superior know-how these designers have access to in Paris. Christelle Kocher, for example, employs the expert handiwork of the *petites mains* from the embroidery house of Lemarié, where she moonlights as artistic director. Her garments, along with most of those produced by her contemporaries, proudly bear the label *Made in France*, a move that causes the price point of these brands to sit on the upper end of the scale. And yet, the argument for cost-per-wear on daily essentials such as jeans and sweatshirts is surely more favorable than pricey special-occasion-only party dresses.

To track down some of these new brands, take a tour of **THE BROKEN ARM** in the Haut Marais or **L'EXCEPTION** near the Canal Saint-Martin, concept stores that are committed to championing the work of emerging French designers, and **ÉTUDES STUDIO**'s own boutique in the Marais.

ALICE CAVANAGH *is a writer/editor living in Paris. She writes about fashion, culture, and travel for* Vogue, W Magazine, *the* Wall Street Journal Magazine, *and* T: The New York Times Style Magazine.

Sept Cinq

WHAT BEGAN AS A business-school project for Lorna Moquet and Audrey Gallier became a bonafide entrepreneurial venture after graduation. Inspired by Polish café–tea salon concepts, the duo created Sept Cinq, a carefully curated collection of lifestyle goods and accessories created by Paris-based designers from Bobbies and Meilleur Ami to Letterpress de Paris. In the back of the shop, a cozy tea salon allows clients to extend their visit. In 2016, they opened a larger, flagship store with a more spacious tea salon underneath the renovated Canopés des Halles in the heart of the city, one of only two independent stores to be given such prime retail real estate.

At Season Paper, makers of the cards seen above, two textile designers create prints and motifs for ready-to-wear fashion that they adapt for paper. The duo attributes the newfound appreciation for paper goods to the DIY movement. Their cards are sold in a variety of specialty shops, including Sept Cinq.

Bobbies

A MIX OF SAINT-GERMAIN chic
and Provençal casual, Bobbies is
the first Parisian line of colored
moccasins, which beautifully updates
an iconic silhouette. Each model
is designed in the team's Parisian
design studio and produced by small
ateliers in Portugal, whose artisans
work each topstitch by hand.

After finding success with
moccasins for men, the Bobbies
collection expanded to include
women's shoes, sandals, derbies,
and boots, and are available at
various points of sale in Paris, in
addition to their flagship boutique
in the Marais.

THE NEW *MODE* AND ACCESSORIES

If there is anyone to credit for changing the face of shopping in Paris it is Sarah Andelman, the co-owner and creative director of Colette, the city's most iconic concept store, which she launched with her mother (Colette) in 1997. "At the time, Paris was in the gutter. Attention was being directed to New York and London, and we had an opportunity to create something special and breathe new energy into the city," Andelman told a curious audience at the *New York Times* TasteMasters conversation series in Paris in March 2016. She and her mother reinvented the concept of retail (since the very beginning, the shop's display and gallery selection has changed weekly to offer perpetual novelty) to give consumers the possibility to discover not only the latest fashions but also emerging names in art, technology, beauty, and design. Colette was the first space to unite fashion—a tight mix of couture and streetwear—and art under the same roof.

"In the beginning, people were afraid to come in. They treated it like a museum and were afraid to touch anything," Andelman recalled during the discussion. But the discomfort in unfamiliarity didn't last long. Andelman is known for giving visibility to up-and-coming artists whose work is exhibited for a month, much like a traditional art gallery. But to appeal to a broad audience, for whom purchasing art (or high fashion, for that matter) is above their means, each artist creates affordable ancillary products or collectibles to be sold in the shop.

And while department stores have had to fight to reinvent themselves for local shoppers as big-box stores (*grandes surfaces*) in nearby suburbs do brisk business,[50] Colette has remained consistently innovative, forever at the forefront of style and design,[51] and able to draw in new shoppers from across the world.

Though decidedly more bohemian chic than Colette, the Haut Marais's concept store Merci, launched in 2009, has been similarly influential in helping new designers and artists get established in a saturated market. A former wallpaper factory, the shop features more than fifteen exhibits and events around a specific theme throughout the course of a year. Sometimes the focus is everyday activities like cycling; other times it puts the spotlight on entire cultures, their traditions, and their fashions. In February 2016, Merci gave the stage to African wax fabric, with a collection of clothing, accessories, and lifestyle goods displayed front and center in the shop's entryway. Headlining the pop-up was Maison Château Rouge, a young label I had discovered the year prior and whose progress I had followed with studied interest.

The vibrant colors, prints, and wax fabrics of Maison Château Rouge are a reflection of the neighborhood in the 18th arrondissement that inspired its name. It's a diverse melting pot of cultures and styles, dominated by the colorful alchemy of traditional African outfits and urban streetwear. The collection, founded in 2015 by brothers Youssouf and Mamadou Fofana, is produced entirely with fabrics they source from the merchants of the Château Rouge neighborhood, in small quantities, and updated according to what the local fabric sellers have on offer.

Youssouf and Mamadou are two of seven children, brought up in a Senegalese household in Seine-Saint-Denis (nicknamed the ninety-three), the underprivileged and largely immigrant suburb of Paris. Considered a scab on the city since the infamous youth riots of 2005 (also

Not hemmed in by one style or technique, jewelry designer Marie Montaud operates by sensations and simplicity. Everything she creates for Medecine Douce emerges from a personal quest for meaning and authenticity in her work. "Marie has always followed her instinct and created collections that reflect her own style and vision of fashion *at the exact moment* when she creates it," said her husband and business partner, Gilles Ballard.

90 €

95 €

90 €

125 €

85 €

"I wanted to create jewelry in a different way than I was taught. . . . My goal was to create small, dainty jewelry that would be more than wearable; [the pieces] would be collectible objects. I included leather, feathers, and embroidery, which, at the time, was uncommon."

—MARIE MONTAUD, JEWELRY DESIGNER
AND COFOUNDER OF MEDECINE DOUCE

the poorest department in the region), the ninety-three is faced with high unemployment and endemic prejudice, leaving locals feeling isolated and relegated to a cultural footnote. It's the area the Republic left behind, some have said. For the Fofanas, the options were either to succumb to the misery or emancipate themselves through education. They chose the latter, went to business school, and took on well-paid jobs in banking. But an interest in fashion persisted. When they understood that Africa was fast becoming the new Eldorado, with companies and investors turning to Sub-Saharan Africa (foreign direct investment in the region was on the rise by 5 percent in 2015[52] according to the World Investment Report produced by the United Nations), they wanted to do their part to help the little guys benefit from this surge in local interest. They created Les Oiseaux Migrateurs (Migrating Birds), an organization that supports small businesses and entrepreneurs in Africa with finalizing and exporting their concepts. The label Maison Château Rouge came after, feeding their interest in fashion and helping to finance their organization.

Their pieces—sold on their website, in their boutique in the Château Rouge neighborhood, and in limited-edition collections like the one produced in collaboration with Merci—has already allowed them to finance their first project: developing and exporting a Dakar-based company that produces bissap, a natural hibiscus juice, with hibiscus flowers cultivated by a women's cooperative in Senegal. Maison Château Rouge is unquestionably poised for big things. "Working in banking didn't change our lives, but it allowed us to see life differently. We want a more equitable and just world. We feel that today, it's urgent that we all take action to make things change," Youssouf says.

Other shops have become shopping destinations by clearly communicating their values, like Centre Commercial, a Canal Saint-Martin multi-brand boutique where sustainable and eco-fashions take pride of place. Labels from France, Great Britain, and Denmark are chosen for their environmentally friendly materials and their local savoir faire. But the space is more than a boutique: It takes on a collaborative role, playing host to various social initiatives, artistic collaborations, art exhibitions, and events.

The world of eco-fashion wasn't new territory for Centre Commercial cofounder Sébastien Kopp. He's one half of the eco–shoe brand Veja, whose mission from day one was to produce shoes ecologically and ethically. Kopp and his partner, François-Ghislain Morillion, realized an opportunity in footwear while traveling and researching for an NGO they created after business school, aimed to help corporations adopt more sustainable business practices. While in Brazil, they observed locals wearing a canvas and rubber shoe that would prove catalytic for the creation of their own brand. As a result, the original Veja shoe was made from organic, fair-trade cotton sourced in Brazil and wild rubber, found in Amazonia. Throughout the 2000s, the brand has developed something of a cult following, making their Centre Commercial venture a natural extension. Veja models in various colors and forms are sold in the boutique, alongside brands like Bleu de Paname, Repetto, Paraboot, Ami, Steven Alan, La Botte Gardiane, Valentine Gauthier, Stanley & Son, and many others.

And of course, leaving one world to enter the craft-driven world of fashion and accessories is an understandable creative shift that many Parisians have made. Claire Rischette of the leather goods brand Fauvette worked for seven years as an optician in Paris when the itch to craft

The vibrant colors, prints, and wax fabrics of Maison Château Rouge are a reflection of the neighborhood in the 18th arrondissement that inspired its name. The collection is produced entirely with fabrics sourced from merchants in Château Rouge.

Atelier Couronnes

ATELIER COURONNES, a boutique-atelier in the 10th arrondissement, represents the union of two talented designers, each with her own successful online shops for her wares: Louise Damas with her namesake line of jewelry and Claire Rischette with Fauvette, her brand of handcrafted leather goods (bags, clutches, and coin purses that can be personalized). Opening a brick-and-mortar shop was born of a desire to contribute to more collaborative spaces in Paris; not only do they display their own goods, but they carry products from other French artisans, such as cards by Papier Tigre and Season Paper, men's skincare by Le Baigneur, Saisons d'Eden natural beauty products, and a range of other accessories.

Behind that eye-catching light fixture (above left) is Julie Lansom, a designer and photographer best known for her handcrafted lampshades, suspension lights, and corner tables. Her graphic Sputnik lampshade, inspired by the retro-futuristic shape of the satellites of the same name sent into space in the 1950s, features hand-painted threads handwoven through wooden, geometric frames. Each tailor-made Sputnik is created in her Paris workshop (her living room!), and they have gone on to add colorful flair to select restaurants and shops like Atelier Couronnes.

something of her own struck hard. She began with the idea of creating her own line of reading glasses and sunglasses that would be sold alongside beautiful leather cases that she would produce herself. She fell in love with the materials she found at the Marché Saint-Pierre in the 18th arrondissement and set forth with the idea, having never sewn before. She began with glasses cases, tried her hand at clutches, and finished with handbags, her object of affection. After completing a training program in leatherwork, she was ready to create Fauvette.

In 2015, she joined forces with young jewelry designer Louise Damas, under the name Atelier Couronnes, and opened a boutique on the rue du Château d'Eau, fast becoming the 10th arrondissement's hotbed of terrific shopping. Louise specializes in jewelry composed of semiprecious pearls, brass, and crystal, and teases inspiration from her love of literature in her designs. "It's an infinite source of inspiration. It allows me to explore various eras, countries, and personalities to create unique pieces with multiple shapes, colors, and materials."

ARTISANAL LIFESTYLE AND HOME GOODS

Fashion and accessories aren't the only goods popping up in new shopping neighborhoods driven by creative upstarts. Artisans in everything from homewares to paper goods have forged their own revival.

Take stationery and paper goods, for instance. France hasn't traditionally been a culture of sending cards for all little events or milestones but you'd never know that from all the cards displayed front and center in concept stores and fashion boutiques. "We have the culture of illustration, art, creations, but paper goods and stationery just weren't in our lifestyle. Letterpress and cards are part of this Anglo-Saxon trend that has spread all over the world. I've done wedding invitations for years, and they used to be very French . . . two pages long! Now, it's the American format that is growing in demand," Letterpress de Paris founder Jean-Frédéric Pouvatchy explained to me when we first met. To create his collection of cards, Pouvatchy works predominantly with young, up-and-coming illustrators based in Paris.

That stationery and paper goods have resurfaced as a fashionable, creative canvas is a testament to the growing backlash to trivial consumption. Letterpress de Paris cards aren't frivolous detritus for the bottom of an office drawer or destined for the forever-untouched pile of mail; they are collectibles meant to be displayed proudly. "We can show the rest of the world that we have the talent and the savoir faire in design and printing," Pouvatchy said as he showed me the atelier. He manages the business side of the operation while his printer, Pascal Pineau, who has thirty years of printing experience behind him, heads up production. Pouvatchy continued, "Moving from minimally designed cards to letterpress splashed with color and illustrations by young artists has given new meaning to Pascal's work. He said it makes him feel like he's cool again! He's proud to work with his hands and sense the value in his work again."

On the day I visited their first printing atelier in the 20th arrondissement, just steps from the Place Gambetta (they have since moved to a newer space), Pouvatchy and Pineau were joined by a handful of the young illustrators they commission to design their cards, who had come to

---

OPPOSITE Centre Commercial is the 10th arrondissement's temple to sustainable fashion.

Comestible Crafts

ANCESTRAL CRAFTS IN COMESTIBLES like honey and jams have also seen a fervent resurgence, and many such products are available at dedicated shops or in gourmet grocers like La Maison Plisson, Causses, and even Galeries Lafeyette Gourmet. My kitchen never goes without Hédène honey and jam from La Chambre aux Confitures. Hédène is the passion project of Cyril Marx and Alexis Ratouis, who were both born into families of beekeepers. After starting their careers in business and marketing, they pursued honey, first by completing a training program at the apiary school Rucher École du Jardin du Luxembourg in Paris, then by creating Hédène. They work exclusively with beekeepers across France who respect traditional harvesting methods and are able to yield the high-quality honey the duo dreamed of producing. From the Jura to Bourgogne, each region's honey boasts its own complex taste profile.

For jams, there is none better than the vast collection by Lise Bienaimé of La Chambre aux Confitures. Bienaimé left an illustrious career at L'Oréal to dip her feet into the world of food. It wasn't entirely unfamiliar to her: Her great-grandfather owned a gourmet grocer, also known as an *épicerie fine*, in Paris, where he confectioned everything from scratch. That love for fine foods was passed down to her grandmother, then her mother, before inspiring her to make the leap. Jam, a condiment as important as butter in the French household, summoned childhood pleasures, conviviality, and sharing, and became the focus of her new homemade pursuit. The majority of Bienaimé's jams and condiments (like chutney and sweet spreadables) are made from French produce. "Each year, I meet with local producers or farming cooperatives, taste their produce, and take the best to make my jams: apricots, prunes, pears, figs, and certain citrus fruits, like lemons from Nice," she said. Any aromas or additional flavors such as violet or rose are sourced directly from Grasse, the famous perfume region. So nostalgic quotient aside, why produce jams, you might ask? "For their versatility and infinite creative possibilities," she explains. Full-size jars may be too cumbersome to bring back as souvenirs, but don't miss the mini packs of three—your breakfasts will thank you!

In a contest of France's most preferred sweet condiment, it would be a toss-up between jam and honey. Both find their way into the daily diet, whether spread across toast or mixed into *fromage blanc*, and are the lifeblood of artisans all across the country. To make Hédène honey, founders Cyril Marx and Alexis Ratouis work exclusively with beekeepers across France who respect traditional harvesting methods.

HÉDÈNE

PARIS

MIEL BOURDAINE

des Landes

ALDER BUCKTHORN
HONEY

"There's nothing better than receiving a card to mark special, or even everyday, moments."

—MAXIME BRENON, COFOUNDER OF PAPIER TIGRE

observe the printing process. As Pineau moved seamlessly, pressing the paper and talking them through each step, the illustrators stood rapt, enthralled to see their art take shape. Letterpress as a technique may be predominantly Anglo-Saxon (Pouvatchy has said so himself) but the brand interprets the product and process in its own way, tapping into the talents and artistic styles of French artists, which results in an object that is wholly unique.

As part of a design agency, the trio behind Papier Tigre was used to designing documents, brochures, and various communication materials for other people, but they wanted to create something for themselves. Self-proclaimed digital geeks, they each had tremendous love for paper and all that can be wrought from it. "As soon as digital began to trump everything, paper goods took on a luxurious quality . . . they were elevated to the role of a keepsake," says cofounder Maxime Brenon. In that way, the digital gave value to the analog, a perfect opportunity to update the idea of correspondence, office accessories, and home decor. What's more, all of their paper goods are made from untreated, recycled paper. The other products they carry in their shop, like Kerzon candles and Le Baigneur men's skincare products, operate under the same ecological standards. The goal, they say, isn't to be a multi-brand shop but to carry a couple of emerging, local designers whose creations are complementary to their own, each with beautiful lettering and paper packaging.

As for accessible art that champions young designers, Slow Galerie in the 11th arrondissement is leading the way. Its founder, Lamia Magliuli, was an engineer in the telecommunications industry for more than ten years before she made a drastic career shift into art curation. A longtime fan of art and culture, she created Slow Galerie with her husband to put the spotlight on the personal work of young illustrators, graphic designers, and silkscreen artists who earn their livings designing for the press, music labels, or brands. "Paris remains an important cultural scene for young artists. So even if our gallery isn't huge, European artists are excited to be exhibited here."

Beyond a collection of art, Magliuli wanted the gallery to be a third space for creatives of all backgrounds. It isn't unusual to see people spilling out onto the sidewalk for events and exhibitions. And while it's an entirely different realm from her previous line of work, she says her background in engineering was tremendously useful. "It really helped in structuring the exhibit schedule and curation, because it requires rigor." Visitors are invited to browse and stay for a tea, coffee, or a snack in the back café nook—to slow down. "That's where the name comes from—I want people to slow down and take the time to savor each piece of artwork and a calm moment in the café."

A MARKET FOR INDIE

With its luxury-lined avenues and world-renowned department stores, Paris will always hold sway among a certain stripe of shopper. But an upsurge in small, independent shops focused on handmade, sustainable, upcycled, or Parisian designs are gaining ground, making the legendary savoir faire à la française something even more special to unearth.

OPPOSITE Papier Tigre design shop that specializes in notebooks, cards, organizers, and other paper goods that help to organize your life.

Slow Galerie

SLOW GALERIE, located in a former apothecary-pharmacy in the 11th arrondissement, looks like an art gallery but is truly a window into the creative minds of young French and European artists. Slow Galerie puts the spotlight on the personal work of young illustrators, graphic designers, and silkscreen artists who make their livings designing for the press, music labels, or brands. On her decision to leave a successful corporate career in telecommunications, owner Lamia Magliuli said, "Life is too short to do the same thing forever." Sometimes, that's the only insight you need.

Shopping Neighborhoods — to Explore —

Today's entrepreneurial leaders in fashion and style—Morgane Sézalory for the label Sézane, Guillaume Gibault of Le Slip Français, Bobbies shoes for men and women, Medecine Douce in jewelry, and many more—have not only opened up the playing field for other designers, crafters, and entrepreneurs but have also carved less-expected neighborhoods into the city's newest shopping destinations: The 2nd, 3rd, 9th, 10th, and 11th arrondissements are vibrant places to begin to explore when looking for goods that show off the best of what Paris has to offer today. Take the 10th arrondissement, for example. You can begin by visiting Atelier Couronnes, Jamini, and La Trésorerie on the rue du Château d'Eau, then cut over the boulevard de Magenta and the rue de Lancry to reach rue de Marseille, where Centre Commercial, Medecine Douce, and a handful of other small shops await. Plan your complete shopping itinerary with a full list of *The New Paris* shops in the guide on page 263.

Q&A

MORGANE SÉZALORY, SÉZANE

IF THERE'S ONE WORD that surfaces time and again in conversation with Morgane Sézalory, it's *obsessed*. The founder and artistic director of Sézane, France's first digital-only fashion label, can't help but profess that she is *obsessed* with caring for her clients, *obsessed* with offering irreproachable customer service, *obsessed* with the quality of her goods, and, perhaps most importantly, *obsessed* with the digital space. It is, after all, the environment that helped her to emerge in a saturated sea of fast fashion and luxury brands. But attentive service and online approachability, rare in the fashion world, are only part of what have made her and her business the talk of the town. For one, her designs—well-edited, feminine basics and statement pieces with unique fabrics, prints, and colors—sit at the nexus of high street and luxury, filling a gaping middle zone. Then there's her polished (but not too polished) girl-next-door mien. Her clients aren't just buying goods she designed; they're effectively buying a piece of her coveted wardrobe.

When Sézalory set out to create her own collections, she didn't lack for loyal fans and customers. Sézane, a contraction of her first and last names, was actually the extension of an existing e-shop called Les Composantes,

where she sold vintage pieces unearthed across France and a small collection of pieces she designed herself. What began as a hobby after her studies became a successful business with ten thousand clients (today, she has well over three hundred thousand). In 2015, she did two collaborations with the American womenswear brand Madewell and opened L'Appartement, a showroom-hangout concept in the 2nd arrondissement (incidentally right in the heart of the Silicon Sentier, the city's tech hub) where clients can try on the collections and place an order (digitally, of course—goods arrive by post) in a space that recalls Sézalory's own home.

Without social media and the word of mouth generated by blogs, Sézalory says there would be no Sézane. I say, without her vision, drive, and unequivocally good taste, there would be no Sézane.

Why do you think your business and concept resonated so powerfully?
People want honesty and greater proximity with the brands or artisans they give their business to. I think some have been drawn to my journey because it's very personal. I taught myself everything and worked hard. I'm attached to what I put out there, and I embody the collections because they truly reflect my own style. I couldn't imagine that my early project would ever lead me here or

OPPOSITE Morgane Sézalory, founder and creative director of Sézane, the first online-only French fashion label.

become viable, and I think my clients sensed that. On top of that, not much was happening in fashion online in France when I started dabbling in designing my own collections. There were a few large multi-brand e-shops but nothing with a creative soul. What I was doing was novel and turned some heads.

When the brand was reborn as Sézane in 2013, I put major emphasis on beautiful photos, elegant, thoughtful packaging (including reusable tote bags), and attentive customer service, because I sensed those elements were missing from the communication and business strategies of some of the companies I shopped with myself. People think we work with a big communication agency for our promotion, but we don't! It's all in-house. The budget we save from not doing any traditional advertising is money we put into improving the quality of our goods, sussing out new, unique fabrics, and building the team internally.

You're a self-taught designer whose small business blossomed quickly and broadly. Did you imagine your career this way?

From the beginning, my goal was to find what made me happy and run with it professionally. I was looking to be free and financially independent. In France, there's this fantasy around advanced academic studies, but there are plenty of people, including within my network of friends, who went to great schools and got the degrees, but they're struggling to find themselves and what they *really* want to do. I spent one year in the United States when I was fifteen and what amazed me, even then, was the extent to which people were encouraged to take action, create their own way. In France, there's a playbook we're all supposed to follow, but it doesn't work for everyone.

I didn't go to business school and come out with a hundred thousand euros to make a project work. I was just trying to pay the rent.

The reaction to what we were producing and how we were producing it was really positive. But there's always a hint of suspicion. We have this culture of the tortured artist where if you're doing something creative, you're meant to be struggling (and you certainly can't have any business acumen). But if you're making money, you're misrepresenting what it means to be an artist. This is slowly starting to change.

Between the government and the media, everyone is championing the *Made in France* label. Was that a consideration for Sézane?

The truth is, you can produce anywhere. It's just a question of being dogged about quality control. There's good and bad everywhere, and that includes in France! We produce our collections where specific skills and materials are renowned. We work with Portugal for jersey, India for embroidery, China for cashmere, among other places, but 95 percent is produced in Europe because we know the ateliers well, they're closer, and we can more easily control production.

Has Parisian style changed since you've been in the industry?

All over the world, people still look to the discretion and femininity of *la Parisienne* as a model they can identify with or aspire to. Effortless chic—a look that's studied but looks completely natural—is still very much the style here; it's just the brands and designers that have changed a bit!

OPPOSITE Inside L'Appartment Sézane, a stunning shopping space featuring the season's clothing and accessories collection as well as a variety of chic lifestyle items.

PARISIAN PERSPECTIVE

MARIN MONTAGUT, 33

WATERCOLOR ILLUSTRATOR AND MULTIDISCIPLINARY ARTIST

Did you always know you would end up in Paris? What drew you to the city initially?

It was a foregone conclusion that I'd end up in Paris. I always felt motivated by art, and Paris was the artistic beacon that called me. I grew up in Toulouse, where everyone knows who you are and you can't go to a café without running into someone you know. The fact that you can be anonymous in Paris was tremendously appealing to me. But I didn't start in Paris. I spent one year in London, but quickly realized it wasn't for me. When I arrived in Paris thirteen years ago, there was no adaptation period; I was immediately at ease. I ended up on the rue de Lancry in the 10th arrondissement, and at the time it was more like Belleville—full of tiny little shops, a chaotic but inspiring mix of people and activities. My instincts led me to the right place!

How do you feel the city has changed the most since you've lived here?

For so long, *rive gauche* was considered the artists' quarter—all the most influential names in art, fashion, and design made it their stomping ground. But today, that creative fiber is on the right bank, where we're seeing more artisans and small shops than ever before. Not only are people interested in handcrafted items but

we've never talked so much about the people and the hands that produce them.

More and more people are dropping traditional professional trajectories for an entrepreneurial lifestyle. Why do you think this is becoming more common?

I'm an example of this. I wanted to learn on the ground because I didn't want to be formatted by traditional training in school. Call it youthful arrogance, but I preferred to shape my own style and let experience in the industry guide my career. At the time, it was very poorly viewed to drop out of school (or not go at all!), even if it was to learn a trade from those with ample experience. I think we're seeing this entrepreneurial lifestyle take off because people have finally realized that advanced studies no longer guarantee job security like they once did. In pursuing their own projects, people get to take back control.

What do you think is most special about Paris today?

I profoundly love this city, more than ten years ago and more than yesterday. It has always been special. But what's certain is that neighborhoods and entire sections of the city are developing in amazing ways. It's far less segmented than before and things are happening all over, which makes every outing a potential experience.

OPPOSITE Watercolor illustrator and multimedia artist Marin Montagut.

the new
PLACES &
SPACES

"There is but one Paris and however
hard living may be here, and if
it became worse and harder even—
the French air clears up the brain
and does good—a world of good."

—VINCENT VAN GOGH

*T*raversing Paris by foot will always trump the experience on public transportation, but there are certain joys in an above-ground métro ride. I've always loved the moment on lines 2, 5, and 6 when the train emerges from an underground station, leaving the darkness of the tunnels behind in one swift move to reveal the city's glow. Once my eyes adjust, they scan the cityscape wildly—left, right, and then below as the train car glides above the din.

Ever since I've lived in Paris, I've taken métro line 2, which connects Nation (12th arrondissement) with Porte Dauphine, its western terminus, because it's the most direct route to Montmartre. Up until 2013, each journey on the line would unfurl the same way. Whether I had my head in a book or was lost in thought, I would naturally jerk to attention as we rode into the Barbès-Rochechouart station. If I didn't already have a clear view from the window, I'd muscle my way through passengers to be able to sneak a glance at a building that had become a focus of fascination. I would have mere seconds to see the abandoned, dilapidated structure lording over a shoddy corner of the boulevard Magenta, but my imagination would run wild long after we zipped ahead to the next station. Visibly a relic of a bygone era, I couldn't help but shudder when I thought of the space's crumbling insides. What had it meant to those who spent time there, and what would its future hold, I wondered. After nearly six years of wondering, I had my answer.

Le Louxor was a neo-Egyptian art deco prewar cinema from 1921 that reopened in 2013 after a twenty-five-million-euro restoration project spearheaded by the city of Paris. After several incarnations, including as a nightclub and gay disco, the emblematic venue had shuttered in 1987 after years of gradual neglect and disrepair. Locals campaigned to restore the gilded masterpiece to its former glory both to boost a neighborhood long perceived as a stronghold for drugs, mischief, and knock-offs and to preserve the seventh art, a term first coined in 1911 by the Italian film theoretician Ricciotto Canudo to refer to cinema. Then-mayor Bertrand Delanoë heeded the call, and the city purchased the cinema in 2003.

Most of the mosaics have been preserved, and the original theater has been reproduced identically, now heated and cooled by geothermal energy. A veritable architectural landmark, Le Louxor is now classified a historic monument and features art-house films. Its greatest asset: the rooftop café and bar with an ideal view of the Sacré-Coeur, accessible only to ticket-holders. To me, it's much more than a cinematic destination; it's one of the city's *many* great revival stories.

PREVIOUS SPREAD The lighthearted spirit of the Canal de L'Ourcq, located past the Canal Saint-Martin. OPPOSITE Le Louxor art-house cinema reopened in 2013 after a twenty-five-million-euro restoration project spearheaded by the city of Paris.

Formerly a covered market dating back to 1863, Le Carreau du Temple now plays host to fashion shows, dance classes, cultural events, and food festivals like the Street Food Temple, shown here.

STRENGTH IN PUBLIC WORKS

If the city has excelled tremendously in one area, it's in public works. And that's a muscle it has been flexing since the seventeenth century, when urban developments like the Pont Neuf bridge and modern sidewalks levitated above the standards in other European nations, making Paris the model of modernity. Within the last ten years, that has translated to a thriving bike-share program with more than forty million journeys per year and between one hundred thousand and two hundred thousand rentals per day (equivalent to about 37 percent of all bicycle journeys in the city), which has been touted as "nothing short of an urban revolution";[53] Mayor Hidalgo's chartered plan to create nearly 250 acres (100 hectares) of vertical and rooftop gardens by the end of her term in 2020 (including an obligation for new constructions to have at least one vegetal wall or rooftop); and a massive push to reduce pollution by curbing dependence on cars and establishing more pedestrian-only sections in the city center.

Urban living improvements and social advancement go a step further with large-scale renewal endeavors and one initiative in particular: the ambitious (and controversial) two-pronged project called Le Grand Paris. The project aims to transform the city into a sprawling metropolis (Métropole du Grand Paris, or Metropolis of Greater Paris), encompassing area suburbs and adjacent regions; establish interconnectedness via the Grand Paris Express, an extended subway network; and provide better access to jobs and resources for populations living on the city's fringes.[54]

It may be years before we see the extent to which this project will change the face of the city, but the impact of the smaller, but no less important, initiatives in the city have already been felt. Aside from the novelty of their revitalization or development, much of the appeal in the types of places and spaces defining Paris today is what they offer Parisians—new opportunities to connect with the cultural fiber of the city and its people. And in many cases, they can be found in areas well off the beaten tourist path.

Formerly forlorn enclaves like the Canal Saint-Martin, the Bassin de la Villette, and La Goutte d'Or have seen an upsurge in creative spaces, independent shops, and artistic and cultural venues. The first to shift was the historically working-class stronghold around the Canal Saint-Martin, a waterway commissioned by Napoleon Bonaparte to provide fresh water for the capital that is perhaps best known to foreigners today for its iron footbridges, from which Amélie Poulain skipped stones in the 2001 film *Amélie*. Though it had already begun shaking off some of its gritty veneer when I moved nearby at the end of 2006, it felt like an at-your-own-risk place to be after the sun went down. And given that it was far removed from where the crux of the city's activity was at the time, it didn't even factor into our list of places to go on weekends. It wasn't until a few years ago that it became a true destination for picnics, strolls, shopping, even dining, among Parisians—a multi-cultural crossroads where Parisians born and bred mingle with expats, immigrants, and smalltown French people who moved to the big city for opportunity.

Marie Montaud and Gilles Ballard of the jewelry label Medecine Douce, whose shop and ate- lier is situated just off the canal on the rue de Marseille, bought property nearby over five years ago because it was all they could afford, a common story. "The mix of people who had to move here, and the existing nonchalance of the neighborhood, made it an attractive home for brands, creative

Rosa Bonheur sur Seine, a *guinguette* (an informal place for eating and drinking) and popular waterfront hangout along the Berges de Seine.

Parisians Reclaim *Rive Gauche*

RIVE GAUCHE (LEFT BANK) Parisians took to Les Berges de Seine, a 1½-mile (2.4-km) stretch of riverbank reserved for pedestrians and cyclists, with a kind of beatific glee that I hadn't ever seen before. Previously a heavily trafficked thoroughfare, the redesigned section (completed in 2013), connecting the banks at the Musée d'Orsay and the Pont d'Alma, gave locals reason to look anew at the city, with greater proximity to its major waterway and exquisite views. It's kitted out with floating botanical gardens, mobile libraries, capsule hotels, boat bistros, bars, children's activities, pop-up cultural exhibits throughout the year, and plenty of space for runners and cyclists to share the road. Some of my fondest memories from spring and summer in the city have been afternoons or evenings along the water, as the sun inches behind the Pont Alexandre III and the serried rows of linden trees that stretch along the river.

Rosa Bonheur sur Seine, a *guinguette* (an informal place for eating and drinking) whose first outpost in the Buttes Chaumont Park in the 19th arrondissement is a veritable institution, infused extra life onto the riverbank when it officially opened for business (opposite). Few can even recall what the left-bank berges felt like before, and by the time you read this, we'll be waxing poetic about the *rive droite* waterfront too, which will have followed in the footsteps of *rive gauche* and undergone its own design metamorphosis.

agencies, artists, and young families," Ballard told me. Once bigger fashion brands came in and leading food critics took notice of inventive restaurants moving in on both sides of the canal, the vibe started to change dramatically. Montaud says the transformation was like night and day. "We certainly don't feel isolated here at all anymore, but there was a time when we had to traverse the city to go out with our friends. Now they all want to come to us!" Living among a progressive population known for its social, ethnic, and religious diversity, the couple is unquestionably at the epicenter of where the city feels most alive.

That rollicking energy and artsy spirit continues up to the Bassin de la Villette, the largest artificial lake in Paris, where two dockside art-house theaters in old warehouses have been joined in recent years by food trucks, the Paname Brewing Company (see page 179), and the Pavillon des Canaux, a quirky third space decked out like an old home, all of which have brought increased interest to the area. The expansive boulevards and frenetic activity of the 19th arrondissement fade from view, leaving behind a lively port-town vibe. Young parents swing their children between them along cobblestone footpaths and rent rowboats to explore the bassin from a different perspective. It's a quiet village in a pocket of the city that never sleeps.

Continue farther and you'll reach the Parc de la Villette, the city's arts and culture center and home to the Paris orchestra at the Philharmonie concert hall, which opened in 2015. Unless Parisians already lived in the neighborhood or were headed to the 19th arrondissement to see a concert; attend a trade show; visit the Cité des Sciences, one of the largest science museums in Europe; or cycle along the Canal de l'Ourcq, rarely did they go out of their way to spend time there. Now, there is a greater energy, with more cyclists, picnickers, and culture-hungry visitors than ever before.

Clear across town in the 16th arrondissement section of the Bois de Boulogne, the city's other cultural bookend gave us all a new reason to venture out to the western extremity. The Fondation Louis Vuitton contemporary art museum lends a futuristic style to an otherwise stately neighborhood with its uniformly Haussmannian-limestone architecture. The hypnotic glass structure, designed by the great Frank Gehry (his first project in Paris since the Cinémathèque Française in 1994), is the first example since the Centre Pompidou in which a museum attracted an audience not strictly for its art but also for the sight of the building itself and the spectacular views it affords (in this case, the Eiffel Tower and the heart of Paris on one side, La Défense business district on the other). In fact, both the Fondation and the Philharmonie have architectural and cultural elements designed to be accessible to all and remind us that art doesn't have to be intimidating or highbrow (the grotto on the lower level of the Fondation Louis Vuitton, for example, doesn't require any appreciation for art installations at all—it is pleasant to stroll through and experience simply *being*).

OPPOSITE Between the Fondation Louis Vuitton in the 16th arrondissement and the Philharmonie de Paris clear across town in the 19th arrondissement (pictured), there are more reasons than ever to cast our eyes upward. Contemporary art and music lovers will rejoice, but so will those who don't have any particular affinity for the cultural arts—the buildings themselves are impressive works in their own right worth experiencing. And both have destination restaurants that offer unparalleled views (TOP). The view of the Parc de la Villette from inside Le Balcon restaurant in the Philharmonie de Paris (BOTTOM).

"Paris has awakened artistically, and that's a driver for everything else."
—MARIE PUGLIESI-CONTI, ARCHITECT

PHILHARMONIE DE PARIS

In the northern section of the city, not far from La Goutte d'Or in the 18th arrondissement, an industrial wasteland became an emblem in sustainable development when the city-led regeneration of the Halle Pajol was completed in 2014. Transformed from an abandoned 1920s freight warehouse (owned by the SNCF, France's national railway company), the low energy *eco-quartier* was created in part to stoke a sense of community in the neighborhood. With nearly 38,000 square feet (3,500 sq m) of photovoltaic solar panels installed on the roof, it is the largest urban solar power center in all of France and is now home to a public library, the city's largest youth hostel, restaurants (including Bob's Bake Shop, see page 66), offices, and gardens. Nearby at La REcyclerie, three little R's wee Americans learn in grade school—Reduce, Reuse, Recycle—act as the space's moral compass and drive DIY workshops and events. A multipurpose concept, the hybrid restaurant, bar, farm, vegetable garden, and upcycling center can be found in the abandoned Ornano train station above the rails of La Petite Ceinture (little belt), a forsaken, fourteen-mile (23-km) rail line from the mid-nineteenth century that circles the city. In its disuse, La Petite Ceinture has become something of a destination; a magnet for flâneurs, who can stroll two walking paths inaugurated by Mayor Hidalgo, and artists for whom the tracks and vacant stations are a canvas. With several hundred species of plants lining the length of the former train tracks, it is also a beautiful sanctuary of wildlife that is rare to see outside the confines of parks and gardens. Restoring the transport line is the subject of much debate between conservationists and the Association Sauvegarde Petite Ceinture, which believes that reviving the railroad will ease traffic congestion on the road and on existing public transportation lines. Until a decision is reached for its future, La Petite Ceinture remains one of the city's most curious treasures to discover.

A NEW WAY TO WORK

There has been a lot of talk in recent years about incubators, fab labs, and co-working spaces around the globe that encourage, guide, and support entrepreneurial pursuits across industries. But for a long time, it seemed as if that collaborative culture had skipped over Paris. Prior to the arrival of spaces like Cantine, the first multipurpose collaborative work space and tech hub in France, launched in 2008; Café Craft, a specialty coffee shop and co-working space that opened in 2012; and Coworkshop, opened in 2014, among a handful of others, the only viable third spaces were the city's many libraries or cafés. But these didn't fit the bill for entrepreneurs looking for environments dedicated to creative exchange.

OPPOSITE Draft Ateliers took the concept of collaborative workspaces a step further, creating an atelier-workshop concept that encourages their creative clients to engage in co-making. At the disposal of freelancers are laser cutters, 3-D printers, woodcutting equipment, sewing machines, and other tools. Anne Gautier, the co-owner, wanted to open a screen-printing workshop with the tools that would allow her not only to test her work but also to produce it from A to Z. Like most of the city's entrepreneurs, the founders of Draft are highly educated, natural-born creatives who left their corporate jobs to create a space that was not only missing in the city but that would benefit the scores of others looking to create with their hands.

View from the tub, one of many quirky spots to sit and have a coffee or snack at the Pavillon des Canaux.

Paris: Global Innovation Hub

CONTRIBUTED BY RAHAF HARFOUSH

IT MIGHT COME AS A SURPRISE to learn that Paris is a global innovation hub, ranked as having one of the best start-up ecosystems in the world. Its central location makes it ideal for connecting to other major European cities like London, only a short train ride away. However, those wanting to enter one of Europe's largest markets (France has a population of nearly 67 million people) must navigate a high tax structure compared to other cities, a language barrier, and a cultural aversion to risk.

France's government has a dedicated Minister of State for Digital Affairs who launched La French Tech, an initiative designed to attract, accelerate, and promote French entrepreneurs both at home and abroad in 2013. Additionally, the government recently announced the introduction of a new type of work visa called the French Tech Ticket that is aimed to encourage foreign start-ups to come to Paris. The government has also announced partnerships with companies like Cisco, who have agreed to invest 100 million euros into France's incubator programs.

From an innovation perspective, France has been strong for decades, helped along by a world-class education system that produces a highly sought-after talent pool, including the École Polytechnique, considered one of the best engineering schools in the world. Parisian entrepreneurs, comprising more than 22,600[55] companies that employ more than 138,000 people, have attracted close to 2.4 billion euros in funding since 2005. In 2015, the European Digital City Index (EDCi), which evaluates how well a city supports digital entrepreneurialism overall, ranked Paris in the top ten (number six, to be precise) outperforming Dublin, Berlin, Madrid, Oxford, and Lisbon. Paris also ranked second in the Index's subcategory of access to funding. That being said, it's important to note that while this is good for Europe, access to late-stage funding[56] in France is quite difficult compared to other international hubs such as Tel-Aviv and Silicon Valley.

One of the biggest changes to the ecosystem in the past few years has been an increase in media coverage both nationally and from around the world. With some highly publicized success stories including BlaBlaCar (which is currently valued at 1.6 billion dollars), Vente-Privee, and Deezer, start-ups are now becoming a regular part of traditional media coverage. In 2011, the launch of Rude Baguette, an English-language blog exclusively covering the French start-up market, helped increase awareness, resulting in more international press and foreign investments.

That's not to say it's all rosy. France has a lower adoption rate of new technologies compared to other European markets. Costs of living, office rent, and labor are quite expensive, and while the rate of English literacy is improving, language remains a significant barrier (Paris was rated 21 out of 35 cities for English Language Skills by the EDCi). The government has also had some missteps including blocking the 2013 sale of DailyMotion by Yahoo in an attempt[57] to keep the French video platform out of foreign hands.

Overall, however, there has been a lot of positive momentum. In the last few years the city has also seen a surge of new co-working spaces—at the time of this writing there are 250! These spaces provide opportunities for early-stage ventures, freelancers, and micro-entrepreneurs to connect to the broader business community and network with other likeminded people.

Accelerators such as NUMA, Microsoft Ventures, and the Family are introducing more sophisticated resources and programs for up-and-coming entrepreneurs, including hack-a-thons, competitions, and educational tools. This is making it easier than ever for French entrepreneurs to launch new businesses and find the needed resources and support to make them successful.

France's rich cultural legacy, strong educational platforms, and investments in ecosystems position it to become one of the world's leading innovative countries.

RAHAF HARFOUSH *is a digital anthropologist, author, and adjunct professor.*

Now, thanks to support within the business community and financial incentives from the city, Paris is becoming a more and more attractive place for starts-ups and entrepreneurs. In 2016, an impressive six-story shared office space called Garage Central opened its doors in a converted garage from the 1930s on the 10th arrondissement's rue des Petites Écuries. Designed as an extension of the home for entrepreneurs in food, tech, and the creative arts, the space's founders were profoundly informed by the neighborhood, itself brimming with doers and entrepreneurs who create, take risks, and innovate in order to shake up the status quo. It is but one of many intimations of a changing work culture, where ambitious upstarts forge the way forward. And while you may not be visiting Paris with workspace needs, the hip coffee shops and mixed-use cultural spaces that have thrived in this newly collaborative environment make prime spots to get a firsthand sense of the city's booming spirit of innovation and creativity.

A NEW HANGOUT: BOUTIQUE HOTELS

C'est vrai! Once-fashionable boîtes like L'Etoile, Le Baron, and the VIP Room, where how much money you flaunted determined entry, have declined in popularity among Parisians. Most clubs today are frequented by wealthy visitors or are members-only, like Silencio. In the wake of the dying club scene, combined with a swing away from impersonal cafés and bars, locals are heading back into hotels to socialize. And not just any hotels but small, intimate, boutique hotels where good vibes reign and quality drinks and food are in ample supply. In speaking with architect Elliott Barnes, a longtime Paris expat and the former partner of acclaimed designer Andrée Putman, I learned this shift had been brewing for ages. In fact, Putman was a driving force behind the boutique hotel concept that developed in New York in the 1980s with Ian Schrager and Steve Rubell (of Studio 54 fame)[58] but was later popularized back in Paris by the Costes brothers, whose Jacques Garcia–designed Hôtel Costes became an atmospheric hotspot for the capital's fashionable top brass. "They brought a new interpretation of *la fête*. You no longer needed to go to a nightclub to party, dance, or have a good time until late; you could do that at the hotel," says Barnes.

Located in a former South Pigalle brothel, Thierry Costes's hippie-chic Hôtel Amour is the first of its kind to truly balance the local hangout vibe—with a restaurant and courtyard garden café—at a hotel. My friend Yoan Marciano, owner of Hôtel du Temps, recalls feeling inspired by the sense of place Costes managed to create and sustain over the years. "Hôtel Amour, and others like it, are more like guest houses than hotels. More often than not, they're frequented by neighborhood people who come in to read the paper or have their morning meetings," he told me over coffee, speaking from experience. In his own hotel, people come for a sort of magical exchange and a familial spirit where everyone can feel at ease. But they also come to him for his stunning, sepia-tinged space, done up by fashion designer Alix Thomsen and set designer Laura Léonard, using the bar-café and private cellar for televised interviews, press events, music album previews, and concerts.

Many others have come along to redefine the role of hotels in Paris as well. One of the most iconic spaces beats wildly once again after an extended closure. Part of the epochal Parisian

nightclubs à la Studio 54, Les Bains was first a high-end bathhouse (then called Les Bains Guerbois) when it opened in 1885 before becoming the ultimate party destination, endowed with a sultry social whirl that attracted the world's VIPs, from Andy Warhol to David Bowie and Kate Moss. It closed in 2010 due to structural hazards but was reborn in 2015 as a five-star boutique hotel with a brand-new restaurant, bar, and spa, but the same epicurean spirit.

On the other side of town, another long-awaited resurgence has come to fruition. The Piscine Molitor municipal swimming pool, just a stone's throw from the Bois de Boulogne, was inaugurated by American Olympic gold medalist (and Tarzan!) Johnny Weissmuller in 1929 and was the most popular swimming pool in the capital for sixty years. A pleasure ground for first-time swimmers, sunbathers, and poolside fashionistas, it made its indelible mark on the collective memory not only as the backdrop to the bikini's first introduction in 1946 but also with its singular design—tiers of art deco changing cubicles, beautiful stained glass, white balustrades, and its "tango yellow" façade, a beacon of summertime insouciance. But the legend took a dive in the 1990s, becoming a derelict artist's squat. It's hard to imagine the resort-like lido pool caked in graffiti, but that chaotic, underground phase of Molitor's history has been cleverly weaved into its present. When it reopened as a hotel-spa, it launched with a rich, artistic program spanning fashion, design, cinema, urban art, and contemporary art, writing a whole new narrative for an incredible icon.

I asked Barnes what he thought was behind this attraction to hotels, aside from a dormant club scene. "It's the 'palace hotel' effect," he began, referring to the distinction given to the country's finest five-star properties. "They usurped the attention from many of the smaller properties dominating the city because spaces flooded with wealthy, foreign tourists. These boutique hotels surf on the wave of larger hotels but develop their own energy. They're more local and Parisians consider them worthy hangouts." And now, they're also places to get genuinely good meals. From French classics at Bachaumont and Hôtel Providence to a more refined, market-driven tasting menu at the Hôtel Particulier Montmartre's Mandragore restaurant, these spots are redefining what it means to sleep, eat, and drink in Paris hotels.

EXPERIENCING THE NEW PARIS

These spaces and neighborhoods are a far cry from the traditional café terraces and immaculately manicured parks of the city center (and aren't likely to make it onto your run-of-the-mill postcard) but they are, without a doubt, the most appropriate reflections of the city's spirit today.

OPPOSITE The Piscine Molitor municipal swimming pool, just a stone's throw from the Bois de Boulogne, was the most popular swimming pool in the capital for sixty years. After falling into disrepair and being taken over by street artists, Molitor was restored to its former glory as a hotel.

East & West: Ideal Itineraries

EAST

HOME BASE: **HÔTEL PROVIDENCE**,
10th arrondissement
BREAKFAST: coffee at **TEN BELLES**
WANDER: **CANAL SAINT-MARTIN**
LUNCH: **HOLYBELLY**
SEE: **THE PHILHARMONIE DE PARIS**
APÉRO: **LE SYNDICAT**
DINNER: **LE 52 FAUBOURG SAINT-DENIS**
DIGESTIF: Drinks on the terrace of **LA
ROTONDE** (ABOVE), 19th arrondissement

WEST

HOME BASE: **MOLITOR**, 16th arrondissement
BREAKFAST: **LA PÂTISSERIE CYRIL LIGNAC**
WANDER: **LES BERGES DE SEINE**
LUNCH: **CLOVER**
SEE: **FONDATION LOUIS VUITTON**
APÉRO: **ROSA BONHEUR SUR SEINE**
(OPPOSITE)
DINNER: **PAGES**
DIGESTIF: gin cocktails at **TIGER**

For additional information on these places and more, see the guide on pages 250–266.

Rosa Bonheur sur Seine, a popular bar along the river, with the Pont Alexandre III and the Grand Palais in the distance.

PARISIAN PERSPECTIVE

DOROTHÉE MEILICHZON, 34
AWARD-WINNING INTERIOR DESIGNER

How do you think Paris has changed in the last ten years, including in design?

In Paris, we used to say that we had to wait for the baguette to be so bad that it was inedible and the espresso undrinkable to notice there was a problem with our "basics." Once Parisians did, we became serious about the flour quality, the origin of the coffee beans, the roasting process . . . it was like Parisians were reborn! I am exaggerating a bit, but the same was true with interiors when I started my company in 2009. Kartell plastic chairs, bistro tables, and baroque chandeliers were all the rage. Decor was either fake (laminated wood, skai synthetic upholstery) or plastic. But since this "awakening" has become global, we gravitate once again toward everything that is authentic. That includes using natural materials (oak, brick, plaster, cotton), making the most of existing architectural elements, and even looking for vintage furniture with stories to tell.

In what ways do you think design has moved away from familiar elements like wicker chairs and zinc bars?

The thing with trends is to know if they will last or not! Red bricks in New York, for example, are a basic. Sometimes they are trendy, sometimes not, but they remain part of the landscape. I think the same is true with French classics: crown molding, boiserie, and chevron wooden floors have been the basics in Parisian apartments for decades. But what will change is the way people update them and make them their own, from wallpapering all the walls twenty years ago to painting walls in acid colors; from dark, wenge furniture ten years ago to lightening everything with white (boucherouite carpets and marble monolith). That is what we, French designers, have to do: renew the codes without disowning the classics.

You pioneered an entirely new style, mixing textures and prints, vintage pieces and modern styles. What inspired this?

I have always been into graphics, so patterns had a natural place in my interiors. Fabrics, carpets, and wallpapers were a great way to play with geometry. Mixing styles and decorative elements makes a place richer, more interesting to look at, and more comfortable.

How would you define Parisian interior style today?

In 2009 when I started using vintage pieces and a variety of fabrics, it was a completely new style. When I spoke about using brass in 2010, people had no idea that it even existed! Now, the brass-marble-Edison-bulb-vintage-furniture-and-reclaimed-wood style seems to be the go-to look all over the world, so I guess it is the end of an era again and time to start something new! That is why I draw and design almost everything myself now, from frescoes painted on walls to handmade patterns on mosaics or marquetry on tables. This is the best way to preserve the past because only craftsmen are able to bring my designs and ideas to life.

lindsey's
NEW PARIS
favorites

Food & Dining

Neo-Bistros / Modern

LE 6 PAUL BERT
The more modern sister restaurant of Le Bistrot Paul Bert, with pedigree ingredients and plates meant for sharing.
6 RUE PAUL BERT, 75011

BISTRO PARADIS
Neo-bistro dishes are inflected with South American flavors at this table helmed by Brazilian chef Alexandre Furtado.
55 RUE DE PARADIS, 75010

CAILLEBOTTE
Thoughtful, contemporary bistro fare from the owners of the popular neighborhood spot Le Pantruche.
8 RUE HIPPOLYTE LEBAS, 75009

LE CHATEAUBRIAND
Basque chef Iñaki Aizpitarte's neo-bistro institution
129 AVENUE PARMENTIER, 75011

CHEZ L'AMI JEAN
This restaurant may have old-world bones, but the cooking is firmly anchored in bistronomy, with chef Stéphane Jégo at the helm.
27 RUE MALAR, 75007

CLOVER
Michelin-starred chef Jean-François Piège's mid-range, modern bistro with an emphasis on fresh, local produce.
5 RUE PERRONET, 75007

LE DAUPHIN
Le Chateaubriand's little sister (and next-door neighbor) serves tapas-style, market-driven small plates and natural wines in a striking space designed by Rem Koolhaas.
131 AVENUE PARMENTIER, 75011

ELLSWORTH
Nouveau Americana fare with a southern bent from Verjus owners Braden Perkins and Laura Adrian.
34 RUE DE RICHELIEU, 75001

FRENCHIE / FRENCHIE WINE BAR
Chef Gregory Marchand's gastronomic table and its wine-bar offshoot (first come, first serve), both must-visits.
5–6 RUE DU NIL, 75002

LE GALOPIN
This is *Top Chef France* winner Romain Tischenko's temple of creative, spontaneous neo-bistro cooking.
34 RUE SAINTE-MARTHE, 75010

MARTIN
The quintessential neighborhood bistro that wows with Frenchified tapas and a superb wine list.
24 BOULEVARD DU TEMPLE, 75011

L'OFFICE
The more formal of Charles Compagnon's trio of restaurants with a modern bistro menu.
3 RUE RICHER, 75009

AU PASSAGE
A relaxed bistro with a menu of shareable plates and natural wines (and a popular hangout among chefs!).
1 BIS PASSAGE SAINT-SÉBASTIEN, 75011

PIERRE SANG ON GAMBEY
The loft-like second restaurant from *Top Chef France* finalist Pierre Sang with a surprise, market-driven menu.
6 RUE GAMBEY, 75011

PIERRE SANG ON OBERKAMPF
The *Top Chef France* finalist's first restaurant, big on surprises. Come early for a seat at the open kitchen.
55 RUE OBERKAMPF, 75011

PORTE 12
Chef Vincent Crepel's thirty-two seat neo-bistro where he inventively plays up seasonal produce in a style greatly informed both by his travels through Asia and Europe and his experience under the tutelage of venerated chef André Chiang.
12 RUE DES MESSAGERIES, 75010

OPPOSITE The South Pigalle municipal basketball court was created out of an initiative led by designer Stéphane Ashpool, the founder of the popular urban streetwear label of the same name, Pigalle. A longtime fan of basketball, Stéphane pushed for the creation of a court as a way to give back to the neighborhood's youth and welcome anyone with a love for the game. It was either that or watch it become a car park. Nestled between two buildings, he refit the court with the help of Nike and LeBron James; it was painted by locals and some of the kids he coaches weekly. This is the second iteration of the court's design and will likely evolve with future artistic collaborations.

SEMILLA

Full- and half-size portions are an added bonus at this left bank favorite where the menu is created by Meilleur Ouvrier de France Eric Trochon.
54 RUE DE SEINE, 75006

SEPTIME

Young chef Bertrand Grébaut's one-Michelin-star neo-bistro with a no-choice menu and beautiful, natural wines.
80 RUE DE CHARONNE, 75011

LE SERVAN

International flavors add a fresh twist to this affordable bistro run by sisters Tatiana and Katia Levha.
32 RUE SAINT-MAUR, 75011

SPRING

Daniel Rose's exquisite restaurant in the 1st arrondissement (reservations required; specify dietary restrictions ahead of time).
6 RUE BAILLEUL, 75001

TANNAT

Produce-driven neo-bistro cooking at affordable prices in a beautiful, mirrored dining room.
119 AVENUE PARMENTIER, 75011

TONDO

Sardinian chef Simone Tondo's modern take on his two favorite terroirs, France and Italy, in a chic, 1920s interior.
29 RUE DE COTTE, 75012

VERJUS

Chef Braden Perkins's nose-to-tail cooking comes to life in this exceptional tasting-menu restaurant. Arrive before your reservation to have a drink in the downstairs wine bar.
52 RUE DE RICHELIEU, 75001

YARD

A neighborhood bistro par excellence, situated in an old ironwork shop. Hearty but sophisticated dishes are prepared by an Anglo chef in an open kitchen. Great for lunch or dinner.
6 RUE DE MONT-LOUIS, 75011

Neo-Brasseries

LE 52 FAUBOURG SAINT-DENIS

Charles Compagnon's third restaurant, with an ever-changing menu and nonstop service from breakfast through dinner.
52 RUE DU FAUBOURG SAINT-DENIS, 75010

CHAMPEAUX

Alain Ducasse's contemporary brasserie under the Canopée at the Forum des Halles serving revisited classics (haricots verts salad, côte d'agneau, steak-frites, and more) nonstop from lunch until late.
LA CANOPÉE—FORUM DES HALLES, PORTE RAMBU-TEAU, 75001

LAZARE

Michelin-starred chef Eric Frechon's modern brasserie inside the Saint-Lazare train station, with all-day service.
PARVIS DE LA GARE SAINT-LAZARE, RUE INTÉRIEURE, 75008

LE RICHER

Charles Compagnon's second neo-brasserie with an ever-rotating menu and a robust list of wines and eaux-de-vie offerings.
2 RUE RICHER, 75009

(New) Classic Bistros

BISTROT BELHARA

Seasonal-driven bistro with modern esthetics and hearty dishes served by old-school servers (suit and tie included!).
23 RUE DUVIVIER, 75007

LE BISTROT PAUL BERT

The best of traditional bistro dishes with hefty portion sizes and a rollicking atmosphere.
18 RUE PAUL BERT, 75011

LE BON GEORGES

Feel-good bistro dishes and a quality wine selection in an inviting, nostalgic dining room.
45 RUE SAINT-GEORGES, 75009

LA BOURSE ET LA VIE

Chef Daniel Rose's first bistro, where he and his team use top-shelf ingredients to revive classic dishes.
12 RUE VIVIENNE, 75002

LE CHARDENOUX

Chef Cyril Lignac's mid-range bistro that showcases classic bistro dishes in an old-world dining room.
1 RUE JULES VALLES, 75011

CHEZ LA VIEILLE

A Parisian bistro institution taken over in 2016 by Chef Daniel Rose, featuring an hors d'oeuvres bar and daily dishes at affordable prices.
1 RUE BAILLEUL, 75001

LE COMPTOIR DU RELAIS

Yves Camdeborde's Saint-Germain bistro institution (stop into L'Avant Comptoir next door for a predinner drink or L'Avant Comptoir de la Mer for seafood tapas).

3, 9 CARREFOUR DE L'ODÉON, 75006

LE PANTRUCHE

The quality bistro that's largely credited for breathing culinary life into the South Pigalle neighborhood—a must!

3 RUE VICTOR MASSÉ, 75009

Japanese Chefs

LE 116

This laid-back wine bar, with a selection of donburi at lunch, meats, and fish grilled by Binchotan (high-heat charcoal) at dinner, is the annex to chef Ryuji "Teshi" Teshima's Pages (see below). Natural wines and cocktails available.

2 RUE AUGUSTE-VACQUERIE, 75016

6036

Matchbox-size izakaya restaurant (Japanese gastro-pub) showcasing the best of French ingredients.

82 RUE JEAN-PIERRE TIMBAUD, 75011

LE 975

Modern French fare with exquisite plating and affordable prices, cooked up by chef Taiki Tamao in the up-and-coming Batignolles neighborhood.

25 RUE GUY MÔQUET, 75017

ABRI

Expect a tasting menu of contemporary French cuisine, prepared full of heart by Katsuaki Okiyama, in a compact space (reservations mandatory!).

92 RUE DU FAUBOURG POISSONNIÈRE, 75010

CLOWN BAR

The best spot in town for natural wine and creative neo-bistro cooking by chef Sota Atsumi in a historic, Belle Epoque interior.

114 RUE AMELOT, 75011

DERSOU

Asian-inspired modern French food and cocktail pairings, all made using local French ingredients. Offers a great Sunday brunch.

21 RUE SAINT-NICOLAS, 75012

LES ENFANTS ROUGES

The feel-good bistro experience run by husband-and-wife duo Dai and Tomoko Shinozuka in the Marais.

9 RUE DE BEAUCE, 75003

NAKATANI

This all-white gastronomic table is the stage for chef Shinsuke Nakatani's incredible talent, blending Japanese technique with a profound love for French seasonal cooking.

27 RUE PIERRE LEROUX, 75007

PAGES

Elegant, contemporary French cuisine from chef Ryuji "Teshi" Teshima, awarded his first Michelin star in 2016.

4 RUE AUGUSTE-VACQUERIE, 75016

RESTAURANT A.T

If the prices at Chef Atsushi Tanaka's gastronomic table make you blanch (95 euros per person for a tasting menu), you can still get a taste of his cooking style at his wine bar underneath the restaurant, featuring natural wines and delicious bar snacks.

4 RUE DU CARDINAL LEMOINE, 75005

Street Food / Comfort Foods

BAGNARD

Lively lunch spot for Pan-bagnat sandwiches, the Niçois specialty.

7 RUE SAINT-AUGUSTIN, 75002

THE BEAST

Texas-style barbecue, craft beer, and the largest selection of Bourbon in Paris, founded by Parisian Thomas Abramowicz.

27 RUE MESLAY, 75003

BLEND

Creative burgers on homemade brioche buns, with several outposts on the right bank.

SEE BLENDHAMBURGER.COM

CAFÉ CHILANGO

Specialty coffee and Mexican tacos and tostadas at lunch, dinner, and weekend brunch.

82 RUE DE LA FOLIE MÉRICOURT, 75011

LE CAMION QUI FUME

The country's first street-food truck; American burgers with French ingredients.

168 RUE MONTMARTRE, 75002
TRUCK STOPS IN VARIOUS LOCATIONS,
SEE LECAMIONQUIFUME.COM

CANDELARIA

The city's first Mexican taqueria and clandestine cocktail bar, still as good as day one.

52 RUE DE SAINTONGE, 75003

CANTINE CALIFORNIA

The permanent outpost from the team behind the city's first organic burger and taco truck.

46 RUE DE TURBIGO, 75003

CHEZ ALINE

The best of French sandwiches on artisanal breads, served up in a former horse butcher's shop.

85 RUE DE LA ROQUETTE, 75011

HERO

Cocktails and Korean street food in a multilevel space that is as intriguing as the food.

289 RUE SAINT-DENIS, 75002

EL NOPAL

No-frills (but mighty delicious) burritos and tacos from a tiny takeaway window.

3 RUE EUGÈNE VARLIN, 75010
5 RUE DUPERRÉ, 75009

PNY (PARIS NEW YORK)

Quality burgers and milkshakes in spaces with great music and a fun crowd (my favorite location is the Miami-inspired Marais outpost).

1 RUE PERRÉE, 75003
50 RUE DU FAUBOURG SAINT-DENIS, 75010
96 RUE OBERKAMPF, 75011

LE RÉFECTOIRE

The popular burger truck's fixed spot for burgers, neo-bistro dishes, and brunch on weekends.

31 RUE DU CHÂTEAU D'EAU, 75010

ROCOCO

A gourmet kebab restaurant where everything, from the condiments to the bread, is homemade. Wash down options like spit-roasted lamb, pork, braised lamb, or falafel (veggie) with craft beers and natural wines.

4 RUE FAUBOURG SAINT-MARTIN, 75010

SAAM

A bare-bones interior keeps the focus on the plate at this fun and flavorful Korean canteen featuring steamed bun sandwiches.

59 BIS RUE DE LANCRY, 75010

STREET BANGKOK

A former chef from the Mandarin Oriental Bangkok brings her hometown flavors to salads, curries, and fish at this funky Thai canteen.

3 RUE EUGÈNE VARLIN, 75010

THE SUNKEN CHIP

Line-caught fish from Brittany served alongside mushy peas or thick-cut fries (chips!) by a friendly staff.

39 RUE DES VINAIGRIERS, 75010

YAM'TCHA BOUTIQUE

Steamed bao buns served in a lovely salon de thé or available for takeaway.

4 RUE SAUVAL, 75001

Other

DESSANCE

The city's first plated dessert bar where each dish showcases the natural sweetness in fruits and vegetables.

74 RUE DES ARCHIVES, 75003

LE FOOD MARKET

Some of the newest and best takes on street food set up shop for this bi-monthly street food market, located on rue de Belleville in the exact location of the weekly farmer's market (between métros Ménilmontant and Couronnes).

WWW.LEFOODMARKET.FR

FOOD DELIVERY Many of these spots also deliver via recent food delivery apps like Deliveroo and Foodora. Access from your mobile device or desktop and have the best of Paris street food come to you!

La Cuisine Healthy / Vegetarian / Vegan / Gluten-Free

BOB'S BAKE SHOP

A quality diner-café run by juice-bar pioneer Marc Grossman, featuring sandwiches, salads, soups, and cakes made fresh daily.

HALLE PAJOL, 12 ESPLANADE NATHALIE SARRAUTE, 75018

BOB'S JUICE BAR

The original Parisian juice bar, made to order, and served with or without a variety of cakes and bagel sandwiches.

15 RUE LUCIEN SAMPAIX, 75010

BOB'S KITCHEN

This healthy canteen in the Marais is vegan-veggie friendly and known for their açaí bowls, futomaki rolls, and fresh juices.

74 RUE DES GRAVILLIERS, 75003

LES BOLS DE JEAN

A collaboration between star baker Eric Kayser and *Top Chef France* winner Jean Imbert, focused entirely on bread bowls (gluten-free available) with market-fresh fillings.

2 RUE DE CHOISEUL, 75002

CHAMBELLAND

Gluten-free baked goods and bread; light and delicious soups and sandwiches are served for lunch. Rice flour is made in the South of France in the co-owner's own mill.

14 RUE TERNAUX, 75011

L'EPICERIE VÉGÉTALE

A produce Eden featuring fruits, vegetables, and wildflowers sourced from the Île-de-France region. Fresh juices available.

51 RUE DE LA FONTAINE AU ROI, 75011

LA GUINGUETTE D'ANGÈLE

The city's cutest gluten-free and veggie counter, open for lunch Monday through Friday.

34 RUE COQUILLIÈRE, 75001

HELMUT NEWCAKE

The city's first gluten-free bakery, with gourmet pastries that easily rival their très-gluten counterparts.

28 RUE VIGNON, 75009

JUICE LAB

Healthy snacks, kale chips, cold-pressed juices, and health shakes all under one roof.

2 RUE DE BÉARN, 75003
83 RUE DES MARTYRS, 75018

JUICERIE

Cold-pressed juices, including three green juices, a beet juice, a carrot juice, and an almond milk smoothie.

2 RUE DE LA MICHODIÈRE, 75002

LA MAISON PLISSON

The Parisian answer to Dean & DeLuca: a gourmet grocer on one side, a bakery-canteen on the other.

93 BOULEVARD BEAUMARCHAIS, 75003

NANASHI

The spot for bento in Paris, with or without meat, and always with a generous dose of healthy grains and vegetables.

57 RUE CHARLOT, 75003

NOGLU

One of the city's first gluten-free restaurants, serving excellent savory and sweet options at lunch and dinner. Several doors down, you'll find their boutique with products offered for takeaway.

16 PASSAGE DES PANORAMAS, 75002
49 PASSAGE DES PANORAMAS, 75002 (TAKEAWAY)

PAPA SAPIENS

A gourmet grocer that puts the spotlight on the small producers and artisans behind the products they carry (each has their biography displayed).

32 RUE DE BOURGOGNE, 75007
7 RUE BAYEN, 75017

RACHEL'S

Healthy salads, breakfast staples, and hearty sandwiches in a space designed by Dorothée Meilichzon.

25 RUE DU PONT AUX CHOUX, 75003

RACHEL'S GROCERY

A Jewish-style deli and grocer across the street from Rachel's, featuring house-cured meats and fish, homemade bagels, dips, salads, and cakes, and a create-your-own hot dog cart.

20 RUE DU PONT AUX CHOUX, 75003

SOL SEMILLA

A haven for superfoods, grains, and vegan dishes just off the Canal Saint-Martin.

23 RUE DES VINAIGRIERS, 75010

SOUL KITCHEN

Healthy soul food like soups, salads, sandwiches, and a slightly hippie vibe make this Montmartre canteen worth the visit.

33 RUE LAMARCK, 75018

TERROIRS D'AVENIR

The city's leading purveyor of high-quality produce, meats, fish, and dairy for top restaurants. Visit the rue du Nil to hop between their various shops.

6–8 RUE DU NIL, 75002

LE TRICYCLE

Vegan hot dogs, soups, salads, and cakes put this funky two-story spot on the Paris street-food/healthy-food map.

51 RUE DE PARADIS, 75010

WILD & THE MOON

Healthy and plant-based salads, soups, snacks, smoothies, and fresh juices take front and center in this indoor-garden spot, as does a commitment to minimizing food waste. Dairy free and gluten free.

55 RUE CHARLOT, 75003

Coffee

L'ARBRE À CAFÉ
Stop in for a coffee or pick up a bag of coffee from this Parisian roaster (boutique only).
10 RUE DU NIL, 75002

THE BEANS ON FIRE
Collaborative roaster and coffee shop next to the Square Gardette park.
7 RUE DU GÉNÉRAL BLAISE, 75011

BELLEVILLE BRÛLERIE
One of the city's leading coffee roasters with cuppings offered on Saturdays (reserve in advance).
10 RUE PRADIER, 75019

BLACKBURN COFFEE
A homey coffee shop serving breakfast and seasonal dishes for lunch.
52 RUE DU FAUBOURG SAINT-MARTIN, 75010

BOB'S BAKE SHOP
All manner of coffee is available in this diner-like shop, brewing Café Lomi coffee exclusively.
HALLE PAJOL, 12 ESPLANADE NATHALIE SARRAUTE, 75018

BOOT CAFÉ
Arguably the city's smallest (and cutest) coffee shop with a rotating roster of roasters from France and beyond.
19 RUE DU PONT AUX CHOUX, 75003

BROKEN BISCUITS
An English-Irish pastry duo whips up delectable cakes and pastries in this coffee shop (filter coffee only).
10 PASSAGE ROCHEBRUNE, 75011

CAFÉ CRAFT
The city's most well-known co-working space that serves specialty coffee, fresh soups, salads, and sandwiches. Not planning to work? Hang out in the front of the space or take your coffee to go and linger by the canal.
24 RUE DES VINAIGRIERS, 75010

CAFÉ LOMI
One of the city's first specialty coffee roasters with a large, multipurpose space in the 18th arrondissement: roastery, training facility, coffee shop open to the public.
3 TER RUE MARCADET, 75018

CAFÉ LOUSTIC
This coffee shop is not only excellent, brewing primarily from Belgian roasters Caffènation, but

also the city's best designed, thanks to the talents of Dorothée Meilichzon.
40 RUE CHAPON, 75003

CAFÉ OBERKAMPF
Beyond the excellent coffee (featuring guest roasters), it's the savory breakfasts and hearty lunches that draw in crowds.
3 RUE NEUVE POPINCOURT, 75011

LA CAFÉOTHÈQUE
The pioneer of the coffee movement in Paris; an artisanal roaster/coffee shop where the beans are sourced from all over the world and roasted in front of you.
52 RUE DE L'HÔTEL DE VILLE, 75004

COUTUME CAFÉ
One of the first specialty coffee shops to open in Paris, serving a full breakfast, lunch, and weekend brunch.
47 RUE DE BABYLONE, 75007

CREAM
A hip coffee shop run by a Franco-English duo in the booming Belleville section of town.
50 RUE DE BELLEVILLE, 75020

LA FONTAINE DE BELLEVILLE
Belleville Brûlerie's café-bar in the 10th arrondissement, a five-minute walk from the Canal Saint-Martin.
31–33 RUE JULIETTE DODU, 75010

FRAGMENTS
Owner Youssef Louanjli is serious about more than high-quality brews; he serves up beautiful food for breakfast and lunch.
76 RUE DES TOURNELLES, 75003

HEXAGONE CAFÉ
Peace and quiet (and excellent coffee!), all at this laid-back specialty shop featuring house-roasted beans exclusively.
121 RUE DU CHÂTEAU, 75014

HOLYBELLY
This is the intersection of great food and great coffee, with an energy that never wavers.
19 RUE LUCIEN SAMPAIX, 75010

HONOR
The city's first outdoor specialty coffee café, situated in the courtyard of the Comme des Garçons boutique, just behind the American Embassy.
54 RUE DU FAUBOURG SAINT-HONORÉ, 75008

KB CAFÉSHOP
The ideal location to people-watch, read, write, or simply take in the motions of one of the city's most dynamic coffee shops.
53 AVENUE TRUDAINE, 75009

MATAMATA
A 2nd arrondissement coffee shop with cozy seating, light fare for breakfast, brunch, and lunch, and cakes served all afternoon.
58 RUE D'ARGOUT, 75002

O COFFEESHOP
Timothée Teyssier's itinerant coffee bike may only hit the road for special events, but he can be found in his new fixed location in the 15th arrondissement.
23 RUE DE LOURMEL, 75015

LE PELOTON CAFÉ
The beating heart of the Marais finally has its coffee shop, run by an American-Kiwi duo with a love for cycling.
17 RUE DU PONT LOUIS-PHILIPPE, 75004

SHAKESPEARE & COMPANY CAFÉ
The café annex to the iconic bookstore. Bob's Bake Shop provides the food (bagels, salads, soups, and desserts) while Café Lomi manages the coffee program.
37 RUE DE LA BÛCHERIE, 75005

STEEL CYCLEWEAR & COFFEESHOP
The concept store–coffee shop from the founder and editor in chief of *Steel* magazine, France's leading authority on urban and outdoor cycling.
58 RUE DE LA FONTAINE AU ROI, 75011

TÉLESCOPE
One of the original and leading specialty coffee shops with bread, financiers, and other homemade treats. Coffee beans available for purchase.
5 RUE VILLEDO, 75001

TEN BELLES
The Canal Saint-Martin's coffee institution, brewing Belleville Brûlerie beans and serving up excellent breakfast items and sandwiches from their own kitchen. Their bakery location is more spacious and with a robust array of baked goods.
10 RUE DE LA GRANGE AUX BELLES, 75010
17/19 BIS RUE BRÉGUET, 75011

TERRES DE CAFÉ
Specialty coffee shop, roaster, and training hub. The flagship space offers tastings and features pastries created exclusively for the shop by Maître Pâtissier Christophe Felder.
40 RUE DES BLANCS MANTEAUX, 75004

Libations

Cocktails

ARTISAN
Natural wines, craft cocktails, and stellar small plates on a quiet corner in the 9th arrondissement.
14 RUE BOCHART DE SARON, 75009

BESPOKE
Cocktails and sliders make an honorable pair at this 11th arrondissement hot spot (which also serves a terrific Sunday brunch).
3 RUE OBERKAMPF, 75011

CAFÉ MODERNE
Meatballs and craft cocktails are the winning formula here, with award-winning mixologist "Mido."
19 RUE KELLER, 75011

CANDELARIA
Push past the unmarked door in this taqueria to reach the hidden, award-winning bar.
52 RUE DE SAINTONGE, 75003

CASTOR CLUB
One of the city's early clandestine cocktail bars with gently priced expert cocktails.
14 RUE HAUTEFEUILLE, 75006

LA CAVE À COCKTAIL
This shop sells a small selection of well-made cocktails by the bottle to go, for shaking and serving at home.
62 RUE GRENETA, 75002

LA COMMUNE
The second bar from the team behind Le Syndicat. Here, they continue with classic French spirits but use them to revive the humble punch bowl, available in different sizes.
80 BOULEVARD DE BELLEVILLE, 75020

COPPERBAY
A nautically themed bar behind the Marché Saint-Martin with creative cocktails and a light food menu.
5 RUE BOUCHARDON, 75010

DIRTY DICK
A smart entry point for novice cocktail drinkers looking to break into the cocktail culture, thanks to their tiki tipples and good-times attitude.
10 RUE FROCHOT, 75009

DISTILLERIE DE PARIS
The city's first legal microdistillery in more than a century. Their bottles are available in various retail locations, wine cellars, and restaurants.
WWW.DISTILLERIEDEPARIS.COM

L'ENTRÉE DES ARTISTES PIGALLE
A two-story cocktail and natural-wine bar with vintage jazz and soul on vinyl until a DJ takes over late at night.
30–32 RUE VICTOR MASSÉ, 75009

EXPERIMENTAL COCKTAIL CLUB
The speakeasy that put inventive (and affordable) craft cocktails on the Parisian map.
37 RUE SAINT-SAUVEUR, 75002

GLASS
Where do locals go to dance, sip cocktails, and nibble on hot dogs until the wee hours? This South Pigalle bar known for its cocktails on tap and awesome music.
7 RUE FROCHOT, 75009

GRAND PIGALLE
The Experimental Group's first hotel is, of course, outfitted with a spacious lounge for craft cocktails and Italian plates crafted by chef Giovanni Passerini.
29 RUE VICTOR MASSE, 75009

GRAVITY BAR
A skate- and surf-inspired cocktail and small-plates bar where the drinks are categorized not by spirits but by sensation. Reservations recommended!
44 RUE DES VINAIGRIERS, 75010

LITTLE RED DOOR
An updated take on the prohibition vibe with high-quality, specialized spirits.
60 RUE CHARLOT, 75003

LOCKWOOD
It's all inventive cocktails, delicious bar snacks, and weekend brunch at this multistory bar in the Silicon Sentier.
73 RUE D'ABOUKIR, 75002

LULU WHITE
A sultry absinthe den that mixes the spirit of nineteenth-century Pigalle nightlife with New Orleans saloons.
12 RUE FROCHOT, 75009

MABEL
Rum gets the attention it deserves at this creative bar, set behind a gussied-up grilled cheese counter.
58 RUE D'ABOUKIR, 75002

MAISON SOUQUET
An award-winning barman shakes up signature drinks for the dimly lit bar in the Maison Souquet, a former pleasure house.
10 RUE DE BRUXELLES, 75009

LE MARY CELESTE
Refined, seasonal small plates pair beautifully with specialty cocktails, craft beer, and natural wines in a space that smacks of California insouciance.
1 RUE COMMINES, 75003

NIGHT FLIGHT
One of the latest Experimental Group cocktail bars, set in an intimate corner of the Hôtel Bachaumont.
18 RUE BACHAUMONT, 75002

OBER MAMMA
A high-energy spot for a spritz and small Italian nibbles at aperitivo hour.
107 BOULEVARD RICHARD LENOIR, 75011

PASDELOUP
Ever-changing cocktail and food pairing options draw in regulars (who know it's worth calling ahead to secure a spot).
108 RUE AMELOT, 75011

RED HOUSE
Students and shoestring travelers will like the laid-back attitude and rowdy fun here, but they'll especially love the 5-euro Negronis.
1 BIS RUE DE LA FORGE ROYALE, 75011

ROSEBUD
An oldie but goodie: Since the 1960s, this spot's unchanging style and service still draw nostalgic crowds and modern-day literati.
11 BIS RUE DELAMBRE, 75014

SHERRY BUTT
A must-visit for whiskey aficionados, a short walk from the Place de la Bastille.
20 RUE BEAUTREILLIS, 75004

LE SYNDICAT
Lovers of all things French come here for modern cocktails made using only homegrown spirits and ingredients.
51 RUE DU FAUBOURG SAINT-DENIS, 75010

TIGER

A left-bank hangout for gin lovers, with creative cocktails and twists on the gin and tonic.

13 RUE PRINCESSE, 75006

LE TRÈS PARTICULIER

A très Twin Peaks–esque cocktail bar in the blissfully secluded Hôtel Particulier Montmartre.

23 AVENUE JUNOT, 75018

Natural Wine

LE BARATIN

The inspiration behind Paris's contemporary natural-wine bistro renaissance, featuring country cuisine and a vast, unlisted wine cellar.

3 RUE JOUYE-ROUVE, 75020

CAFÉ DE LA NOUVELLE MAIRIE

This is ground zero for natural wine in Paris, with three generations of proprietors who still frequent the bar and bistro for its deep wine list and wide terrace.

19 RUE DES FOSSÉS SAINT-JACQUES, 75005

LE CAVE

The wine shop from Iñaki Aizpitarte (Le Chateaubriand), featuring foreign natural wines only.

129 AVENUE PARMENTIER, 75011

CLOWN BAR

See Food & Dining.

114 RUE AMELOT, 75011

LA DERNIÈRE GOUTTE

A left-bank institution for organic and biodynamic wines from small producers, run by Juan Sanchez of Semilla (see Food & Dining).

6 RUE DE BOURBON LE CHÂTEAU, 75006

MA CAVE FLEURY

The wine bar of Champagne Fleury, the pioneering biodynamic champagne estate.

117 RUE SAINT-DENIS, 75002

AUX DEUX AMIS

A neighborhood favorite that is good for a quick predinner glass of obscure, natural wine or for one of each stunning small plate at lunch and dinner.

45 RUE OBERKAMPF, 75011

LA POINTE DU GROUIN

Chef Thierry Breton's 100-percent Breton wine bar, featuring small plates, homemade bread, and natural wine. Patrons are expected to pay in "grouins," the bar's own currency (not to worry, there's a change machine!).

8 RUE DE BELZUNCE, 75010

LA QUINCAVE

Frédérick Belcamp's Montparnasse wine shop and wine bar with a superlative selection of more than two hundred menu options.

17 RUE BRÉA, 75006

SEPTIME LA CAVE

A cozy wine shop and bar from the team behind Septime and Clamato, with delectable small dishes and earthy natural wines.

3 RUE BASFROI, 75011

Caves à Manger

LA BUVETTE

Camille Fourmont's popular right-bank cave à manger—a wine shop that serves food—showcases beautiful produce, meat, and cheeses along with a smart edit of natural wines.

67 RUE SAINT-MAUR, 75011

LA CAVE À MICHEL

The cave à manger annex to Le Galopin (see Food & Dining), with stunning small plates and expertly selected natural wines.

36 RUE SAINTE-MARTHE, 75010

LA CAVE DU PAUL BERT

Le Bistrot Paul Bert's Bertrand Auboyneau cast a wider net on the rue Paul Bert to open a small-plates bar with wines from small producers (standing room only).

16 RUE PAUL BERT, 75011

LA CHAMBRE NOIRE

Natural wines and farm-to-table small plates with a crowd that spills over from next-door Café Chilango.

82 RUE DE LA FOLIE MÉRICOURT, 75011

CLAMATO

The no-reservation seafood bistro and wine bar that's as popular among locals as it is among chefs after their shifts, run by the Septime crew.

80 RUE DE CHARONNE, 75011

FREDDY'S

Excellent small plates and a solid wine list make a delicious alternative to dining at this cave à mager's sister restaurant next door, Semilla.

54 RUE DE SEINE, 75006

LE VERRE VOLÉ

This canal-side natural-wine destination (and the first cave à manger in Paris) serves a mix of delicate, Asian-inflected small plates and more rustic country classics.

67 RUE DE LANCRY, 75010

VIVANT CAVE

No matter who owns it (it used to be Pierre Jancou—see page 167), this spot is known for its exceptional natural wines and comforting nibbles.

43 RUE DES PETITES-ÉCURIES, 75010

Craft Beer (Shops, Bars, Taprooms & Brewpubs)

A LA BIÈRE COMME À LA BIÈRE

A cave à bières stocking more than three hundred artisanal beers and offering regular tasting ateliers.

20 RUE CUSTINE, 75018

BIÈRES CULTES

A specialty shop carrying international craft beers and glassware, and hosting tasting workshops.

14 RUE DES HALLES, 75001
44 RUE DES BOULANGERS, 75005
25 RUE LEGENDRE, 75017
40 RUE DAMRÉMONT, 75018

BREWBERRY

A beer shop and bar geared toward both novices and more experienced specialty-beer drinkers.

18 RUE DU POT DE FER, 75005

BREW UNIQUE

The city's first DIY brew center/workshop space for beer lovers.

1 RUE DES JEUNEURS, 75002

LA CAVE À BULLES

The institution for craft beer in Paris with a curated selection of bottles by owner Simon Thillou.

45 RUE QUINCAMPOIX, 75004

DEMORY

The spacious bar from the duo that revived the historic Parisian beer brand.

62 RUE QUINCAMPOIX, 75004

EXPRESS DE LYON

It may look like the identity-free bars on the street, but inside you'll find French and European craft beers on tap.

1 RUE DE LYON, 75012

LA FINE MOUSSE

One of the city's first beer bars with a rotating selection of twenty craft beers on tap.

6 AVENUE JEAN AICARD, 75011

LA FINE MOUSSE RESTAURANT

The best place to discover how well craft beers pair with food (small, shareable plates).

4 BIS AVENUE JEAN AICARD, 75011

THE GREEN GOOSE

Irish craft beers pair perfectly with elevated pub food: scotch eggs, meat pies, and a renowned brunch, all lovingly made in-house.

19 RUE DES BOULETS, 75011

PANAME BREWING COMPANY

A Parisian brewery and brew bar on the Quai de la Loire, the perfect spot for a predinner drink outdoors.

41 BIS QUAI DE LA LOIRE, 75019

LE SUPERCOIN

With its focus on French microbrews, this is the ideal spot to taste and learn about French ales, IPAs, and stouts.

3 RUE BAUDELIQUE, 75018

EL TAST

One of the city's caves à bières, with a top-notch selection of craft beers from Île-de-France, served alongside meat-and-cheese platters.

70 RUE DUHESME, 75018

LE TRIANGLE

One of the rare restaurant-microbrewery hybrids in Paris, featuring seasonal cooking and a craft beer pairing with their house beer and guest brewers.

13 RUE JACQUES LOUVEL-TESSIER, 75010

LES TROIS 8

A rollicking bar specializing in craft beers and natural wines.

11 RUE VICTOR LETALLE, 75020

Sweets

ARNAUD LARHER

A colorful spectrum of pastries and baked goods await in this Meilleur Ouvrier de France's must-visit shop.

93 RUE DE SEINE, 75006

BONTEMPS PÂTISSERIE

The sablé (shortbread cookie) in all its forms is on beautiful display in this charming shop run by two sisters.

57 RUE DE BRETAGNE, 75003

CARL MARLETTI

A colorful array of pastries from Carl Marletti. In summer, try his fraisier (strawberry shortcake), which has been named best in Paris.

51 RUE CENSIER, 75005

CÉDRIC GROLET AT LE MEURICE HÔTEL

The young, award-winning pastry chef of one of the city's oldest luxury hotels. Go for tea at Le Dali lounge and try a sampling of his magnificent creations.

228 RUE DE RIVOLI, 75001

CHAMBELLAND

See Food & Dining, La Cuisine Healthy, page 255.

14 RUE TERNAUX, 75011

LA CHOCOLATERIE CYRIL LIGNAC

Chef Cyril Lignac's design-forward foray into chocolate is meant for lingering. Come for hot chocolate and chocolate pastries and leave with one of his luscious bars in a multitude of flavors.

25 RUE CHANZY, 75011

LE CHOCOLAT ALAIN DUCASSE

It's bean to bar at Alain Ducasse's chocolate lab and boutique. See the action as you browse the selection.

40 RUE DE LA ROQUETTE, 75011

CHRISTOPHE MICHALAK

The celebrity chef's first namesake pastry shop with riffs on classics served in clear containers for easy takeaway.

16 RUE DE LA VERRERIE, 75004

COLOROVA

A colorful salon de thé and pâtisserie with a stunning selection of elegant pastries available daily.

47 RUE DE L'ABBÉ GRÉGOIRE, 75006

LA COMPAGNIE GÉNÉRALE DE BISCUITERIE

Gilles Marchal's Montmartre-based ode to le biscuit with seriously good shortbread cookies, financiers and macarons à l'ancienne, each named after a 19th century dancer.

1 RUE CONSTANCE, 75018

L'ÉCLAIR DE GÉNIE

Christophe Adam's temple of éclairs in all their forms and flavors.

32 RUE NOTRE DAME DES VICTOIRES, 75002
14 RUE PAVÉE, 75004

LES FÉES PÂTISSIÈRES

Fairy-like, portable, and ever-changing: Miniature versions of classic French pastries are easy to eat on the go and make excellent gifts.

21 RUE RAMBUTEAU, 75004
105 AVENUE VICTOR HUGO, 75016

FOU DE PÂTISSERIE

The first concept shop dedicated to the top names in pastry. Expect signature treats from Philippe Conticini, Jonathan Blot, Boulangerie Bo, and more, delivered fresh daily.

45 RUE MONTORGUEIL, 75002

DES GÂTEAUX ET DU PAIN

A fruit-lover's paradise! Try one of everything in season at Claire Damon's sleek pastry shop.

89 RUE DU BAC, 75007
63 BOULEVARD PASTEUR, 75015

GILLES MARCHAL

The first Parisian outpost for the former head pastry chef of the hotels Plaza Athénée and Le Bristol, known especially for his madeleines.

9 RUE RAVIGNAN, 75018

UNE GLACE À PARIS

Artisanal ice creams and desserts, for takeaway or to be enjoyed in the tea salon at the back of the shop.

15 RUE SAINTE-CROIX-DE-LA-BRETONNERIE, 75004

GONTRAN CHERRIER

The young baker made waves with his squid ink baguettes and unique loaves and now he's dabbling in supremely good pastry, all incorporating grains like oats, flaxseed and black cumin.

22 RUE CAULAINCOURT, 75018

HUGO & VICTOR

Between luscious, seasonal pâtisseries, ice creams, and an array of chocolates, Hugues Pouget's elegant shop is an indulgent must-visit destination.

40 BOULEVARD RASPAIL, 75007

JACQUES GENIN

The king of chocolate, candied fruits, and flavored caramels. The 3rd arrondissement location also has a tea salon where you can order pastries like his award-winning Paris-Brest.

133 RUE DE TURENNE, 75003
27 RUE DE VARENNE, 75007

JEAN-PAUL HÉVIN

One of the chocolate industry's most innovative and respected chocolate masters puts his emblematic chocolate, bars, ganaches and macarons on display. For the best experience, visit his chocolate cellar.

231 RUE SAINT-HONORÉ, 75001
41 RUE DE BRETAGNE, 75003

LIBERTÉ

Benoît Castel's minimalist sanctuary for star-quality loaves and pastries, made from an open kitchen.

39 RUE DES VINAIGRIERS, 75010

LA MAISON DU CHOCOLAT

The temple of chocolate ganache with unique creations by head chocolate master Nicolas Cloiseau. See website for additional locations.

225 RUE DU FAUBOURG SAINT-HONORÉ, 75008

8 BOULEVARD DE LA MADELEINE, 75009

LA MAISON DU CHOU

The cream puff in its simplest and freshest form. You choose from four fillings, and the staff fills the puff pastry in front of you.

7 RUE DE FURSTENBERG, 75006

AUX MERVEILLEUX DE FRED

It's all about airy, flavored meringues at this elegant single-product pastry shop that originated in Lille.

24 RUE DU PONT LOUIS PHILIPPE, 75004

2 RUE MONGE, 75005

94 RUE SAINT-DOMINIQUE, 75007

MICHEL CHAUDUN

The legendary chocolate maker may have retired, but he passed the reins to an equally brilliant talent: Pâtissier Gilles Marchal is at the helm of this high temple of exquisite chocolate-making, bringing its singular savoir faire into the future.

149 RUE DE L'UNIVERSITÉ, 75007

MON ÉCLAIR

Why choose a ready-made éclair when you can customize your own? That's the concept of this 17th arrondissement éclair shop.

52 RUE DES ACACIAS, 75017

MORI YOSHIDA

Just call this boutique Japanese pastry chef Mori Yoshida's homage to French pâtisserie.

65 AVENUE DE BRETEUIL, 75007

PAIN DE SUCRE

From macarons to luscious lemon tarts, the selection is vast at this colorful shop run by a duo who cut their teeth in the kitchens of triple-Michelin-starred chef Pierre Gagnaire.

14 RUE RAMBUTEAU, 75003

PAIN PAIN

A beautifully decorated boulangerie-pâtisserie from Sébastien Mauvieux, whose baguette was named Best in Paris in 2012.

88 RUE DES MARTYRS, 75018

PASCADE

Everything is dedicated to the pascade, a crêpe soufflé specialty from the Aveyron region of France.

14 RUE DAUNOU, 75002

LA PÂTISSERIE ACIDE

Original twists on classic recipes like the tarte au citron and the macaron, best enjoyed in the dessert bar alongside a cup of specialty coffee or tea (but also available to go).

24 RUE DES MOINES, 75017

LA PÂTISSERIE CYRIL LIGNAC

An array of French breakfast classics and more-refined pastries by chef Cyril Lignac.

133 RUE DE SÈVRES, 75006

24 RUE PAUL BERT, 75011

PATRICK ROGER

The worlds of art and chocolate collide for Patrick Roger, the most artistic of Parisian chocolatiers.

2–4 PLACE SAINT-SULPICE, 75006

3 PLACE DE LA MADELEINE, 75008

199 RUE DU FAUBOURG SAINT-HONORÉ, 75008

PIERRE HERMÉ

From exceptional macarons to cakes and his signature Ispahan series of desserts, it's no wonder M. Hermé is nicknamed the "Picasso of pastry."

4 RUE CAMBON, 75001

39 AVENUE DE L'OPÉRA, 75002

18 RUE SAINTE-CROIX-DE-LA-BRETONNERIE, 75004

72 RUE BONAPARTE, 75006

PIERRE MARCOLINI

The most French of Belgian chocolatiers! Don't miss his iconic fruit-filled ganache hearts.

235 RUE SAINT-HONORÉ, 75001

89 RUE DE SEINE, 75006

POPELINI

The cream-puff mecca, with seasonal and classic flavors ranging from salted caramel to pistachio and orange flower.

29 RUE DEBELLEYME, 75003

44 RUE DES MARTYRS, 75009

PROFITEROLE CHÉRIE

Meilleur Ouvrier de France Philippe Urraca's ode to his favorite French pâtisserie: the profiterole! Each is made to order.

17 RUE DEBELLEYME, 75003

SADAHARU AOKI

The most iconic of Japanese pastry chefs in Paris. Don't be surprised to find Japanese flavors like yuzu, matcha, and sesame woven into his creations.

35 RUE DE VAUGIRARD, 75006

YANN COUVREUR

The first solo haute patisserie from this young pastry chef, formerly of the Prince de Galles luxury hotel.

137 AVENUE PARMENTIER, 75010

Shopping

Clothing & Accessories

ATELIER COURONNES
Atelier-boutique featuring handmade leather goods by Fauvette and handmade jewelry by Louise Damas.
6 RUE DU CHÂTEAU D'EAU, 75010

BLUNE
This French label for women and children (the name combines brune and blonde) revisits classic silhouettes with unique prints.
6 RUE D'AMBOISE, 75002

BOBBIES
Moccasins, loafers, and boots get a colorful, artisanal treatment at this Marais shop.
1 RUE DES BLANCS MANTEAUX, 75004

THE BROKEN ARM
A sharp selection of designer fashion and accessories dominates one half of this North Marais concept store, while on other, a specialty coffee and market-driven canteen.
12 RUE PÉRRÉE, 75003

CENTRE COMMERCIAL
Eco-minded fashions and accessories from French and European brands.
2 RUE DE MARSEILLE, 75010

CENTRE COMMERCIAL KIDS
Eco-minded fashions and accessories from French and European brands . . . for kids!
22 RUE YVES TOUDIC, 75010

COLETTE
The city's most successful and iconic concept store, featuring fashion, lifestyle goods, and art.
213 RUE SAINT-HONORÉ, 75001

COMMUNE DE PARIS 1871
Six years after shaking up men's fashion, this dandy-chic menswear label continues to offer quality garments, all made in Europe, in their North Marais flagship.
19 RUE COMMINES, 75003

CUISSE DE GRENOUILLE
Inspired by 1960s surf culture, this shop is dedicated to casual-chic menswear and lifestyle accessories.
5 RUE FROISSART, 75003 (FLAGSHIP)
71 PLACE DU DOCTEUR FÉLIX LOBLIGEOIS, 75017

ETUDES STUDIO
A fashion collective producing modern men's streetwear and accessories.
14 RUE DEBELLEYME, 75003

L'EXCEPTION
A multi-brand concept boutique with an ever-rotating collection from emerging designers.
24 RUE BERGER, 75001

LA GARCONNIÈRE
A well-edited men's lifestyle shop featuring clothing, beauty accessories, high-tech gear, and comestible goods, all displayed in a beautiful space beneath a living green wall.
40 RUE DES PETITS CARREAUX, 75002

MAISON CAULIÈRES
An artisanal skincare label made from natural oils sourced in the Loire Valley.
39 RUE DURANTIN, 75018

MAISON CHÂTEAU ROUGE
An African wax-printed clothing and accessories label with a philanthropic commitment to supporting new businesses in Africa.
40 RUE MYRHA, 75018

MEDECINE DOUCE
Sophisticated and feminine handcrafted jewelry, using materials like brass, semiprecious stones, and string.
10 RUE DE MARSEILLE, 75010

MERCI
The Marais's bohemian-chic concept store with a regularly rotating thematic focus and three on-site cafés.
111 BOULEVARD BEAUMARCHAIS, 75003

LA PANOPLIE
Contemporary men's fashion brand with a clean-cut selection of separates, from sweatshirts and chinos to windbreakers.
126 RUE VIEILLE DU TEMPLE, 75003

SEPT CINQ
A multi-brand boutique featuring goods made by Paris-based designers. Also available: Letterpress de Paris and Season Paper greeting cards, Bobbies shoes, Meilleur Ami scarves, and more.
54 RUE NOTRE DAME DE LORETTE, 75009

SÉZANE (L'APPARTEMENT)

A showroom/shopping hangout. Try on the clothes, place your order, and have your items delivered to your hotel within approximately 48 hours.

1 RUE SAINT-FIACRE, 75002

LE SLIP FRANÇAIS

100 percent French-made undergarments for men and women in patriotic blues, whites, and reds.

137 RUE VIEILLE DU TEMPLE, 75003

46 RUE DES ABBESSES, 75018

LA TONKINOISE À PARIS

Jewelry made from recycled and repurposed materials, including timepieces, bangles, and accessories.

80 RUE JEAN-PIERRE TIMBAUD, 75011

VERBREUIL

A family-run leather-goods and handbag brand that's big on subtle luxury and utility.

4 RUE DE FLEURS, 75006

Comestibles

CAUSSES

A gourmet greengrocer with quality products and a selection of prepared foods ready for takeaway.

222 RUE SAINT MARTIN, 75003

55 RUE NOTRE DAME DE LORETTE, 75009

LA CHAMBRE AUX CONFITURES

Artisanal jam, chutney, and sweet spreads made primarily from French ingredients (and with little or no added sugar).

60 RUE VIEILLE DU TEMPLE, 75003

9 RUE DES MARTYRS, 75009

FROMAGERIE GONCOURT

My favorite local cheesemonger in the 11th arrondissement, whose selection is served in a number of local restaurants, including Le Chateaubriand.

1 RUE ABEL RABAUD, 75011

HÉDÈNE

Artisanal honeys produced exclusively in collaboration with beekeepers across France who respect traditional harvesting methods.

AVAILABLE AT BHV/MARAIS DEPARTMENT STORE AND FROMAGERIE GONCOURT (SEE ABOVE).

LA MAISON PLISSON

The Parisian answer to Dean & DeLuca: A gourmet grocer on one side, a bakery-canteen on the other. See Food & Dining, La Cuisine Healthy, page 255.

93 BOULEVARD BEAUMARCHAIS, 75003

Lifestyle Goods

LE BAIGNEUR

Men's skincare products. See Papier Tigre.

L'ILLUSTRE BOUTIQUE

Stationery, prints, and illustrations from French artists in a tiny shop in the charming Passage du Grand Cerf.

1 PASSAGE DU GRAND CERF, 75002

JAMINI

A Franco-Indian lifestyle shop brimming with cushions, quilts, scarves, and other accessories made by artisans in the designer's native Assam.

10 RUE DE NOTRE DAME DE LORETTE, 75009

10 RUE DU CHÂTEAU D'EAU, 75010

KERZON

Fragrances and candles. See Papier Tigre.

KLIN D'OEIL

Handcrafted decorative pieces, lifestyle accessories, and affordable art in a colorful shop meant for lingering.

6 RUE DEGUERRY, 75011

OFR.

Bookstore and gallery in the Haut Marais with a broad selection of foreign magazines, international art and fashion books, and other lifestyle accessories like candles, notebooks, and bags, updated daily. Weekly events are held in the space's back room.

20 RUE DUPETIT-THOUARS, 75003

PAPIER TIGRE

Design-forward paper goods and office accessories that add a creative touch to the world. Also carried: lifestyle goods from other small, Parisian labels like Kerzon and Le Baigneur.

5 RUE DES FILLES DU CALVAIRE, 75003

PARIS PRINT VAN

Local artists' work is silkscreen printed onto T-shirts, totes, and cards, all from inside a vintage ice cream van.

VARIOUS LOCATIONS, SEE PRINTVANPARIS.COM

SLOW GALERIE

A gorgeous graphic arts gallery and tea salon, located in a former apothecary.

5 RUE JEAN-PIERRE TIMBAUD, 75011

LA TRÉSORERIE

A stunning space to source all of your homewares, from dishes and linens to sustainable cleaning products and storage accessories.

11 RUE DU CHÂTEAU D'EAU, 75010

Places & Spaces

Places to Visit

BASSIN DE LA VILLETTE, 75019
The largest artificial lake in Paris plays host to two dockside art-house theaters, food trucks, the Paname Brewing Company (see page 179), and other creative spaces.

CANAL SAINT-MARTIN, 75010
Once Napoleon's main source for supplying fresh water to the city, the 2½-mile (4.5-km) canal is now one of the most popular spots to stroll, shop, eat, and picnic.

LES DOCKS: CITÉ DE LA MODE ET DU DESIGN
A neon-green serpentine building overlooking the Seine dedicated to innovation in fashion, design, and art with frequent exhibits and installations. Wanderlust and Nüba are two resident nightlife venues that share the space.
34 QUAI D'AUSTERLITZ, 75013

LA BELLEVILLOISE
A quirky multipurpose venue in the 20th arrondissement where locals gather for brunch, attend concerts, share a drink, or participate in many events organized year-round.
19–21 RUE BOYER, 75020

LA CANOPÉE DES HALLES, 75001
The city's former central market ("belly of Paris"), then a run-down shopping center called the Forum, is now La Canopée, after six years of construction and redesign. The new urban epicenter, surrounded by a garden, features a new shopping mall, conservatory, library, chef-driven restaurants, offices (like those for BlaBlaCar and Facebook), and easier access to underground transportation.

FONDATION LOUIS VUITTON
A contemporary art museum at the edge of the Bois de Boulogne, designed by Frank Gehry.
8 AVENUE DU MAHATMA GANDHI, 75116

LA PETITE CEINTURE
A fourteen-mile (23-km) rail line from the mid-nineteenth century that circles the city. Sections of the line have become a nature trail open to the public.
2 RUE CAUCHY, 75015

LA PHILHARMONIE DE PARIS
Concert hall of the Paris orchestra (Parc de la Villette).
221 AVENUE JEAN-JAURÈS, 75019

LA RECYCLERIE
A restaurant-bar, vegetable garden, and upcycling center that hosts a "troc party" (bartering party) on the first Friday of every month, where skills and goods are traded.
83 BOULEVARD ORNANO, 75018

LA ROTONDE
Originally a tollhouse at the gate of the city, the space today is part restaurant, bar, co-working space, contemporary art gallery, and outdoor event space.
6–8 PLACE DE LA BATAILLE DE STALINGRAD, 75019

LE CARREAU DU TEMPLE
Formerly a covered market dating back to 1863, this cultural space now plays host to fashion shows, dance classes, cultural events, and food festivals.
4 RUE EUGÈNE SPULLER, 75003

LE COMPTOIR GÉNÉRAL
A funky, bohemian event space and café along the Canal Saint-Martin.
80 QUAI DE JEMMAPES, 75010

L'IMPROBABLE
A clandestine café–third space serving Belgian sandwiches.
5 RUE DES GUILLEMITES, 75004

LE LOUXOR CINÉMA
A neo-Egyptian art deco cinema (and protected monument) from 1921 that shows art-house films.
170 BOULEVARD DE MAGENTA, 75010

LE PAVILLON DES CANAUX
A creative third space kitted out like the inside of home. Locals gather here for the quirky experience, the good vibes, and the comfort in homemade cakes and coffee.
39 QUAI DE LA LOIRE, 75019

Boutique Hotels

BACHAUMONT
Designer Dorothée Meilichzon's signature retro style brings this forty-nine-room hotel to life, with a cocktail bar managed by the Experimental Group and the restaurant menu overseen by chef Gregory Marchand.
18 RUE BACHAUMONT, 75002

LES BAINS

The hottest nightclub in Parisian history has come back to life as an elegant hotel, bar, spa, and (more restrained) source of nightlife.

7 RUE DU BOURG L'ABBÉ, 75003

GRAND AMOUR HOTEL

After Hôtel Amour came even bigger love, this time in the 10th arrondissement. As quirky in design as the first, this space comes with a library, restaurant, bar, wine cellar, sauna, and forty-three rooms.

18 RUE DE LA FIDELITÉ, 75010

GRAND PIGALLE HOTEL

The Experimental Group's first foray into hospitality is considered a "bed and beverage"—find cocktails in the rooms or have them delivered to you. Rub elbows with locals in the downstairs lounge.

29 RUE VICTOR MASSÉ, 75009

HÔTEL DU TEMPS

A sepia-tinged boutique hotel with a ground-floor lounge/bar that is popular among locals for morning meetings or quiet afternoons with a book.

11 RUE DE MONTHOLON, 75009

HÔTEL PANACHE

A smartly designed forty-room boutique property in one of the liveliest neighborhoods of Paris. Its neo-bistro, Panache, is a popular dining spot for locals.

1 RUE GEOFFROY-MARIE, 75009

HÔTEL PARTICULIER MONTMARTRE

This five-room private mansion and restaurant is ideal for those in search of privacy. Stay anonymous or mix with locals in the downstairs cocktail bar.

23 AVENUE JUNOT, PAVILLON D, 75018

HÔTEL PROVIDENCE

English country manor meets Parisian pied-à-terre in this 10th arrondissement property, featuring a fireplace sitting room, a spacious restaurant, and a cocktail bar in each of the rooms.

90 RUE RENÉ BOULANGER, 75010

MOLITOR

The most popular swimming pool in the capital for sixty years. Molitor was restored to its former glory as a hotel, with a Clarins spa and rooftop bar.

13 RUE NUNGESSER ET COLI, 75016

LE PIGALLE

South Pigalle's bon vivant spirit is alive and well at this forty-room property with rooms dressed up in Nouvelle Athènes style and a lively wine bar managed by Camille Fourmont of La Buvette.

9 RUE FROCHOT, 75009

LA RÉSERVE

A sumptuous luxury property tucked behind the Champs-Elysées with Jacques Garcia–designed interiors, a double-Michelin-star restaurant (Le Gabriel), and an incredible spa.

42 AVENUE GABRIEL, 75008

For an even broader selection of *The New Paris* establishments and updates, please visit www.thenewparisbook.com.

References

BOOKS

Belau, Doni. *Paris Cocktails: An Elegant Collection of over 100 Recipes Inspired by the City of Light.* Kennebunkport, ME : Cedar Mill Press, 2015.

DeJean, Joan E. *How Paris Became Paris: The Invention of the Modern City.* New York: Bloomsbury, 2014.

Fielding, Raymond. *The Lumière Cinematograph: A Technological History of Motion Pictures and Television: An Anthology from the Pages of the Journal of the Society of Motion Picture and Television Engineers.* Berkeley: University of California Press, 1979.

Haine, W. Scott. *The World of the Paris Café.* Baltimore and London: The Johns Hopkins University Press, 1996.

Lobrano, Alexander. *Hungry for Paris: The Ultimate Guide to the City's 109 Best Restaurants.* 2nd ed. New York: Random House Trade Paperbacks, 2014.

McQuire, Scott. *Visions of Modernity: Representation, Memory, Time and Space in the Age of the Camera.* London: SAGE Publications, 1998.

Meynink, Katrina. *Bistronomy.* New South Wales: Murdoch Books, 2014.

Oumamar, Emmanuel. *La Bière à Paris.* Saint-Avertin: Editions Sutton, 2014.

Pendergrast, Mark. *Uncommon Grounds: The History of Coffee and How It Transformed Our World.* New York: Basic Books, 2010.

ARTICLES / ESSAYS

2015 Global Startup Ecosystem Ranking. http://blog.startupcompass.co.

Deloitte Technology Fast 500. http://www2.deloitte.com/global/en/pages/technology-media-and-telecommunications/articles/technology-fast-500-emea.html.

Fickling, David. "Australia is Exporting Its $3.2 Billion Café Culture to the World." *Bloomberg,* May 26, 2015. http://www.bloomberg.com/news/articles/2015-05-26/coffee-gurus-tout-2-000-courses-where-starbucks-stumbled.

Kimmelman, Michael. "Paris Aims to Embrace Its Estranged Suburbs." *New York Times,* February 12, 2015.

Labro, Camille. "Le Pain Superstar." *Le Monde* (Paris), October 25, 2013. http://www.lemonde.fr/m-actu/article/2013/10/25/le-pain-super-star_3501984_4497186.html.

Ross, Annabel. "A New Wave Is Brewing." *The Age,* October 13, 2009.

Stein, Sadie. "Amuse-Bouche." *T: The New York Times Style Magazine,* April 12, 2015. http://www.nytimes.com/2015/04/02/t-magazine/aux-merveilleux-de-fred-pastries.html

Wells, Patricia. "Vive la Baguette: As French as Paris." *International Herald Tribune,* October 9, 1983. http://www.nytimes.com/1983/10/09/travel/fare-of-the-country-vive-la-baguette-as-french-as-paris.html?pagewanted=all.

Endnotes

1   "Bleak Chic," *Economist,* December 21, 2013, http://www.economist.com/news/christmas-specials/21591749-bleak-chic.

2   Ibid.

3   Joan E. DeJean, *How Paris Became Paris: The Invention of the Modern City* (New York: Bloomsbury, 2014), 18.

4   DeJean, *How Paris Became Paris,* 3.

5   Richard Florida, *The Rise of the Creative Class: And How It's Transforming Work, Leisure, Community, and Everyday Life* (New York: Perseus Book Group, 2002).

6   DeJean. *How Paris Became Paris,* 3.

7   "Bleak Chic."

8   Semilla and Freddy's chef (and Meilleur Ouvrier de France) Eric Trochon said this seemed to coincide with the decline of the Paris party scene. Instead of a raucous good time at night with friends, Parisians gathered around a table for hours.

9   Alexander Lobrano, *Hungry for Paris: The Ultimate Guide to the City's 109 Best Restaurants,* 2nd ed. (New York: Random House Trade Paperbacks, 2014), 353.

10 The term itself wasn't coined until 2003 by French food journalist Sébastien Demorand, then the host of *Master Chef France.*

11 Katrina Meynink, *Bistronomy* (Australia: Murdoch Books, 2014), 208.

12 The second and only remaining Spring restaurant has been located in the 1st arrondissement since 2009.

13 On my first lengthy visit to Paris in 2006, friends advised me to tell people I was Canadian, not American, should I be asked about my origins. The transgressions of the Bush administration had apparently left an unsavory impression on the French, and it was wise to tread carefully. Omid Tavallai, one half of the American catering duo Emperor Norton (who won over Parisians with their cowgirl cookies, banana bread, donuts, and granola) distinctly remembers the attitude couching distaste for the Anglo-Saxon population in general. "When I first visited France twelve years ago, it was not cool to speak English. In fact, if they heard you speaking English in line for a club, there was a good chance the bouncer wouldn't let you in. Now it's the opposite; being foreign is cool. Modern Parisians are more international," he said. The broad availability of cheap Internet certainly helped, as did Barack Obama winning the presidential election, and later, a strong euro that spurred a wave of tourism to postcard cities like New York. This was key, said Omid's wife Alannah, to the shift in Parisian perspective. "They'd go to shop, of course, but they'd also eat and then realize the things they were having were both good *and* hard to come by in France." Jump ahead several years and "street food" is the blanket term for both food that can be eaten in the street or on the go and food served in fast-casual eateries. When I think of street food, I imagine rows of stalls and ramshackle carts lining a warren of narrow streets and alleyways in Asia. In the United States, I think of food trucks and mobile carts that sell creative and often unexpected combinations like Korean tacos at Kogi BBQ in Los Angeles or Native American cuisine with a Mexican twist like Navajo-style grilled flatbread with carne asada in Phoenix. In Paris, "street food" traditionally defined the men roasting chestnuts or corn in giant, round makeshift grills outside métro stations and in front of major department stores. Technically, the many open-air markets and the vendors selling roasted chicken, sandwiches, and crêpes across the city form a version of street food as well. But fast food and foreign imports have come to define the category. For esteemed chefs and food entrepreneurs on the rise in Paris, "street food" snacks were an opportunity to shake things up and add their own stamp to the genre. Which is to say, lowly street fare went the way most things in Paris go—a bit fancy.

14 "Obesity and the Economics of Prevention: Fit Not Fat—France Key Facts," OECD (The Organisation for Economic Co-Operation and Development), accessed March 13, 2016, http:// www.oecd.org/els/health-systems/obesityandtheeconomicsofpreventionfitnotfat-francekeyfacts.htm.

15 Patricia Wells. "Vive la Baguette: As French as Paris," *International Herald Tribune,* October 9, 1983, http://www.nytimes.com/1983/10/09/travel/fare-of-the-country-vive-la-baguette-as-french-as-paris.html.

16 Camille Labro, "Le Pain Superstar," *Le Monde,* October 25, 2013, http://www.lemonde.fr/m-actu/article/2013/10/25/le-pain-super-star_3501984_4497186.html.

17 W. Scott Haine, *The World of the Paris Café* (Baltimore and London: The Johns Hopkins University Press, 1996), 1.

18 Ibid, 131.

19 Mark Pendergrast, *Uncommon Grounds: The History of Coffee and How It Transformed Our World* (New York: Basic Books, 2010), 242.

20 Commodity coffee describes coffees that are not traded on their quality but as a cost-effective daily good.

21 Bernard Ruyant, "Les Evolutions des 60 Dernières Années et Leur Influence Sur le Futur" (presented at the 28th Roasting Congress in Colmar, France, September 29–30, 2013).

22 Author Simran Sethi said it best in her book *Bread, Wine, Chocolate: The Slow Loss of Foods We Love* (New York: HarperOne, 2015), 82: "An over-roasted coffee is like charring a high-quality steak: Doing so means that what you taste is something burnt—the heavy roast, instead of nuances in the bean."

23 Single-origin coffee, compared to blends that are commonly used by large coffee brands.

24 First wave describes the post–World War II proliferation of low-quality coffee. Second wave is exemplified by companies mass-producing higher-quality espresso coffee for cafés and supermarkets. Third-wave coffee makers are distinguished by their dedication to extracting the best from coffee in its purest, unadulterated form. Annabel Ross, "A New Wave Is Brewing," *The Age,* October 13, 2009.

25 David Fickling, "Australia Is Exporting Its $3.2 Billion Café Culture to the World," *Bloomberg,* May 26, 2015.

26 Half-washed, half-natural beans. Both refer to methods of coffee production.

27 Today, the blog lives on with updates about their growth, their renovation to accommodate more clients than they anticipated in their previsions, and miscellaneous stories from the 'Belly. And in the same spirit of transparency as the blog, the website itself is informative. Take the "Facts" page, which answers questions

such as "Why do you communicate in English?" (simply: "Because it's the common tongue and it's incredibly fun to write and speak") and, my favorite, "Why is your coffee better and more expensive than anywhere else?" Perhaps a bit overzealous, but their explanation is smart: "There are a few reasons why the coffee tastes good. First, we look after the main component of your cup of joe, the water. Ours goes through a reverse-osmosis system calibrated to give us precisely the water we need to make the best coffee possible. Second, we buy the best beans in town from la Brûlerie de Belleville. They source in-season, high-grade beans and then roast them just right. Finally, we set the ego aside and use the amazing tools at our disposal to not only be good sometimes but be good all the time. We don't pull shots manually, only relying on our eyes to decide when a shot is fully extracted—we let the volumetric paddle measure the right amount of water going through the bed of coffee so that your espresso tastes invariably delicious, whether I'm watching it pour or not. It's called consistency and it matters to us. As far as the price goes, Belleville buys great beans from farmers who work hard to deliver that level of quality so it only make sense they pay the big bucks for it and, as a result, so do we, and, as a result, so do you. That being said, a double espresso in a no-name brasserie serving filthy Café Richard from a dirty machine on rue Rivoli goes for 6 euros so...."

28 "Les Meilleurs Éclairs au Chocolat de Paris," *Le Figaro*, April 2015, http://www. lefigaro.fr/sortir-paris/2015/03/04/30004-20150304ARTFIG00054-les-meilleurs-eclairs-au-chocolat-de-paris.php.

29 Marie-Anne Suizzo, "Pleasure is Good: How French Children Acquire a Taste for Life," *The Conversation*, January 4, 2016, https://theconversation.com/pleasure-is-good-how-french-children-acquire-a-taste-for-life-51949.

30 Dorie Greenspan, *Paris Sweets: Great Desserts from the City's Best Pastry Shops* (New York: Clarkson Potter, 2002), 57.

31 Like most chocolatiers, Jacques Genin is a *fondeur*, which means he uses high-quality chocolate from companies that process the beans so that the chocolate is ready to work with.

32 Pierre Marcolini works bean-to-bar but produces his chocolates in Belgium, not in Paris where he has four shops.

33 "The word *merveilleuse* is associated in France with the Directoire regime, when it referred to dashing society ladies in scandalous, transparent gowns who romped through the salons of late-eighteenth-century Paris. Riffing on the theme, Vaucamps has given the flavors of his "collection" vaguely Directoirish noms de guerre: *Incroyable* (made with Belgian-inflected speculoos cream and shaved white chocolate), *Impensable* (coffee), *Excentrique* (cherry), and *Magnifique* (praline)." Sadie Stein, "Amuse-Bouche," *T: The New York Times Style Magazine*, April 12, 2015, http://www.nytimes.com/2015/04/02/t-magazine/aux-merveilleux-de-fred-pastries.html?_r=0.

34 The recipes aren't the only things with an Anglo tilt—the name Bontemps is a nod to Bon Temps, Louisiana, the fictional town from the popular American vampire series *True Blood*.

35 Nate Freeman. "A Few Rounds With Colin Field, Bartender Extraodinaire at the Ritz in Paris." *Observer*. October 15, 2014, http://observer.com/2014/10/a-few-rounds-with-colin-field-bartender-extraodinaire-at-the-ritz-in-paris/.

36 Doni Belau, *Paris Cocktails: An Elegant Collection of Over 100 Recipes Inspired by the City of Light* (Kennebunkport, ME: Cedar Mill Press, 2015), 13.

37 http://www.cognac.fr/cognac/_fr/2_cognac/index.aspx?page=histoire.

38 http://www.snooth.com/articles/why-organic-and-biodynamic-wines-matter/?viewall=1.

39 Emmanuel Oumamar, *La Bière à Paris* (Saint-Avertin: Editions Sutton, 2014), 115.

40 Ibid, 113.

41 Ibid, 177.

42 Nick Fletcher, "MPs' Vote to End Beer Tie Wipes £350M Off Britain's Big Pub Companies," *Guardian*, November 19, 2014, https://www.theguardian.com/business/2014/nov/19/mps-vote-end-beer-tie-wipes-350m-britains-big-pub-companies.

43 Sethi. *Bread, Wine, Chocolate*, 118.

44 Zara is a good example of this. The brand "only locks in 50 to 60 percent of its line by the start of the season, meaning that up to 50 percent of its clothes are designed and manufactured smack in the middle of the season. If a certain style or design suddenly becomes the rage, Zara reacts quickly to get them into stores." Clara Lu, "Supply Chain Analysis—The Secret Behind Zara's Retail Success," *TradeGecko*, December 4, 2014, https://www.tradegecko.com/blog/zara-supply-chain-its-secret-to-retail-success.

45 "La Revitalisation des Commerces de Proximité Par la Ville de Paris," *Atelier Parisien d'Urbanisme*, April 2013, http://www.apur.org/sites/default/files/documents/revitalisation_commerces_proximite.pdf.

46 Mike Doherty, "The Story Behind the Stuff:

Consumers' Growing Interest in 'Real' Products," *Fast Company*, October 18, 2012, http://www. fastcompany.com/3002249/story-behind-stuff-consumers-growing-interest-real-products.

47 RetailMeNot, Inc., "Study Shows United States Continuing to Lead E-commerce Sales as Mobile Commerce Shifts Transactions Away From the Desktop Computer," *PR News Wire*, March 31, 2015, http://www.prnewswire.com/news-releases/study-shows-united-states-continuing-to-lead-e-commerce-sales-as-mobile-commerce-shifts-transactions-away-from-the-desktop-computer-300058184.html.

48 "In France, Multichannel Shopping Habits Affect Small Retailers, Too," *eMarketer*, January 23, 2015, http://www.emarketer.com/Article/France-Multichannel-Shopping-Habits-Affect-Small-Retailers-Too/1011885.

49 "L'évolution des Commerces à Paris: Inventaire des Commerces 2011 et Évolutions 2007–2011," *Atelier Parisien d'Urbanisme,* January 2012, http://www.apur.org/sites/default/files/documents/APBROAPU556.pdf.

50 Adam Gopnik, "The View from a Bridge," *New Yorker*, December 8, 2014, http://www.newyorker.com/magazine/2014/12/08/view-bridge.

51 Reaffirming the shops's importance and legitimacy in the world of style, art, and design, Colette was the first shop in the world to reveal the new Apple Watch. This exclusivity was not only a first for Colette, but a first for Apple.

52 World Investment Report, http://unctad.org/en/PublicationsLibrary/wir2015_en.pdf, 18.

53 Luc Le Chatelier, "Le Vélib' Taille sa Route, Huit Ans Après le Lancement," *Télérama*, January 13, 2016, http://www.telerama.fr/scenes/le-velib-taille-sa-route-huit-ans-apres-son-lancement,136863.php.

54 Michael Kimmelman, "Paris Aims to Embrace Its Estranged Suburbs," *New York Times*, February 12, 2015, http://www.nytimes.com/2015/02/13/world/europe/paris-tries-to-embrace-suburbs-isolated-by-poverty-and-race.html.

55 http://www.startuphubs.eu/.

56 Mark Bivens, "The Billion Dollar Startup Club," *Rude Baguette*, November 25, 2014, http://www.rudebaguette.com/2014/11/25/rudevc-billion-dollar-startup-club.

57 Eric Pfanner, "French Efforts to Block Sale of Stake in Video Site to Yahoo Are Criticized," *New York Times*, May 1, 2013, http://dealbook.nytimes.com/2013/05/01/french-efforts-to-block-stake-sale-of-start-up-to-yahoo-is-criticized.

58 Pierre Perrone, "Andrée Putman: Acclaimed Designer Who Helped Pioneer the Concept of Boutique Hotels," *Independent*, January 30, 2013, http://www.independent.co.uk/news/obituaries/andree-putman-acclaimed-designer-who-helped-pioneer-the-concept-of-boutique-hotels-8473832.html.

Acknowledgments

THIS PROJECT WOULD NEVER have come to life without the help and support of some incredible individuals.

Heartfelt *remerciements* go to my agent, Judy Linden, who believed in my idea from the very first email and worked with me to find it a wonderful home at Abrams (and to Will Taylor for introducing me to her!). Thank you to my editor, Laura Dozier, whose excitement, encouragement, and confidence in me and this project propelled me forward and made it an absolute joy to produce. And producing it wouldn't have been possible without the talents of Charissa Fay, whose photography took the book to another level; and Sarah Gifford, who took our words and photographs and brought them to life on the page. To my best girls Lauren and Lisa, and my "word nerds" Sara and Amy, who read sections of the manuscript and cheered me on at each step of the process. To my mentor from the start of my writing career, Amy Thomas—I am forever grateful for each piece of advice that you have so generously offered me over the years; this book is, in large part, thanks to you. To my friends: Jennifer, for your sharp eye for detail and your invaluable assistance; to Rahaf and Jesse for advice, check-ins, and words of encouragement; Cody, for your masterful research skills; Bryan, for always challenging me; and Elle, for lending an ear and offering your help when I needed it most. To Nichole Robertson, if not for our brainstorming sessions, *The New Paris* may have remained in my mind and never put onto paper. To my family: thanks to your urging me to travel, I was able to imagine a different life for myself; consider this my expression of love for the city you gave me the space to explore on my own. To my Cédric, your patience throughout this journey was a greater gift than you will ever realize and I cannot thank you enough.

And to Paris: This is for you.

Editor: Laura Dozier
Designer: Sarah Gifford
Production Manager: Denise LaCongo

Library of Congress Control Number: 2016945903

ISBN: 978-1-4197-2403-9

Text copyright © 2017 Lindsey Tramuta
Photographs copyright © 2017 Charissa Fay

Photograph, page 18, taken from the rooftop of the former offices of BETC.
Photograph, page 175 (top left) © Arnaud Andre. Photograph, page 175
(bottom) © Alexandre Martin. Photograph, page 232. Le Carreau du Temple.
Photograph, page 237 (bottom) © Elodie Dupuis. Photograph, page 248 ©
Hervé Goluza. Photograph, 250, taken with permission of DJS/Mairie de Paris.

Printed and bound in the United States
10 9 8 7 6 5 4 3 2

Abrams books are available at special discounts when purchased in quantity
for premiums and promotions as well as fundraising or educational use.
Special editions can also be created to specification. For details, contact
specialsales@abramsbooks.com or the address below.

ABRAMS The Art of Books
115 West 18th Street, New York, NY 10011
abramsbooks.com